# THE AMERICAN REVOLUTION

# The American Revolution

COLIN BONWICK

MACMILLAN

First edition 1991

Published by
MACMILLAN EDUCATION LTD
Houndmills, Basingstoke, Hampshire RG21 2XS
and London
Companies and representatives
throughout the world

Typeset by Footnote Graphics
Warminster, Wiltshire

Printed in Hong Kong

British Library Cataloguing in Publication Data
Bonwick, Colin, *1935*–
The American revolution.
1. War of American Independence
I. Title
973.3
ISBN 0–333–37680–3
ISBN 0–333–37681–1 pbk

# CONTENTS

# Contents

For Jonathan and Andrew

# Acknowledgements

I wish to thank Mr Jim Potter for his many helpful comments on the economic and demographic sections of Chapters 1 and 2, though responsibility for them remains with me.

I also thank Mr D. C. Jones for permission to reprint Tables 3.1 and 6.15 from A. H. Jones, *Wealth Of A Nation To Be*, and Mr Andrew Lawrence of the Department of Geography, University of Keele, for drawing the maps.

Last, but certainly not least, I thank my wife, Mary Rand Bonwick, for her many contributions to this book.

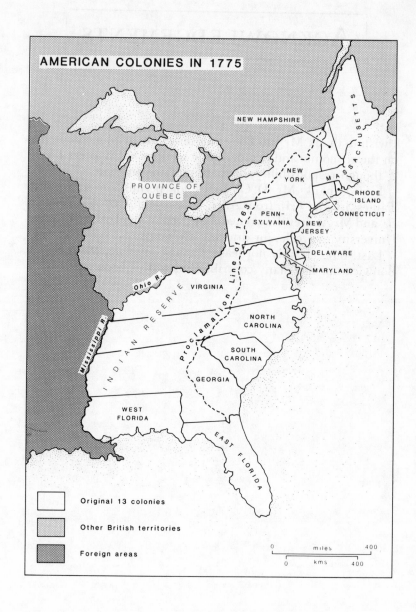

AMERICAN COLONIES IN 1775

NEW HAMPSHIRE

PROVINCE OF QUEBEC

MASSACHUSETTS

NEW YORK

RHODE ISLAND

CONNECTICUT

PENN-SYLVANIA

NEW JERSEY

DELAWARE

MARYLAND

Ohio R.

Proclamation Line of 1763

VIRGINIA

INDIAN RESERVE

NORTH CAROLINA

Mississippi R.

SOUTH CAROLINA

GEORGIA

WEST FLORIDA

EAST FLORIDA

Original 13 colonies

Other British territories

Foreign areas

0    miles    400

0    kms    400

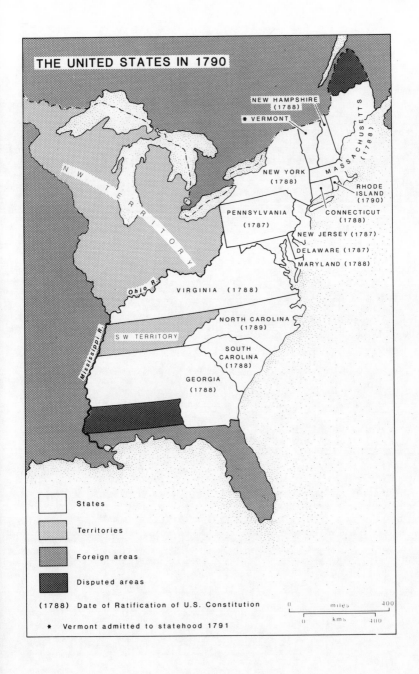

# THE UNITED STATES IN 1790

NEW HAMPSHIRE (1788)

* VERMONT

MASSACHUSETTS (1788)

N W TERRITORY

NEW YORK (1788)

RHODE ISLAND (1790)

PENNSYLVANIA (1787)

CONNECTICUT (1788)

NEW JERSEY (1787)

DELAWARE (1787)

MARYLAND (1788)

Ohio R.

VIRGINIA (1788)

NORTH CAROLINA (1789)

S W TERRITORY

SOUTH CAROLINA (1788)

MISSISSIPPI R.

GEORGIA (1788)

☐ States

▒ Territories

▓ Foreign areas

█ Disputed areas

(1788) Date of Ratification of U.S. Constitution

* Vermont admitted to statehood 1791

0        miles        400

0        kms        400

# INTRODUCTION

The American Revolution, after two hundred and more years, is superficially well-known and inadequately understood. General narratives mostly treat it as a colonial rebellion. They equate it primarily with the growing resistance to imperial policy that led to an outbreak of hostilities at Lexington in April 1775 and concluded with British recognition of the United States eight years later. The achievement of political independence was its grand objective, besides which all other matters paled in importance. According to this familiar story, the Revolution came to its climax with the Declaration of Independence in 1776; thereafter it was almost synonymous with the war. At its most extreme, Daniel Boorstin has declared that 'properly speaking, 1776 had no sequel, and needed none. The issue was separation, and was accomplished.'[1] In other respects, it is argued, the Revolution was scarcely revolutionary at all.

Such judgements are misconceived. They imply either that the internal debates and processes which gave birth to the United States from 1776 onwards were little more than necessary consequences of independence, or treat them as matters of secondary importance. Their belittling of domestic developments is profoundly misleading. Separation from Britain was only a prerequisite beginning: independence and military victory were necessary to the Revolution, but were not sufficient for its achievement. The accompanying internal revolution was what shaped the United States and moulded its future development. It created a republican system of government based on the supremacy of the people in place of traditional monarchic society, drastically altered the relationship between elites and their social inferiors, and introduced a sequence of major reforms. It also constructed a federal union out of thirteen distinct and separate colonial communi-

1

ties. Founding a republican regime created a nation very different from contemporary European societies, set an ideological agenda for the future, constructed a political framework sufficiently strong and supple to meet the needs of later generations, and propelled the United States in a democratic direction. These developments were the heart of the Revolution.

This assessment of the relative importance of its principal elements forms the basis of the present account. The common conflation of the Revolution with the War of Independence is rejected in favour of focusing primarily on the founding of the republic. From this perspective the Declaration of Independence is important principally for its internal significance, and the war becomes an enabling process which had considerable influence on civilian behaviour. Independence and military victory did not by themselves create a republican society. As Canada, South America and twentieth-century emergent nations demonstrated later, self-government and even democracy itself could lead to many different political forms.

Such an approach is not entirely novel. Several leading participants also uncoupled the Revolution from the war, though they disagreed over when the crucial phase took place. John Adams (later to be second President) argued in 1818 that a 'radical change in the principles, opinions, sentiments, and affections of the people was the real American Revolution'; he insisted that this crucial change had taken place long before the war began.[2] Conversely Benjamin Rush (a signer of the Declaration of Independence) declared in 1787, only a few years after the republic had been founded and the peace treaty concluded, that 'nothing but the first act of the great drama is closed. It remains yet to establish and perfect our new forms of government, and to prepare the principles, morals, and manners of our citizens for these forms of government after they are established and brought to perfection.'[3] Each view contains elements of truth. The Revolution was rooted in colonial society, politics and intellect at a particular stage, but it took far longer to complete the structure of republic government than to win the war; the development of republican culture was continuous and unending.

In one respect traditional mythology is correct and Adams and Rush were mistaken. The war years were indeed a crucial phase of the internal revolution, for they saw the establishment of republican government in the states and the first attempts at constructing national authority. Furthermore, emphasis on the formation of a viable republic reinforces rather than diminishes the significance of the Revolutionary War. Construction of a successful alternative model of political legitimacy made worthwhile American resistance to the apparently authoritarian tendencies of British policy after 1763, justified the risk involved in challenging the military strength of the strongest world power outside continental Europe, and vindicated (if only in part) the ideological principles enunciated in the preamble to the Declaration of Independence. Moreover, the need to marshal as much support as possible for the struggle with Britain had important domestic consequences. Just as the pre-war dispute stimulated the articulation of libertarian principles which in turn shaped the formulation of national ideology, so the manifest need for popular support if military victory was to be won heightened the aspirations of the middle and lower ranks in American society and demonstrated that government authority could be effective only with their support.

The direction taken by these changes was far from inescapable. Only in the longest term was separation of the colonies from Britain a virtual certainty. It was far from certain until the last minute that any colonies would seek independence during the eighteenth century, or that if they did so their attempt would succeed. Interpreting the process by reference to maps of the modern United States is especially misleading, for it obscures the fact that many British colonies in North America remained loyal during the Revolutionary War and did not gain legal or *de facto* independence until much later. Similarly, the political culture created by internal revolution was more than a predictable minor modification of late-colonial British American practice. Many new forms were certainly related to those that preceded them, but their ideological fabric, network of political and social values, and structure of legitimate authority were strikingly different. Above all, a new continental community had emerged where none had previously existed – for the federal union of 1800 was far from a direct lineal descendant of the old British-American empire.

It took almost twenty years to complete the internal revolution. Beginning even before the Declaration of Independence, as Adams argued, and continuing after the war, as Rush insisted, a network of disparate yet interactive processes transformed American society and institutions, drastically altered the political principles on which they operated, and created a nation from a collection of separate and diverse colonies. Whether the Revolutionary achievement could survive over many years necessarily remained an open question, but there can be no doubt that the United States which entered the nineteenth century was very different in many, if not all, respects from the colonial America from which it emerged.

These complex developments took place at several levels of activity and over differing periods of time. Some were deeply embedded in the fabric of American social evolution and to a considerable extent they were independent of government policy. Population growth, economic development and western expansion were largely secular continuations of long-term processes dating back to the earliest days of colonial settlement. They accelerated after a sharp dip during the war and provided much of the context for the Revolution by sustaining the political processes of founding the republic without being totally determinative. Superimposed on these economic and social processes were two tiers of political action. The thirteen states which rebelled against Britain acted individually to form the first tier, and collectively acted as a nation to form the second. Revolutionary change began simultaneously at each level but whereas it was substantially complete in the states within a decade, it came to a climax at national level only after 1787.

Of these two tiers the Revolution at the lower level was in many ways more important during the war years. The states had developed as separate colonies for several generations before the outbreak of war at Lexington in 1775, and remained largely autonomous primary spheres of political

action until the federal government began asserting its authority towards the end of the century. Their initial primacy
meant that the task of erecting the apparatus of republican
society rested firstly with them. Each was obliged to address
individually a series of fundamental problems including the
need simultaneously to construct an effective government,
implement grand ideological principles, and redefine relationships between its governing elite and their social inferiors.
Though compelled to tackle them separately, the states collectively established important general principles on such
matters as constitution-making and the rights of citizenship.
At the same time the Revolution generated opportunities for
social change and other political reforms that could be
implemented only at state level.

Beginning several months before the Declaration of Independence, each of the thirteen original states constructed a new
system of government by drafting a formal written constitution
to replace British authority. Rhode Island and Connecticut
found it easy to adapt their colonial charters to the new
republican situation, others found it more difficult. Most
completed the task before the end of 1776, and by 1780 the initial
phase of constitution-making was over. Although local circumstances dictated important variations, the constitutions
shared a high degree of ideological and structural commonality.
Their authors built on political principles, institutions and
experience derived from their colonial past yet translated
them into a distinctively American system. In particular, they
redefined the relationship between the members of society and
their government: the people ceased to be subjects and
became citizens. They also became the sole source of legitimate political authority. Governments were required to be
their servants rather than their masters. In institutional terms
the constitutions attempted to define the limits of lawful
government as well as its powers. They separated government
into its three elements of legislature, executive and judiciary in
order to frustrate any tendencies each might have towards
acquiring excessive power. A majority also included a declaration of rights which proclaimed the people's fundamental
rights and the principles of republican government.

Social changes were interwoven with political processes and

took longer to mature. Each state moved at its own pace but although advances were slower in some places than others, important developments were visible everywhere by the end of the century. Some changes went to the heart of American social organisation, for the Revolution was as much a struggle over who should rule at home as one against Britain. Deployment of natural rights theories in defence of American interests before 1775, the experience of manning the army and new offices created by the states, and the broader demands of self-government all served to raise the expectations of those who had not previously aspired to share in government. Claims to continuing social hegemony and political supremacy made by the established and often conservative patriot elites were challenged by men of lower social status who argued that they were entitled to share in the direction of a nation they were helping to create. The outcome was a significant realignment of relations between elites and their social inferiors at state level. New men were enabled to enter public life, both as voters and as elected officials. They demanded that their interests be considered even if they conflicted with those of the rich. Elites were forced to share their power.

Independence also created other opportunities for change. In a few areas, land confiscated from large landlords loyal to Britain was transferred to their tenants or small landowners, though this was not usual; more importantly the acquisition of territory west from the Appalachian mountains to the Mississippi river created opportunities on a vast scale for small farmers to obtain land. The states began legislating for a self-consciously different future. All substantially reduced – and in the case of Virginia eliminated – religious discrimination. All except Massachusetts and Connecticut dismantled their church establishment if they had one. Such changes were matters of substantial importance in societies where membership of a particular church was a prime determinant of a citizen's place in the community. Similarly, but less extensively, all northern states starting with Pennsylvania began the slow task of abolishing black slavery, and simultaneously white indentured servitude faded out. Several states also began modernising their property and inheritance laws and ameliorated their penal legislation. Some recognised the need for public education, and a few practical steps were taken to satisfy it.

Creation of a national union greater than the sum of its individual communities formed the second tier of the internal revolution and took far longer to complete. Such a union was vital if the states were to profit from the introduction of republicanism and enjoy the reciprocal advantages of their diversity; it could also bring fuller collective benefits than those attainable by each individually. Although essential to the Revolution's long-term success, the emergence of a vigorous national union was far from inevitable especially since communications were currently poor. In particular a strong central government was required if the nation was to develop cohesion, but since such a government would necessarily diminish the states' authority many contemporaries resisted it as being a repudiation of the Revolution itself. After a considerable time and much uncertainty a permanent continental union and effective federal government were finally established – long after the states had constructed their own governments.

Only a rudimentary central government was erected during the war. The circumstances from which it developed were far from promising. As subordinate members of the empire, before 1776 each colony had formal connections with Britain but none with its fellow provinces; elements of potential unity undoubtedly existed in colonial America but any sense of American community or nationality was at most embryonic. Opposition to British policy after 1763 stimulated continental unity, and the outbreak of fighting made collaboration imperative. Yet the demands of war had only limited effect. Only an embryonic national government operated until the war was won. Congress began life in 1774 as an extra-legal protest body and was poorly fitted to exercise national authority. It consisted of delegates from states eager to load it with responsibility but reluctant to cede it effective power. Though permitted by the states to exercise limited power, Congress functioned more as a conference of their representatives than as an autonomous government. It achieved victory largely by synchronising their efforts; in Adams's vivid phase, 'thirteen clocks were made to strike together'.[4] Efforts to devise a national constitution began simultaneously with the Declaration of Independence in 1776, but by the time the war ended and Britain conceded American independence there was still more hope than substance in the states' claim that they had formed a perpetual union. When eventually ratified in 1781, the Articles of Confederation, as the first United States Constitution was entitled, rested on the explicit principles that the states were sovereign and retained all powers not expressly delegated to Congress. Thus Congress continued to depend on them for revenue and possessed only those limited powers the states chose to grant. In spite of notable successes such as the Land and Northwest Ordinances which provided templates for territorial expansion, evidence that problems attributed (often mistakenly) to Congress's deficiencies were solvable, and hints that government under the Articles was capable of gradual improvement, the union remained frail during the immediate post-war years. Many men came to believe that it could survive only if drastically restructured.

The Revolution's second national phase took a further decade to complete. Politically it comprised three elements: construction of a second federal constitution, implementation of an effective national government, and evolution of a system of political parties. Critics had insisted even before the Articles of Confederation were ratified that greater central authority was necessary for the satisfactory conduct of foreign policy and other national affairs. These demands were intensified in the mid-1780s by a growing belief among conservatives that what they considered as democratic excesses in the states would have to be curbed. For both reasons, they argued, a stronger national government was essential if the Revolution was to succeed. In 1787 Congress was persuaded to summon a Convention authorised to propose amendments to the Articles. It met at Philadelphia and immediately jettisoned its instructions in favour of drafting a fresh document. The new federal constitution constructed a complex framework of republican government. It derived its legitimacy directly from the authority of the people, guaranteed a republican form of government to the states, separated the three elements of government (legislature, executive and judiciary) in an effort to frustrate excesses in any one branch, and made provision for the protection of citizens' rights. Simultaneously it met the pragmatic need for stronger central authority by assigning substantial but not unlimited powers to the federal government while protecting the states within their own diminished sphere of jurisdiction.

Yet even ratification of the Constitution and its inauguration in 1789 failed to complete the Revolution and secure the republic, for it was no more than an institutional skeleton which needed muscles and a nervous system if the national union was to mature. George Washington's policy as first President from 1789 to 1797 played a crucial role in giving substance and vigour to the newly created federal government by developing the machinery and procedures necessary to apply in practice the new Constitution's principles. Besides dealing with day to day problems he laid down principles of organisation and conduct for the executive, created a new level of effective authority partly above and partly parallel to that of the states, encouraged his subordinates to formulate programmes designed to strengthen national supremacy, and achieved legitimacy for the regime by gaining public acceptance.

One last element was needed to complete the national system and consummate the Revolution. Unexpectedly the device that met the requirement for a nervous system was a system of political parties. Ironically, it emerged out of opposition to policies which though intended to promote national unity had provoked sharp divisions and bitter debate. To government supporters and critics alike such a system seemed to threaten the integrity of the Revolution, yet party formation proved to be the key to its consolidation. The first parties provided a structure capable of articulating the relationships between citizens and state and federal governments, harnessing and taming the potentially dangerous consequences of conflicting interests in a diverse and extensive society, and channelling disagreements between opponents and supporters of government at all levels. By integrating individual, local and national concerns with the formulation and execution of public policy, they completed a federal structure of politics which coupled the requirements of substantial local autonomy to the imperatives of national interest.

It would be wrong to exaggerate the extent of Revolutionary change. Americans did not face the same social challenge as the French after 1789 and the Russians in 1917. Principles announced in the Declaration of Independence were not fully implemented, American republicanism was not synonymous with radical egalitarianism, and the United States did not immediately become a democratic society. Also, the benefits of revolution were distributed unequally. Rich supporters of independence retained their property and much of their power. Many white men made substantial gains, but many others remained poor and were still excluded from partici-pation in politics and government; white women scarcely benefited at all. Much discriminatory legislation remained in place, especially on religious grounds. Above all, the logic of the Revolution extended human rights to blacks only to a very limited degree. Most continued to be enslaved, and those who were freed were not granted the customary rights of citizen-ship; in white eyes they were still inferior. In these and other matters much business remained for future generations to complete.

Nevertheless, what happened in the United States was indeed a revolution. The changes it generated were neither evolutionary nor inevitable: they were optional, sudden and progressive. Republicanism rested on different principles from those of the royal regime that preceded it and the *anciens régimes* of continental Europe. Government in America de-rived its authority from its citizens and possessed only limited powers; it no longer ruled over subjects, nor did it enjoy the absolute supremacy claimed by parliament in Britain. Yet it was sufficiently powerful to provide vigorous administration, flexible enough to adjust to nineteenth-century expansion, and tough enough to survive a major rebellion. Previously dominant elites were obliged to admit their social inferiors to a share of political power, and important reforms were introduced in many states. In comparison with colonial America social relationships and community values had changed dramatically. The Revolution also created machinery

by which its benefits could be extended to those who currently
did not enjoy them, and established processes whereby further
reforms could be implemented. It could not, however, guarantee that the opportunities it had created would be seized.
Above all, it provided a platform for the future: democracy
was well on the way to acquiring prescriptive authority.

# 1
# LAND, PEOPLES AND THE ECONOMY

Thirteen colonies were developing and maturing rapidly in mid-eighteenth-century America. Their European and African populations were multiplying at a pace far more rapid than in the old world – though at the expense of the indigenous population. Their economy was expanding, and increasingly it included highly profitable engagement in overseas trade. This development was a product of human enterprise, and derived from the colonists' ability to exploit the potential of a rich and extensive natural environment.

I

The United States land mass at the moment of independence was already vast by European standards. Its 867,980 square miles of territory stretched about 1500 miles from a northerly point on the frontier with modern Canada to a disputed southern border with Florida (which reverted to Spain in 1783 after twenty years of British control, and was not acquired by the United States until early in the following century), and up to 1200 miles from the Atlantic Ocean westwards to the Mississippi river. Topographically the country was dominated by the Appalachian mountain system. Formed by a series of parallel ridges and valleys measuring between 20 and 80 miles wide and rising to above 6000 feet in places, it ran down the coast from close to the shore at its northeastern end to about 300 miles inland in the south before fading into a coastal plain some 200 miles short of the Gulf of Mexico. Until the Louisiana Purchase of 1803 extended American territory to the Rockies, the mountains bisected the country into a zone of effective white occupation east of the watershed, in which rivers drained into the Atlantic, and a western zone of negligible white settlement where rivers drained into the Mississippi and the Gulf.

This land was rich in natural resources. Once its extensive forest cover had been cleared, the soil was generally fertile, and the combination of hot summers and substantial rainfall throughout the year (between 32 and 48 inches, and more in some areas) which make the geographers' term 'the humid east' an apt description of its climate, created very favourable conditions for agriculture. Winters brought considerable variety in temperature. Values dropped to a January mean of freezing point or lower in the northeast of the country and were accompanied by heavy snow; further south winters were milder and growing seasons commensurately longer.[1] During the eighteenth century development was still limited, even in the occupied area, and much of the continent's latent wealth, especially west of the mountains, lay unexploited. All densely inhabited areas lay close to the coast: the white population thinned out further inland, especially in the south. Moreover, according to Samuel Blodget writing in 1806, no more than 20,800,000 acres of land (roughly 8 per cent of the present seaboard states from Maine to Georgia, together with Vermont and West Virginia) had been improved by 1774.[2]

Within this general framework the settled area was divided physically into three regions. To the north, four New England colonies – New Hampshire, Massachusetts, Rhode Island and Connecticut – constituted a unified region east of the Hudson river. As yet Vermont and Maine were not separate communities: Vermont was not admitted as the first new state until 1791, and Maine continued as a district of Massachusetts until it achieved statehood in 1820. For the most part, New England's landscape consisted of wooded mountains and hills. An indented shoreline provided many small harbours, but its restricted coastal and riverine plains and valleys offered only limited agricultural land of good quality.

To the south and west, New York, New Jersey, Pennsylvania and Delaware formed a second region. Known collectively as the middle or Mid-Atlantic colonies (and later states), and sometimes in association with New England as the northern states, it enjoyed somewhat shorter and milder winters and possessed extensive fertile land and excellent large harbours on the Hudson and Delaware rivers. On the eve of the Revolution the Appalachian mountain ridges limited the extent of immediately cultivable land and diverted the thrust of white settlement north and southwards instead of directly westwards. In New York it was possible to travel north up the Hudson and turn west along the Mohawk Valley for about 100 miles before reaching the limit of significant settlement.[3] Similarly the mountains deflected settlers from Pennsylvania southwestwards into the southern backcountry during the years preceding independence; few crossed the watershed into the Mississippi basin before the Revolution.

Everywhere south of Pennsylvania formed the third region. This area can be usefully subdivided into an upper and a lower South, each bigger than either of the other two regions. Together they formed more than half the colonies' total land area east of the mountains. Maryland, Virginia and parts of North Carolina were grouped round Chesapeake Bay to form the upper South; the remainder of North Carolina, South Carolina, and Georgia constituted the lower South. Climate and terrain progressively underwent considerable modification as one moved southwards. The weather became milder, growing seasons lengthened in the increasingly hot and humid summers, and it became possible to grow crops unsuited to northern areas. Counter-balancing its benign climate, the disease regime deteriorated in coastal areas and the lower South was especially unhealthy; a seventeenth-century visitor described South Carolina as 'in the spring a paradise, in the summer a hell, and in the autumn a hospital'.[4]

The southern landscape also changed from east to west. A broadening strip of flat land known as the Tidewater stretched from Chesapeake Bay and the coast to a so-called and barely visible 'fall line' which notionally connected the first set of falls or rapids on each of the rivers that crossed it. These rivers, such as the Potomac, Rappahannock, and James and their tributaries, provided useful if limited means of transportation into the immediate interior. Further inland the terrain rose gradually to form an undulating region known as the Piedmont which gave way in turn to the foothills and frontal ridge

of the Appalachians. At their northern end, in Maryland, the
Tidewater and Piedmont together were no more than a few
miles wide; at their southern extremity, where they turned
west to merge with the Gulf plains, each was considerably
more than 100 miles wide. Beyond the frontal ridge lay the
Great Valley of Virginia. Easily accessible only at its northern
end, it was topographically linked more with Pennsylvania
than the rest of Virginia. Piney barrens, swamps and mountain areas apart, southern soil was generally, if modestly,
fertile.

A fourth region, west of the Appalachians, was an area of
great interest to whites but had attracted few settlers before
the Revolution. Its landscape dropped away from the mountains until reaching the rich valley bottom of the Mississippi
to the west and the Great Lakes to the north. Much of the
land was wooded and provided a favourable habitat for
wildlife, but the fertility of its soils remained untapped.
Colonial speculators purchased large tracts of land in anticipation of future profits, though as yet its prime resource in
the eyes of many was the fur-bearing animals whose pelts they
purchased from the Indians. When the west is taken with the
three seaboard regions, this huge territory offered a diverse
and attractive physical environment. Development, however,
depended on the capacity of human inhabitants to exploit its
potential.

## II

Three races – native Americans, Europeans, and Africans –
populated North America on the eve of the Revolution. First
to arrive and still greatest in number were indigenous native
Americans known by Europeans as 'red Indians'. They had
crossed the Bering Strait from Asia to Alaska some 10,000 to
20,000 years earlier and trickled slowly southwards; by the
time European explorers, conquerors and settlers arrived in
the New World their numbers had risen to an estimated
100 million. Most lived in central and south America, where
they developed highly sophisticated cultures. Archaeological
evidence and modern demographic analysis suggest that

immediately prior to the establishment of the first permanent English settlements in 1607 about 10 million or so Indians inhabited the area of the present contiguous United States, of whom approximately 500,000 lived in the eastern part including 300,000 within 150 miles of the Atlantic seaboard.[5] Stone age technology, divisions among themselves, and a debilitating incapacity to resist European diseases made it impossible for Eastern tribes to prevent the expropriation of their lands by predatory settlers. By 1776 their numbers had shrunk by two-thirds, they had lost control almost everywhere from the coast to the Appalachians and were in retreat elsewhere: it was already clear that the future would be directed by whites. Even so, the Indian challenge was far from fully extinguished. European governments and settlers alike continuously exploited tribal rivalries as they manoeuvred among themselves for control of the continent. Throughout the Revolutionary era those tribes located immediately beyond the settled area posed a potential threat to many frontier communities and ensured that Indian relations would remain an important element in state and national politics. Indians fought on both sides of the War of Independence but were not mentioned when the articles of peace were negotiated.[6] Thereafter the pressure on them to cede their lands resumed.

European command of North America began with a chain of English colonies founded during the seventeenth century. After several unsuccessful attempts, bridgehead settlements were established at Jamestown, Virginia, in 1607, Plymouth (later incorporated into Massachusetts) in 1620, and around Boston, Massachusetts, in 1629–30. Ironically, advice from the Indians was crucial to their survival, particularly in Virginia where mortality rates were especially high. By 1650 three further colonies – Connecticut, Rhode Island and Maryland – had been added and the European population had risen to 50,000; the English position was secure and the colonies were capable of self-sustaining development. Colonisation, interrupted by the English civil wars and Cromwellian interregnum, resumed after the restoration of Charles II in 1660. New York was captured from the Dutch in 1664, New Jersey and the Carolinas were founded during the 1660s and Pennsylvania during the 1680s. Infilling and secondary extensions took place continuously, and the establishment of Georgia in 1732 completed the thirteen colonies which later separated from Britain to form the United States.[7] In contrast, the French colony of New France in the St Lawrence Valley of modern Canada (founded 1609) grew far more slowly, and the Spanish town of St Augustine, Florida (founded 1565), was little more than a military settlement. A few French settled in the Mississippi Valley, and even fewer Spaniards settled in the southwest.

Rapid population growth was central to American development throughout the eighteenth century. Thomas Malthus, the English political economist, estimated in 1798 that numbers were doubling every 25 years; modern demographers concur with his judgement.[8] A population of approximately 275,000 including blacks but excluding native Indians in 1700 rose to approximately 2,500,000 by 1775, to 3,929,214 by 1790 (the year of the first federal census) and 5,296,990 in 1800. This rate of increase of total population from all causes, roughly 3 per cent per annum or 34 to 35 per cent per decade, fluctuated from decade to decade and area to area but was far higher than in any European country at its most rapid. Numbers increased especially rapidly in the peaceful years of the 1720s and 1760s and again during the 1780s, which proved to be the decade of fastest natural growth in American history, but more slowly during war decades such as the 1750s and 1770s.[9] Growth was fastest in newly developing areas just behind the leading edge of settlement, and lowest in long-settled coastal counties. Region by region, it was highest in the middle colonies, where population increased 5.5 times every 50 years between 1690 and 1790, and slackened to 4.5 times in the south. At 3.5 times growth was lowest in New England. Even so, population growth failed to keep pace with the extension of territory during the second half of the eighteenth century. By British standards America was not densely populated. A coastal strip from southern New England to Pennsylvania and around Chesapeake Bay was the most thickly settled area, largely because it contained most of the larger towns; outside them, population density only rose as high as 45 persons per square mile in Rhode Island and eastern Massachusetts. Overall the country had only 2.88

persons per square mile in 1775 and no more than 6.1 per square mile by the end of the century.[10]

Natural increase accounted for most of this rise, and the family provided its essential framework. A favourable sex ratio (a small majority of 50.9 per cent were male), marriage on average at 24–25 for men and 21–22 for women followed by childbirth every two years for 15–20 years ensured a high birth rate. Sufficient good food high in protein, generally favourable health conditions, low mortality rates in rural areas (even in the less healthy Chesapeake) and urban mortality rates low by the standards of large British towns produced an exceptionally high survival rate of 75 per cent; in the words of Walter Nugent, Americans lived longer, married younger, had more children and saw more of them grow to maturity than Europeans did. This combination of high fertility and low mortality augmented existing population by 28 per cent every decade, with regional variations shaped by environmental factors and internal migration. It also generated a very young population. At the end of the century the median age of whites was 16, and one in three of the population were under 10 years old. Since fewer than 40 per cent of the population was in the prime working ageband between 16 and 45, every productive worker was obliged to support two or perhaps three other persons.[11] In the particular environment of eighteenth-century America this imperative was stimulating rather than onerous.

Immigration raised this already high natural increase in the white population to about 32 per cent every decade. Between 1700 and 1790 about 350,000 to 370,000 white immigrants arrived.[12] Their influx ran as high as about 15,000 every year during the 1760s. Many came from Ireland and continental Europe. Their entry substantially modified the colonies' ethnic structure; by the time of the Revolution many inhabitants of the British colonies were not English by origin. Among these new arrivals were as many Scotch-Irish as English, 100,000 Rhineland Germans, and smaller numbers of Swiss, Huguenots (as French Protestants were known), Swedes and Sephardic Jews. Of those who arrived from the British Isles about a quarter were convicts and most were men.[13] Many from continental Europe came in family groups, thus encouraging non-British demographic growth.

In addition estimates suggest that the immigrants included approximately 350,000 Africans. Captured from virtually every tribe south of the Sahara but principally from those communities inhabiting the immediate hinterland of the west coast, all had been forcibly transported across the Atlantic. About 5000 to 25,000 were brought in between 1619, when the first cargo entered Virginia, and 1700. By far the great majority arrived during the eighteenth century as the American economy expanded. As with whites, more entered during the 1760s – when about 75,000 were imported – than in any previous decade. Natural increase, especially when the sex ratio approached parity, combined with importation produced a black rate of natural increase higher than that among whites during the sixty years before 1770.[14]

Eighteenth-century immigration converted the relatively simple ethnic structure of the original settlements into a considerably more complex society as the United States achieved independence. Calculations based on the first national census recorded that people of English stock had already fallen to only 47 per cent of total population. When the Welsh (3 per cent) and Scots (4 per cent) are added, the British still formed only a bare majority of 54 per cent of total white and black population. Even when the Scotch-Irish from Ulster (8 per cent) and southern Irish (4.5 per cent) are included, the proportion of Americans originating from the British Isles still added up to only 67 per cent of the whole. Though continental European ethnic groups individually formed only small components of the whole, collectively they added up to one-eighth of total population: Germans (about 8 per cent) were the largest continental group, followed by the Dutch, some French and Swiss, and a few Swedes, Finns and Jews. Outnumbering the continental Europeans and native Indians, but themselves outnumbered in the settled areas only by the English, were the African Americans. Forming a little more than one-fifth of the non-Indian population, their numbers reached about 500,000 by 1775 and grew to 757,208 in 1790.[15]

Regional distribution of the multitude of ethnic groups was very uneven. Among whites, New England was ethnically the most homogeneous area since its inhabitants were more than 80 per cent English by origin. In contrast the middle colonies of New York, New Jersey, Pennsylvania and Delaware were by far the most heterogeneous. The Dutch were strongly represented along the Hudson river and on Long Island in New York and in New Jersey where they formed 20 per cent of the population; there were also Germans and Scots in both colonies, especially along the Hudson and Mohawk valleys. Pennsylvania had the most diverse population of all the colonies. Only one-third of its people were English, and Germans matched their numbers so closely that at one time they demanded that German should be recognised as an official language; the residue was made up by Scotch-Irish, Welsh and others including a few descendants of the Swedes who had settled on the Delaware river in the previous century. In the south more than half the white population was English by origin except in South Carolina. Considerable numbers of Germans lived in western Maryland and the Great Valley of Virginia, and others lived throughout the south. Even more Scotch-Irish inhabited the developing backcountry from Maryland southwest to the Carolinas and Georgia. The region also contained some Irish in Maryland, where they formed about a tenth of the population, Scots and Swiss in North Carolina, and some French Huguenots in South Carolina. A few Sephardic Jews lived and traded in major towns from New England to the south.[16]

Africans were also distributed unequally across America, though for a different reason. Whereas the pattern of European settlement was the consequence of essentially free choice by voluntary migrants (apart from convicts), blacks were forcibly distributed in accordance with white requirements for their labour. New England, Pennsylvania and Delaware had little need for their services and consequently had populations that were 3 per cent or less black. The proportion rose to 10 per cent in New York and New Jersey as a whole and to 18 per cent around New York City, on western Long Island and in northern New Jersey. But taken together these northern blacks formed only a small element of the African-American population, for 89 per cent lived in the South to which they had been directed in response to urgent white demands for their labour. The effect of this concentration on the ethnic structure of the South was striking. Of the populations of Maryland and Virginia 39 per cent were black, as were 35 per cent of North Carolina, 45 per cent in Georgia and a massive 61 per cent in the coastal parishes that formed the principal populated area of South Carolina.[17] A by-product of this demand for black labour was a rise in the region's demographic growth during the 1760s from about 35 per cent of the colonies' total population to 44 per cent. Unlike the native Indians, Africans formed an important component of American society during the Revolutionary era. Almost all were slaves.

Variations in growth rates resulted in a markedly unequal regional distribution of population. By the close of the colonial era, almost half the people lived in the South, where the regional growth rate had reached 33 per cent per decade. At 38 per cent, the growth rate in the middle colonies was even faster. By 1770 they had about a quarter of the population and were overtaking New England, whose relative lack of attractive areas for development coupled to significant out-migration had reduced its growth to 27 per cent per decade shortly before the Revolution.[18] Similar variations marked the populations of individual colonies. Virginia, with over 500,000 inhabitants, was by far the largest in population as well as land area; next came Pennsylvania with over 275,000 and Massachusetts with just under 275,000. Maryland, a bene-ficiary of expansion around the Chesapeake, and North Carolina, whose backcountry was filling rapidly, were the only other colonies with many more than 200,000 inhabitants. Con-necticut just touched the 200,000 mark, and New York, South Carolina and New Jersey were the only remaining colonies to have more than 100,000 people. By contrast, at the lower end of the scale only New Hampshire and Rhode Island had more than 50,000 inhabitants; Delaware, with about 40,000, and Georgia, the newest colony whose 27,000 people were scattered along its coast and up the Savannah river, brought up the rear. Across the Appalachians the west was a sparsely settled region: about 17,000 white people occupied modern Kentucky and Tennessee, a few others inhabited the Mississippi valley, and virtually none lived north of the Ohio river.[19]

## III

The economic growth of pre-Revolutionary America more than matched its vigorous demographic development. Its most striking feature was its overwhelmingly agricultural character, and this continued long after independence. Apart from specialised activities such as ironmaking, shipbuilding, modest developments in textile production, shoemaking, printing and other small-scale workshop activities directed towards domestic markets, manufacturing was conducted in the home. A second feature was a diversity so great from region to region that it can be better described as a collection of local economies than as a single continental system; transport difficulties greatly accentuated this variety. Expansion was powered by two interactive motors. The first was the rapid increase in population; the second was increasing overseas demand for staple products such as tobacco, grain, flour and bread, rice and indigo, and forest products.

Both motors were essential to growth, though their consequences were different. Rapid population growth encouraged cultivation of fresh land within existing areas of occupation, extension of settlement on the frontier, and formation of new communities. When added to the output of previously settled areas, this new production accounted for the bulk of American economic activity. Necessary though it was, however, growth in this sector of the economy was restricted in character. Production of staples for export had far more dynamic effects, even though only 9 to 12 per cent of gross output was directly engaged in overseas trade, and much of the expansion attributable to it was achieved by opening fresh lands. There were improvements in commercial organisation, cheaper and more efficient transport and slowly rising productivity, though improvements in agricultural productivity were limited.[20] Access to markets far wider than those offered by local consumers, and the generation of new lines of trade when necessary greatly encouraged domestic growth; its effects were felt throughout the colonies if only at second or third remove in remoter areas where near subsistence farming was still common. Growth in trade was considerable during the fifteen years before the Revolution in spite of political turbulence during the 1760s. Demand for American agricultural products increased and prices received for tobacco, rice, indigo and grain rose more rapidly than those of goods purchased. More capital became available for internal expansion, manufacturing increased and intercolonial trade increased to supplement overseas commerce.[21]

The effects of this staple production differed from region to region, and from crop to crop. They included shifts in agricultural production in response to market opportunities, such as the beginning of a switch from tobacco to grain in the Chesapeake shortly before the Revolution, and the development of overseas trading networks. More important in the long run, staple production encouraged diversification and stimulated that sophisticated economic development which was essential for future prosperity. Mercantile and financial services expanded, as did construction of ironworks and processing plant such as flour mills and rum distilleries; similarly, shipbuilding, textiles, shoemaking and workshop manufacturing increased considerably. Most notably the requirements of overseas trading led to urban growth, mainly in coastal areas, and the emergence of several towns with more than 10,000 inhabitants in all regions except the upper South.

Deficiencies in available statistical evidence cannot obscure the general features of American economic growth during the third quarter of the eighteenth century. Agricultural production was amply keeping up with the demands of a rising population for food. The quality of diet was high, providing the strength necessary for child-bearing and hard physical work. It also generated a substantial surplus of goods and services for export in response to the demands of overseas markets. A cross-section of trade figures in 1770 illustrates the broad pattern and scale of American exports. Tobacco worth £724,186 was the most valuable commodity, followed by wheat, flour and bread which together were worth £605,840, rice worth £266,708, dried fish worth £147,342, timber products at £135,132 and indigo at £103,925. Other commodities such as whale oil, iron, meat, forest products, flaxseed and rum together were valued at £469,665. A five-year run of statistics reveals yet another dimension to the pattern. In

every year from 1768 to 1772 the colonists paid on average
£3,920,000 for imported goods and £280,000 for slaves and
indentured white servants; they also paid £40,000 in taxes and
duties to Britain. On the credit side, however, they earned
almost enough to meet the entire cost. Exports of commodities
brought in an average of £2,800,000 each year to meet the
bulk of the import bill. Additionally, Americans sold ships
valued at £140,000 and earned £600,000 from the carrying
trade and £220,000 from commission, leaving a manageable
deficit of only £40,000 each year.[22]

Long-term economic trends were highly favourable in spite
of cyclical fluctuations which sometimes had important short-
term consequences. By comparison with contemporary British
standards, American growth was rapid. Between 1650 and
1770 the colonial gross product grew annually by 3.2 per cent
on average, though growth rates varied from region to region.
Rural New England grew more slowly than other regions
because it had few agricultural products suited to export
markets, and the South grew faster, especially for slave-
holders who appropriated the surplus wealth generated by
their black slaves. The middle colonies both diversified most,
as their exports of grain, iron and ships demonstrated, and
grew fast. Much of the overall increase is attributable to rising
population and territorial extension, but not all. Incomes per
capita rose by at least 0.3 per cent per year for much of the
colonial period, and by 0.5 per cent after 1750; if slaves and
indentured servants are discounted as consumers, the increase
for free whites becomes even higher.[23] By 1774, Americans
possessed non-human wealth (that is, counting servants and
slaves as potential consumers not as property) of £37 per
capita, giving the large majority higher real incomes than
those enjoyed by any European community – and greater
than those received by more than half the world's population
in the late twentieth century. If colonial wealth is divided only
among those entitled by law and convention to own it, and
slaves and servants are considered as property, the figure
rises substantially to £252. If slave property is excluded and
since almost all wealthholders were heads of household, this
figure is roughly equivalent to the average wealth of free
families, both white and black, which was £222.[24] Such

statistics of wealth can be helpful, even if they are tentative in nature.

Of itself, however, no general model provides an adequate description of the American economy or a sufficient basis for discussion of its political implications. For economic activity in the eighteenth century consisted less of an integrated national unit than a collection of local economies which partly followed and partly overlapped the geographical structure of the Atlantic seaboard. Regional differences in exports are especially revealing. The upper South colonies around Chesapeake Bay were most productive. Over five years from 1768 they earned £1,046,883 per annum from commodity exports; in contrast the lower South earned £551,949, the middle colonies £526,545 and New England only £439,101. Differences in the ratio of exports to population are also striking. In 1774 the upper South exported goods to the value of £1.82 per capita, compared with £1.78 from the lower South and £1.03 from the middle colonies; New England managed to export only £0.84 per capita – less than half the amount exported in the South.[25] Variations in economic activity such as these both influenced the distribution of wealth and structure of society in each region, and interacted with broader cultural and ideological imperatives to create regional and local communities possessing distinctive characteristics as well as shared common qualities. Both the similarities and the diversity of the American economy had great importance for the establishment of an independent United States.

New England was poorer than the other regions. Lacking extensive rich soils, it was populated largely by small farmers whose engagement with a trading economy through a chain of small towns was limited. Boston, however, was a well established commercial centre, and evidence suggests a high level of domestic comfort. Little agricultural produce other than horses shipped from Rhode Island to the West Indies went onto the overseas market; more important were forest products such as timber from the less well-settled district of Maine. The region's most substantial exports came from the sea. They included fish exported to the West Indies and southern Europe, and whale oil which together with potash was its only major export to Britain. The only area with which

New England had a trade surplus was southern Europe; elsewhere it was in deficit by £16,400 with the West Indies and a mammoth £593,200 with Britain. So great was its dependence on the outside world that it was obliged to import foodstuffs from the middle colonies in order to feed, especially in the Boston area, its rising population. What enabled New England to finance its trade deficits was profit earned from providing shipping, insurance and financial services in North Atlantic trade. In 1772 the northern colonies combined earned £740,000 in invisible earnings.[26]

There were, however, considerable local differences. In the better farming areas such as the Connecticut Valley the more successful farmers had aggregated increasing acreages to themselves. Recently founded communities in northern areas of the region and along the Maine coast were much more commercially oriented than older agricultural areas in the interior, and Boston had become a regional metropolis whose economic attention was principally focused on business with the outside world. Nevertheless, its economic limitations had a profound effect on New England's wealth. With 26 per cent of the colonies' total population its people possessed only 20 per cent of their private physical wealth, that is, counting real estate, slaves and indentured servants, livestock, crops and other portable physical assets, and adding financial assets after deduction of liabilities.[27]

To cross the Taconic mountains into New York and the middle colonies was to enter another country. Agriculture was more advanced, more commercial and more prosperous than in New England, and there were more important urban centres than in either New England or the South. The Hudson Valley was unusual in that much of its land was owned in great patroonships of thousands of acres – a Dutch pattern continued by British speculators – and farmed by tenants. The developed area of Pennsylvania contained perhaps the richest soils in the northern colonies, as well as a milder climate. It quickly became a major area for family farmers (both as landowners and large-scale tenants) and its exports of flour, bread and wheat ensured its substantial trade surpluses. Two other elements also benefited the region's economy. Pennsylvania virtually ignored British imperial legislation to become a major producer of bar and pig iron, and Philadelphia and New York profited from the development of their respective hinterlands to become major entrepots. Shipbuilding and fisheries were also well developed. Thus the region could feed itself amply as well as export foodstuffs to Britain, southern Europe, the West Indies, and sometimes to its neighbours. It could augment its profits still further by providing shipping and financial services. Its broad range of activities was a source of great economic strength.

This diversity also had importance for the scale and distribution of wealth. The inhabitants of the middle colonies were richer than those of New England. They formed 27 per cent of the population, and possessed 25 per cent of the colonies' net wealth, partly because of the higher value of their land and its crops, and partly because their commercial success brought in a substantial surplus of financial assets over liabilities. Also, if slaves and servants are treated as property and the region's wealth is divided among free persons, the average wealth was £42. Since there were not many slaves the figure only drops to £40 if divided among all inhabitants.[28]

The South was different again, not only because it was geographically more extensive, and even more rural and agricultural than other regions. Land and slave labour were the keys to its economy. Development was most advanced in the Tidewater, where population was densest, tobacco cultivation at its highest and wealth at its greatest – and 50 to 60 per cent of the population were black slaves. Nevertheless the pressure of population on existing land and the constant search for higher profits among the rich ensured that the backcountry was filling rapidly as the country approached independence. Initially its mode of agriculture and size of holding were comparable to those in other family farming areas, but as fresh areas were developed so tobacco and slavery expanded. On the eve of the Revolution, white settlement, staple crop agriculture and with them black slavery had extended well into the Piedmont in Virginia and South Carolina and to a lesser extent in North Carolina. Yet the upper South as a whole was not irrevocably committed to this pattern. As tobacco culture expanded into the Piedmont and took slavery with it, so the older-established areas diversified into grain. In 1738–42 the ratio of value of tobacco to grain exports was 14 to 1; by 1768–72 it had fallen to 4 to 1. The change had extensive ramifications. Since tobacco was a product of high value relative to bulk which was destined for a single primary market, it was most efficient to collect it through great planters or Scottish merchants resident in America and perform other entrepreneurial services in Britain. Wheat, in contrast, could be more economically concentrated in the colonies before being distributed to a variety of markets in America itself, the West Indies, or Europe. With this change came development of the first towns of any size in the upper South – Baltimore, Maryland, and Norfolk, Virginia – though their growth had not gone very far before the outbreak of war.[29]

The second centre of southern society was the lower South. Here the principal cash crops were rice and indigo, and to a lesser extent deerskins and naval stores. During the period 1768 to 1772 the annual value of indigo exports, which were encouraged by a British bounty, stood at £111,864, but they were outpaced by rice, exports of which were valued at £305,533, even though substantial quantities were consumed at home.[30] Both crops were highly profitable, and their voracious appetite for slave labour made South Carolina unique as the only colony with a black majority; it was also the richest province per free person, had the highest standards of living among whites and the greatest concentration of wealth. In Charleston it possessed the only southern town of note; it attracted much of North Carolina's trade as well as that of its own interior. Heat, humidity and disease along the coast encouraged sea-island planters to spend their summers in its somewhat healthier and more comfortable climate, thus endowing it with a high level of cultural sophistication. The town's prosperity was such that even artisans commonly owned slaves. By comparison, the backcountry was far less affluent since it was still in its settlement phase.

Every southern colony was deeply engaged in overseas trade through production of staples such as tobacco and later of wheat in the upper South and rice and indigo in the lower colonies. If southern exports are compared with those of other regions, the contrast is striking. Those from the upper South alone equalled those from the northern colonies combined, and sales of the lower South added a further 50 per cent: this extensive cultivation of cash crops was its economic motor. There was, however, an important qualification to the rule that agriculture was the source of southern wealth. The highest individual profits were often made by providing services such as trade and local services, and above all in land speculation. It was almost a matter of definition that great Chesapeake planters owned land in at least two counties, and most had invested heavily in undeveloped land to the west, including in some instances land west of the mountains.[31]

The importance of land and slavery as components of southern wealth was substantial. The region as a whole possessed half the population but only about one-third of the white population. This minority owned 55 per cent of the colonies' total wealth, including half the land and 95 per cent of the slaves. If the capital value of the slaves (estimated at about £20 million) is discounted the South's share of colonial wealth drops sharply to 46 per cent. The effect of slavery on the distribution of wealth is similarly striking. If non-human physical wealth is divided only among free inhabitants the average holding is £61 per capita. If it is divided among the slaves as well, it drops to £36 – much the same as New England. Conversely, if the slaves are treated as property and their value divided only among wealthholders, the physical wealth of southerners rises to £395.[32] On this basis the South was almost three times richer than New England and more than twice as rich as the middle colonies.

Yet if land was the prime source of wealth and agriculture engaged almost all the workforce throughout the colonies, it is arguable that the towns were the most dynamic sector in the colonial economy. In its early stages each was a product of the particular needs of its immediate hinterland, but the largest towns had diversified and achieved a measure of economic autonomy. All five major towns were ports providing mercantile services for import and export trade, financial services, entrypoints for immigrants, and limited manufacturing; they also served as centres of government and cultural activities. Philadelphia, with at least 24,000 and perhaps more than 30,000 inhabitants, and New York with about 22,000, were the largest. Boston and Newport, Rhode Island, were handicapped by New England's lack of agricultural exports. Instead, they depended largely on fishing, the carrying trade, and (in the case of Newport) the slave trade. By 1775 their populations had reached 16,000 and 11,000 respectively. The only substantial town in the South was Charleston, South Carolina, but in spite of the area's great wealth its population was no more than 16,000. A second tier of towns were much smaller in size. Most, like Portsmouth, New Hampshire, Baltimore, Norfolk, and Savannah, Georgia, were also ports, but there were several interior towns, notably Albany, New York, which served as an entrepot for the northern fur trade, and Hartford, Connecticut. Even smaller were numerous towns that were barely more than villages. Here the level of economic specialisation was higher. In Essex County, Massachusetts, for example, Salem and Ipswich were trading centres, Marblehead and Gloucester were small ports, and interior towns like Andover, Rowley and Wenham were producers of grain, cattle and timber for sale in the surrounding area. Williamsburg, the seat of royal government in Virginia, was one of the few other southern communities to have any claim to urban status. Its year-round population was only 1500, and only rose substantially during sessions of the Assembly; it decayed rapidly after the state capital was removed during the Revolution.[33]

On the eve of the Revolution the colonies were well set. Their population was increasing rapidly without overreaching the capacity of the land to sustain it. Their economy was growing and developing, and provided a sturdy infrastructure for social growth. Like other communities they were susceptible to disruption, but the long-term prospects were highly favourable – whether they remained members of the British empire or became an independent nation.

# 2

# SOCIAL, POLITICAL AND
# INTELLECTUAL PATTERNS

Within a common underlying pattern social mores varied. Contemporary Europeans were mistaken in believing that American society was more or less homogeneous. Unquestionably there was no counterpart for whites to the stark contrast between the degradation of the poor and the gross wealth, privileges and power of the aristocracy that was evident in many parts of the old world. Yet substantial differences in wealth and income were clearly visible, and the existence of social hierarchy was generally acknowledged by all, if frequently resented by the less fortunate. In some areas the social faultlines were blurred, in others sharp and steep; the rivalries they provoked contributed significantly to the outcome of the Revolution. Ironically the evidence suggests that American society was becoming more differentiated, and in some ways closer to English society as it moved towards independence.

## I

The distribution of property is one good indicator of general and regional structures. Throughout the colonies as a whole the richest tenth of the population owned more than half the total physical wealth of the community, and within that fortunate group the richest 1 per cent owned almost 15 per cent. At the other end of the scale the bottom fifth of the population were themselves a species of property and could legally own nothing, and the next 30 per cent above owned no more than 3 per cent of the total.[1]

Within this general picture there were significant variations.

31

New England's wealth was notably unequal although its richest citizens were not as rich as those elsewhere. Its inhabitants' overall per capita wealth was only £36, and that of its free population rose to no more than £38 even if the few slaves are counted as property. Yet in spite of this relative poverty, the top tenth of free wealthholders still possessed 47 per cent of the region's total physical wealth.[2] Better agricultural conditions well suited to large-scale family farming and cultivation of commercial crops produced more equally distributed wealth in the middle colonies than in either of the other regions. In the cities some men, like William Bayard and John Cruger in New York, and Thomas Willing and Israel Pemberton in Philadelphia were worth from £50,000 to £100,000 but on average the rich owned relatively less than elsewhere. Thus the top 10 per cent of wealthholders possessed only 35 per cent of total physical wealth (including slaves and servants as property), and the middle 30 per cent owned 36 per cent.[3]

The South possessed the greatest concentration of wealth, though since it was the richest region its whites enjoyed the highest standard of living in colonial America. Here the concentration is especially striking if slaves are also included as potential wealth holders. The top 1 per cent owned 29 per cent of the region's wealth and the top 10 per cent owned 69 per cent; the bottom 40 per cent owned nothing since they were slaves.[4] Its inhabitants also included many of the richest men in the colonies. Charles Carroll of Carrollton in Maryland was estimated to be worth £100,000. The greatest concentration of the rich was to be found among the sea-island planters of the coastal parishes of South Carolina. A comparison between the relative wealth of rich and poor farmers in the North and South confirms the latter's far greater inequality. In the North the richest farmers (those owning property worth £400 or more) on average owned ten times the amount possessed by poor farmers (those owning £99 or less); in the South they owned twenty-two times as much as their poor neighbours.[5]

One reason for variations in the distribution of wealth lay in differences in each area's stage of development. Jackson Turner Main's typology is a useful device for measuring this. He discerns four stages of development from equality to economic and social stratification. The earliest stage was

characterised by considerable equality. Most settlements conforming to this form were on the western edge of white
habitation, but examples existed in virtually every colony.
Land prices varied considerably but it could be purchased for
3 shillings an acre in the wilderness areas of Maine, £5 per
hundred acres in the Wyoming Valley of Pennsylvania and as
little as 2 or 3 shillings per acre in parts of the South. In some
places where land was owned in large tracts by absentee
landlords the structure of pioneer society remained. A second
stage was subsistence farming in areas where there was a high
proportion of small farmers, as in parts of New England,
Pennsylvania and the southern backcountry, and the third
was the stage at which commercial farming was usual, as it
was around Chesapeake Bay, the area around New York City,
and the coastal areas of the lower South. The final stage was
the development of distinct urban centres. By the eve of the
Revolution a broad picture of social diversity and differentiation had emerged.[6]

Starting at the bottom there was one point at which the
dividing line between social strata was sharp and clear. By
the mid-eighteenth century slavery existed in every colony
and enslavement had long been the normal, though not
universal, condition for African Americans. Its basic principles were clear, though the law was complex. Slaves were a
form of property. They were bound for life, subject to the will
of their owners and could be bought and sold; their condition
was transmitted to succeeding generations through the female
line. The law offered limited protection against maltreatment
but no rights. Race provided the crucial determinant of status.
All whites were free or would become free; all slaves were
blacks or in rare instances native Indians. Fewer than 5 per
cent of blacks had benefited from manumission or uncertainties concerning their status during the previous century and
had gained their freedom. Most of these lived in the North,
where they comprised up to 10 per cent of the African
American population; in the South fewer than 3 per cent were
free.[7] Everywhere they suffered legal and informal racial
discrimination. No matter how essential blacks were to
economic development, whites controlled American society
and expropriated the proceeds of their labour. Fears of a slave

uprising were constantly in white minds, but a careful policy of frustrating the growth of African solidarity by mingling members of different tribes, coupled to ruthless coercion and calculated rewards prevented the outbreak of rebellions. Revolts in New York in 1739 and South Carolina during the 1740s were notable for their rarity – and the brutality with which they were suppressed. Among blacks malingering, indiscipline and sullen insubordination were common expressions of protest, and in spite of their predicament they sustained a measure of social and cultural life not controlled by their masters.[8]

Just as whites decided where slaves should be directed, so they determined the employment to which they would be put. In the South, where the demand for labour was greatest, they were deployed in large numbers as agricultural labourers. Around Chesapeake Bay little more than half the planters owned slaves, and two-thirds possessed fewer than 5 slaves, but gangs of 20 or more were increasingly common, and the richest planters owned more than 100; conversely, almost half the blacks lived in units of more than 20 slaves. In the lower South 50 to 60 per cent of white households owned slaves; more than half owned between 3 and 18 slaves, and almost one-third owned 26 or more.[9] The only northern areas to use slaves in substantial numbers were the lower counties of New York, including western Long Island, where the proportion of blacks ranged from one-fifth to over one-third and northern New Jersey where about 12 per cent of the population was enslaved. About 3000 lived in the city of New York, 750 in Boston and 670 in Philadelphia, where they formed a significant component of the labour force in urban commerce and industry and as sailors and dockworkers.[10] They were also used as farmworkers as well as in the workshops and distilleries of small towns like Providence, Rhode Island, Lancaster, Pennsylvania, and New Brunswick, New Jersey. With the growing sophistication of the southern economy, increasing numbers were trained as skilled artisans, whether on plantations or in towns, particularly Charleston. Everywhere they were used as domestic servants.

Within white society the bedrock was a large number of landless labourers. It included perhaps a fifth of adult males.

Together with the slaves they formed about 30 per cent of the population. Many were immigrants who had arrived as indentured servants or redemptioners bound to service for three to seven years. They endured frequent exploitation during their servitude, but their numbers had shrunk to below 5 per cent of the population by 1774.[11] Others included a substratum of marginal people who found work difficult to obtain, northern agricultural labourers who performed the physical work largely done by slaves in the South and around New York City, and a comparable proportion in the South of whom between a quarter and a half might eventually obtain a small property. Some in the North were also young men waiting to obtain land of their own; for them landlessness was usually a temporary condition.

Many landless whites lived in the major towns. Here the critical distinction was between those who worked with their hands and formed up to two-thirds of the population, and those who did not. Merchant seamen, day labourers and other unskilled workers were the urban counterpart of the rural landless; they were about a quarter of the total. Many were poor – between one-fourth and one-third in Philadelphia – and their vulnerability to economic fluctuations made it difficult for them to meet basic family needs without resorting to charity.[12] Artisans, most of whom were self-employed craftsmen, formed the remainder of the mechanic community. They, too, had their hierarchy. At the bottom were coopers, weavers and shoemakers who possessed limited and easily learned skills and needed little capital. Immediately above them were artisans such as cabinet-makers, silversmiths and bakers who possessed high skills but required only low amounts of capital. At the top of the mechanic hierarchy were highly skilled artisans who required large volumes of capital and who needed to coordinate the work of several trades; they included shipwrights, housebuilders, printers and ironmasters. Many of these men, and occasionally women, employed up to two dozen workers, including slaves, and owned substantial property.[13]

Above the artisans in status were those who did not work with their hands, including ministers of religion, doctors, lawyers and particularly traders. Here, too, there were hierarchies. Among professional men schoolmasters were lowest in status and poorest, receiving salaries as little as £20 a year.

At the opposite end of the scale, the practice of law also gave access to political influence, in rural colonies as well as towns. Lawyers sometimes earned more than £500 a year; their ranks included many leading Revolutionaries, ranging from John Adams of Massachusetts to Alexander Hamilton of New York, John Dickinson of Pennsylvania, and Thomas Jefferson, George Mason and James Madison of Virginia. Traders ranged from small shopkeepers engaged in local retail markets to wealthy merchants with sufficient resources to take financial risks and finance trade with Europe. The great merchants had incomes which probably averaged £500 per annum; shopkeepers probably earned half that amount or less.[14]

Yet about two-thirds of all white men were farmers. Throughout the colonies as little as 50 or even 25 acres could provide a minimal living for a family, though much would depend on the location, quality and tenure of the land. All but about 10 to 15 per cent of landholders farmed between 50 and 500 acres. Most owned their land but tenancy was common in some areas. In the developed areas of New York, Pennsylvania and the Chesapeake perhaps up to one-third were tenants. In areas such as the Hudson Valley, where there were between 6000 and 7000 tenants, the arrangement could provide a route to upward mobility for men who lacked capital, but the opportunity depended everywhere on the attitudes of landlords. On some Maryland manors it worked to the mutual advantage of both parties. On others, especially in the older areas, tenancy was a condition of poverty for those lacking sufficient funds to move to the frontier or leave agriculture; such men were effectively bound to the cultivation of tobacco in regions where its profitability was declining. Outright ownership of land was much more common. Ordinary farms in New England were seldom more than 100 acres, though the more successful Connecticut Valley farmers built up larger holdings. In the middle colonies and especially the South, farms were generally larger. Small farmers owned 50 to 500 acres in Virginia; unlike New England their produce was directed towards overseas commercial markets.[15]

Even in the South, small farmers preponderated numerically, but the social effects of staple crops and slavery were profound. Tobacco was a crop that could be grown on a variety of soils in the upper Tidewater and Piedmont, and could be profitable for small producer and great planter alike. An owner of as little as 50 acres who depended entirely on family labour could grow 3 acres of tobacco and devote the remainder of his land to food crops, wood-lot and fallow fields. Possession of slaves greatly increased profitability: two could double a family's net income, and a gang of twenty or more gave disproportionately greater benefits.[16] During the 1760s and early 1770s, when tobacco prices were high, men who owned both land and slaves could obtain a disproportionate share of available credit, and use it to improve their holdings. Poor men were cut out of the market for slaves and land, and had to go to the frontier to improve their situation – if they could. In Virginia about 30 per cent of farmers owned 100 to 500 acres, with an average of 230 acres. The richest planters – those in the Northern Neck between the Potomac and Rappahannock rivers – owned on average 3000 acres each, and some much more. These great planters and their families formed no more than about 5 per cent of the white population, and the richest of them a tiny fraction, but they dominated society. And the population was 50 to 60 per cent black and enslaved.[17]

The consequences of commercial agriculture were even more pronounced in South Carolina. Efficient production of rice, the principal staple crop, required substantial capital investment and a minimum of 5 to 10 workers. It was known as the aristocratic crop for that reason. Individual family farmers could not afford to enter a market dominated by large plantations employing 50 to 100 workers – all of them black and enslaved. Charleston and adjacent parishes were populated by men of great wealth – nearly 30 per cent of men left £1000 or more – far fewer whites of modest wealth than other towns, and very large numbers of slaves: 60 per cent of whites were farmers, of whom half owned 300 acres of land and perhaps nearly half owned slaves; only one-tenth were artisans and one-twelfth were merchants or shopkeepers. Only in the backcountry, which was not fully developed, were there large numbers of smaller farmers similar to those found in the interior of other southern colonies. In the South as a whole, the richest 10 per cent of the population (including slaves) owned 69 per cent of its wealth.[18]

## II

Hierarchies of a different type existed among communities. Individual families were the core ingredient of American society. Family farms were primary social as well as economic units throughout the colonies, and in the South the large plantations extended the family to include slaves and servants. Many settlers migrated in family groups, and from the Wentworths of New Hampshire to the Hutchinsons and Olivers of Massachusetts, the De Lanceys and Livingstons of New York and the Lees, Randolphs and Carters of Virginia, family networks among the rich were prominent in every colony. Churches also played an important social as well as spiritual role, but the lowest stratum of political organisation was townships in the North, counties in the upper South and parishes in South Carolina. Their responsibility was to maintain law and order, arrange for poor relief when necessary and provide limited local services such as highway maintenance. Especially in New England the townships were more than political aggregations of inhabitants. Their government overlapped with membership of churches and thus became the focus of social cohesion and enforcer of traditional moral values. Thus inhabitants of rural areas in particular were usually members of at least three overlapping communities: family, congregation and township or county. Harmony required subordination of individual interests to those of the community. Local pressures to conform were often intense, but lacking powerful instruments of coercion the townships depended ultimately on consent to sustain harmony and the results were uneven. Stability was strongest in areas that were ethnically, theologically and economically homogeneous, as in many Connecticut towns. Townships in the middle colonies were far more heterogeneous by these criteria and in commercial towns like Germantown (just outside Philadelphia) individual self-interest was far more powerful. In the South the obvious need to maintain racial solidarity in the face of black slaves was a potent imperative towards white harmony – for those who owned none as well as those who owned many.[19] These local communities were the most important level of social and political organisation as far as day-to-day life was concerned.

Above them were two higher levels of community. First came the thirteen individual colonies; internal diversity at this level made harmony far more difficult to achieve. Secondly, in the absence of any continental union before the Revolution, the final level of community was the empire. In theory the British government was expected to administer imperial affairs in the general interest. Definition of this general interest became increasingly contentious, and rivalries among local interests, especially between Britain and the thirteen colonies, became more difficult to resolve after 1763. Ultimately it proved impossible to maintain Anglo-American union on terms acceptable to all parties.

Social hierarchies and the unequal distribution of property generated powerful and self-conscious elites at every level. It is hardly surprising that elitist pretensions were common among southern gentry, but they were also to be found among the great families of the middle colonies and even in New England. Each township in the North and county or parish in the South had its local elite and above them each colony had its provincial elite. There was no America-wide continental elite, but a superior tier of men possessed profound social and political influence in the colonies: the imperial elite located in England and virtually synonymous with the English aristocracy. Its authority operated throughout the empire and was therefore an integral part of the colonial social hierarchy. Each tier of elite comprised those who exercised influence and authority appropriate to the level concerned, together with their associates; they also provided cultural and behavioural role-models for social inferiors. Political power was closely correlated with wealth, status and social connections so that, put crudely, the elites were the rich and their supporters in each community. At the lowest level of a small New England town the elites were often no more than prosperous farmers and local shopkeepers who served as selectmen subject to the ultimate authority of town meetings whose members sometimes included all adult males. Old-established southern communities were usually dominated by the richest planters. In mid-century Maryland and Virginia the gentry were firmly in the saddle. They self-consciously aped the behaviour and social values of the English aristocracy, and their wealth, their dominance of the local economy and above all their ownership of blacks (the richest 100 planters owned an average of 80 slaves each) gave them massive superiority over their white inferiors. The great rice planters were even more dominant over South Carolina. A similar situation existed in the large towns such as Boston, Philadelphia and New York, where great merchants formed the core of the elite and were powerful in local politics as well as trade.

The supremacy of the rich was even more evident in colony government. It was common for a local 'court' consisting of great planters, merchants and officials to revolve around the royal governor, especially in the South. The gentry were usually paramount in provincial as well as local affairs, and the choice of candidates at elections was generally made from among their ranks. Membership of one of the 'first families' was almost essential for a political career in Virginia, and in Massachusetts the mid-century House of Representatives drew its leaders from a small group of men.[20] The supremacy of gentlemen was almost total in South Carolina, and qualified by a cautious recognition of their need for broader white acquiescence in Virginia. Great families such as the Livingstons, Schuylers, Van Rensselaers and Morrises owned huge estates in the Hudson Valley and dominated New York; further north families such as the Hutchinsons and Olivers were increasingly influential in Massachusetts and the Wentworths dominated New Hampshire. By contrast, in Pennsylvania the elite, especially those allied with the proprietor, was powerful in Philadelphia but also fragmented and constantly quarrelling among itself, and in Rhode Island there was bitter rivalry between rural and commercial factions which diminished the influence of rich merchants.

Elitist pretentions were rationalised by reference to the principles of harmony, order and community. Numerous distinctions existed in American society, among them being education and talent as well as wealth. The conclusion was drawn that social order required the recognition of the supremacy of the community over individual interests, social hierarchy and differentiation of functions. The connection had been long recognised. Thus when the Connecticut township of Wallingford was founded in the 1730s land was distributed according to social rank in preference to any other criterion: men of high rank were assigned 476 acres, men of middle rank 357 acres and those of 'Loer [sic] Rank' only 238 acres.[21] It was presumed that authority should rest in the hands of the elite since they possessed the education, breadth of vision and experience to execute their responsibilities. Above all, in what was a self-justifying circular argument, the elites claimed they had a greater stake in society than their social inferiors since they owned more of its property; this in turn gave them the political independence deemed necessary to define, identify and promote the general welfare. By contrast, according to the elites, the lower orders, even if free, were totally self-interested and lacking in moral capacity, intellect, understanding and independence. They were, as Peter Oliver (a member of one of Boston's most distinguished families who later became a loyalist exile) argued 'perfect machines, wound up by any hand who might first take the winch'.[22] Elites went on to argue that there was a natural reciprocity of interest between ruler and ruled. The lower orders could be permitted limited political rights – provided they internalised the deferential values deemed appropriate by their social superiors and made their choice of representatives from among the gentry. Otherwise, their function was to labour. In return, gentlemen had a duty to consider the welfare of the community as a whole and protect the interests of its inferior members.[23]

Numerous devices were employed to overawe social inferiors. Throughout the colonies the rich imitated the English gentry by building opulent houses in the English style, as William Byrd did at Westover, Virginia, or having their portraits painted by artists such as John Singleton Copley in Boston. Virginian gentlemen indulged in high-stake gambling and horse racing to demonstrate their great wealth, and displayed condescending generosity to subordinates in order to reinforce their social supremacy; everywhere their status was flaunted by retinues of liveried black slaves. Courthouse rituals, service on the bench and election to the legislature demonstrated and reinforced political supremacy.[24] Close ties bound established churches to the structures of secular authority and provided spiritual legitimacy whether they were the Anglican churches of the South or the Congregational standing order in New England. In Virginian churches and New England meeting-houses alike, social hierarchy was sustained by seating congregations according to social rank.

Yet colonial elites were by no means wholly secure or totally self-confident. None were aristocratic in the English or continental European sense. They lacked the titles, privileges and above all the possession of high family status over generations that gave automatic social prestige and political authority across the Atlantic; neither was their economic superiority over other whites, great though it was, comparable to that enjoyed by great landed aristocrats over other Englishmen. When Arthur and William Lee, members of a leading Virginia family, visited Britain they were not accepted as equals by the landed aristocracy but mixed in middling rank circles. The wealth of the American elites was relatively new. Moreover, in spite of self-serving insistence on the superiority of community welfare over individual interests and the desirability of maintaining social hierarchy in the interests of all, status was the product of aggressive individual enterprise in open competitive markets, whether it derived from commerce or the land. By this measure elite claims to superiority were not self-justifying, but could be challenged by competitors operating on the same individualistic principles within the same economic markets.[25] And perhaps most significant of all, though elites claimed supremacy within their own provinces they were themselves subject to regulation by imperial authority. At the pinnacle of colonial society, royal governors represented the cultural supremacy of British society as well as the political authority of the crown.

## III

Any discussion of the fabric of American society would be incomplete without reference to the centrality of religion. Church membership in eighteenth-century America was high, ranging from about 56 per cent of the population in the South to as much as 80 per cent in the North.[26] Maryland was the only colony to possess a substantial Roman Catholic minority, partly because it had been founded in the previous century as a Catholic refuge, and partly because it had subsequently received a disproportionate number of Irish Catholic indentured servants. Apart from miniscule numbers of Jews, all other Americans were Protestants – a fact that shaped their cultural, social and political attitudes as well as defined their theological principles.

Within the ranks of Protestantism there was great diversity. The principal denominations were Anglican, Baptist, Congregationalist, Lutheran, Presbyterian, Dutch and German Reformed, Mennonites and the Society of Friends, known as Quakers. In addition there were numerous smaller sects such as Methodists, Moravians, Rogerenes, Sandemanians, Separatists and French Huguenots.[27] Several larger denominations were divided into splinter groups. Among this multiplicity of sects, two enjoyed the legal privileges of establishment which included allocations of land and support from taxation. The Congregational Church was established in Massachusetts, Connecticut and New Hampshire where it benefited from the colonies' descent from the original Puritan settlements. The Church of England was weakly established in the five counties round New York City, more substantially in Virginia, and weakly in the other southern colonies. The privileges of both churches coincided with areas in which they were numerically dominant. Quakers were numerous and influential in Pennsylvania in spite of their lack of legal privilege, and to a lesser extent in Rhode Island where the Baptists were especially powerful. As was to be expected, Presbyterians were numerous among the Scotch-Irish, though New England had also generated Presbyterian churches whose main difference from Congregationalism lay in church organisation. Once again the middle colonies were more heterogeneous than the other regions, since German settlers, like the English, were divided among several sects, and other ethnic groups also had their own churches. Religious affiliations were a significant contributor to social cohesion. Shared philosophical values were indications of commitment to the principles of secular society, and establishments could provide valuable support for colonial elites as the Congregational Church did in New England. Under other circumstances, however, sectarianism could be divisive. In Pennsylvania the rivalry between Quakers and their associates, Anglicans and Presbyterians was an important ingredient in pre-revolutionary political rivalries, and in Virginia growing numbers of non-Anglicans resented the privileges enjoyed by the established church.

## IV

The framework of colonial government was well articulated. Its prime unit was the individual colony or province, but political activity took place at every level from town and county meetings upwards. Each province was a microcosmic community in itself. Maryland, Pennsylvania and Delaware were proprietary colonies in which the crown had vested political authority in the Calvert family (in Maryland) and the Penn family (in the other colonies), though it continued to supervise the proprietors' administration. At the other extreme, Connecticut and Rhode Island possessed charters which gave them extensive autonomy, including the right to elect their own governor; in practice they were virtually republics long before the Revolution though their small size gave them little influence elsewhere. All other provinces were royal colonies in which legal authority flowed from the crown – in Massachusetts through its charter, and in others technically through the authority granted to its governor by virtue of his royal commision.[28] In every colony the structure of government superficially replicated its British counterpart, with traditional functional divisions between executive (the governor), legislature and judiciary, and distinctions between governor, upper house (except in Pennsylvania and Georgia) and lower house that mimicked the social balance of monarchy, aristocracy and democracy manifested in England by the king, lords and commons. But these similarities were misleading, for colonial politics functioned differently from English practice in several important respects.

The disparity between institutional structure and actual practice was especially acute in the case of the governors. Formally they represented the dignity and authority of the crown; nominally they possessed far more legal power. They were responsible for internal administration, enforcement of customs laws, granting lands, and acting as military commander-in-chief with considerable authority. They also possessed broader prerogative powers than the crown currently did in England, including the right to veto legislation and dissolve the assembly, as well as the right to nominate members of the upper house in most colonies and appoint members of the higher judiciary. But reality was different. As royal officials they could be dismissed at will by the British government, and their average term of office was only five years. As executive heads of government they lacked sole control of appointments to office and were often hobbled by the appointment of councillors who functioned partly as advisers, partly as second houses of legislature, and even as judiciary. Above all, they were dependent for political support, revenue and even their own salaries, on lower houses of assembly which they could seldom influence by patronage in the way that enabled British prime ministers to control the House of Commons.[29] Benning Wentworth used his power to distribute timber contracts to considerable effect in New Hampshire, but this was unusual. Much depended on individual talents and the constraints of particular circumstances. Most governors were obliged to cooperate with their assembly if they wished to achieve anything. Francis Fauquier and Lord Botetourt were successful in Virginia but Francis Bernard failed to establish a satisfactory relationship with the Massachusetts legislature. Talent was no guarantee of political success if it was deployed towards objectives unacceptable to the legislature – as Thomas Hutchinson, the native-born but tory governor of Massachusetts, discovered to his cost.

Neither house of a colonial assembly exactly replicated the two houses of parliament. Upper houses, being appointed by the governor (except in the charter colonies) could also be dismissed and thus lacked independence. They could neither persuasively claim to be a political balance between the governor and the lower house since they straddled the executive and legislature, nor could they claim to represent a distinctive aristocratic social estate since they were not as socially distinct from their fellow colonists as was the landed aristocracy from other Englishmen. By comparison, the lower houses were in some respects more powerful within their own sphere than was the House of Commons in England, even though most could be summoned, prorogued and dissolved at the governor's will and their legislation could be vetoed by the governor or disallowed by the Privy Council in London. The extent of their political power varied from colony to colony but was considerable in all cases. In particular the lower houses claimed and asserted complete control over money bills and in some instances the disbursement of funds; they also set fees, paid governors' salaries, appointed treasurers, and regulated the establishment of new boroughs and counties, together with their representation.[30] The presence of large numbers of gentry among their ranks, especially in southern colonies such as Virginia and South Carolina, persuaded most governors to negotiate with them. But the core of the lower houses' political influence lay in the simple fact that they represented their provincial communities in a way that neither of their partners in government did. This practice of politics allowed powerful interest groups (especially urban merchants and great southern planters) an influence disproportionate to their numbers.

The suffrage was far less restricted than in England. The medieval proposition that those who were to pay taxes should be invited to give their consent, but those who were not to be taxed need not be represented was present in attentuated form. Other considerations were more important. Two principal criteria determined eligibility for the franchise: the degree to which a potential voter displayed commitment to the interests of the community, and the extent to which he possessed a will of his own and an ability to exercise independent political judgement. It was also implicitly argued that good government depended on a good measure of ethnic, religious and social homogeneity. Thus Massachusetts originally defined the right to vote by membership of the Congregational church, but in 1691 its new charter established a property qualification instead. Elsewhere, doubts over their allegiance to the community were sufficient to exclude Jews in seven colonies and Roman Catholics in five, including Maryland which had been founded as a haven for Catholics but had come under Anglican control at the end of the seventeenth century; lack of citizenship was exploited as a means of excluding some Germans in Pennsylvania. The requirement to possess the capacity for independent judgement was automatically deemed to exclude all women, young men not living in independent households, servants and slaves, though not necessarily free blacks.[31]

Possession of property was the primary qualification for the franchise. Ownership of freehold land had triple merit. It demonstrated possession of a stake in society, in an agricultural society it was held to demonstrate particularly admirable social virtue, and it gave its owner independence in the broader economic, social and therefore political sense. From Pennsylvania southwards voters were required to own 50 acres (100 acres unsettled or 25 settled in Virginia): elsewhere they needed land worth £50, £40 or 40 shillings a year in value. Several colonies, notably Massachusetts where it was very important, had alternative financial criteria which enabled propertied townsmen to vote. These requirements were sufficiently low to enable virtually all heads of farm households to vote, but in towns such as Philadelphia they excluded at least a third of all adult males, including the mass of the poor. In some small New England towns practical considerations extended the vote in local elections well beyond the legal limits, and there was considerable variation of practice within as well as among the colonies. But the probable range of voting was between 50 and 80 per cent of all free white adult males. When expressed the other way round, the statistics demonstrate that many potential voters were excluded.[32]

Participation in politics was uneven. Voting was less common in colony-wide than local elections, but if apathy was common, the electorate displayed considerable interest in major issues. Higher property qualifications for office, custom, and perhaps deference towards men of high social standing, dictated that representatives were drawn from much more limited social strata than were voters: more so in colony elections, less so in small towns. Although two-thirds of voters were farmers or artisans, only one-fifth of representatives came from the same background. Most were great planters, merchants or lawyers drawn from the upper tenth of the population. In certain colonies such as Virginia they were obliged to curry favour with their social inferiors, but in all colonies they expected to be re-elected, or at least replaced by men of similar status.[33]

By comparison the judiciary was less independent and less developed than the legislature. Local justices were often elected, and in practice expressed the views of the communities over which they exercised their authority. Much court business was administrative rather than judicial in the customary sense, and criminal business was frequently concerned primarily with enforcement of prevailing religious and moral values. Juries were also normally expected to represent the values of their communities. Even the highest judges were often professionally unqualified, and most were closely connected with the local structure of political power. They were not appointed on good behaviour as demanded by New York and other colonial legislatures, but at the crown's pleasure and could be removed by the governor. Vice-Admiralty courts, which adjudicated on overseas trade and navigation as well as other important maritime matters, were composed of single royal judges who sat without a jury; they were accordingly much disliked, especially by traders.[34]

At mid-century the apparatus of local control from townships and counties to provinces seemed generally to work well. Political turbulence which had characterised the 1720s and 1730s had settled down, and certain colonies such as Connecticut and South Carolina were particularly renowned for domestic harmony.[35] Government machinery and political processes were sufficiently inclusivist to include most white interest groups, without being democratic in the later sense.

## V

Like the people themselves, the American mind was diverse and maturing rapidly. Literacy was high and schooling widespread if erratic. Public education for boys was usual in New England. Elsewhere education was largely left to the churches or to individual families; in the South rich planters often sent their sons abroad, as did the Lees of Virginia. Little care was taken over women's education and none over that of black slaves. Two-thirds of American white men were literate, ranging from about a quarter in the South to almost universal literacy in New England. The third quarter of the eighteenth century saw a burst of college founding to supplement the few that previously existed. By 1775 there were nine: to use their modern names they were Harvard, Yale, Dartmouth and Brown in New England, Columbia, Rutgers, Princeton and Pennsylvania in the middle colonies, and the College of William and Mary in Virginia – the only southern institution. Rising levels of education had extensive ramifications. Printing presses and booksellers were common, especially in major towns. Thirty-six newspapers were published in 1775. Several towns had chartered libraries by the time of the Revolution, and the American Philosophical Society was founded in 1743 to promote scientific enquiry.[36] Educated Americans were keenly interested in European culture, but their own music, imaginative literature and painting were still at an early stage of development, and architecture was the preserve of gentlemen amateurs such as Joseph Brown of Providence and Thomas Jefferson.

On the eve of the Revolution the American mind was already capacious. Its principal concerns were theology and the exploration of the natural universe, though politics came to occupy a central location as the crisis developed. No single intellectual system reigned supreme, for important elements were in competition with each other: some men's belief in the power of human reason and the possibility of progress was matched by the pessimism of others and an awareness of the frailty of human nature. Already the colonies had produced two men of substantial intellectual achievement. Benjamin Franklin made important contributions to electrical theory and had been elected to the Royal Society in London, and Jonathan Edwards, a Massachusetts minister, developed the most powerful eighteenth-century theology by incorporating Calvinist theology with the principles of Newtonian physics and Lockean psychology.

Many Americans devoted great attention to exploring and comprehending the natural world. They observed the transit of Venus across the sky in 1769, David Rittenhouse constructed an orrery to demonstrate the planetary system, and John Bartram and many others explored the continent. Much of

their effort was devoted to the recording and classification of
flora and fauna, but they also attempted to identify and
interpret the significance of what they observed. They concluded that God had created a logical, orderly world that
functioned according to rational principles and that God's
purpose and intentions towards man were benevolent.
Furthermore, they believed that it was within the capacity of
human reason to comprehend the nature of both the universe
and God's intentions for man. In particular they concluded
that the eighteenth century was a period highly favourable for
human development and insisted on the possibility of progress. This conviction that man possessed the capacity to
understand and command the world in which he lived, and
that America offered an especially favourable environment for
social advancement was a powerful driving force, but it must
be emphasised that even the most optimistic Americans did
not believe that progress was certain. A strain of pessimism
ran through colonial political attitudes and belief in the
possibility of progress was increasingly tempered by a fear
that it might not be achieved. They noted that the ancient
republics of Greece and Rome had advanced only to collapse,
and their experience during the worsening dispute with
Britain reinforced fear that the future could bring the anti-
thesis of progress.[37]

Theology provided another alternative challenging the
rationalism and optimism that were such notable features of
the secular mind. Most churches and sects had rejected the
rigours of much early Protestantism in favour of rational
Christianity which had much in common with secular theories
of the universe, but although the commanding authority of
seventeenth-century Puritanism had diminished in New England as elsewhere, it was by no means dead. The Great
Awakening, which swept the colonies in the 1730s and 1740s
and split Congregational, Presbyterian and Baptist churches
alike, was clearly Puritan in character. The theological arguments of Jonathan Edwards, its greatest preacher, emphasised
the depravity of human nature and the supremacy of God.
They placed the doctrines of original sin (whereby all humans
are considered to have been tainted by Adam's ultimate sin
of defying God's will in the Garden of Eden), predestination

(whereby God chooses an 'elect' few for salvation, leaving all others to eternal damnation) and God's irresistible grace at the centre of revivalist theology and insisted on man's total dependence on God's will for salvation.[38] The ramifications of the Awakening rumbled on for more than a generation and were especially influential among settlers filling the southern backcountry during the decades immediately before the war.

## VI

As the American people moved towards the Revolution they developed a political ideology which provided a philosophical basis for the new regime. It was never completely systematic nor always consistent, and was drawn from many sources. Besides Puritanism, the rational universe of the Enlightenment and English legalism, they included the traditional doctrine of the putative Anglo-Saxon ancient constitution which allegedly had provided a model system of representative government before being overthrown by the Norman conquest in 1066. Another major element was republicanism, which many scholars currently regard as the central organising principle of American Revolutionary theory. It originated with the classical tradition of Greece and Rome, which was later reinterpreted for modern use by Niccolo Machiavelli, the renaissance Florentine writer, and James Harrington, the theorist of the seventeenth-century English civil war. The theory was transmitted to the colonists partly through their reading of classical texts, but more through the eighteenth-century commonwealthmen or 'real whigs' who were the contemporary exponents of English radicalism. To a much lesser extent American Revolutionary ideology was influenced by the economic individualism associated with the operation of a free competitive market.[39] Together they provided a general theory of citizenship, social behaviour and authority. Before the Anglo-American crisis it was latent rather than active, and initially it was neither inherently anti-monarchical nor totally inconsistent with loyal membership of the British empire. But its imperatives were unleashed by the dispute and

quickly dominated the intellectual processes involved in forming independent governments.

American republicanism was especially concerned with the
moral integrity of the people since it was considered vital to
every community's welfare and prosperity.[40] The theory
recognised that civil society was frail and easily damaged, and
conceded that men had a natural tendency towards self-
centredness; the example of the fate of Greece and Rome in
this context was instructive and deeply alarming, for the
colonists concluded that both had collapsed not in face of
external attack but in consequence of internal decay and
moral turpitude. At the core of republican theory was concern
over the private integrity of the individual citizen: his honesty,
frugality, self-control, and moral self-responsibilty. Here it
came close to and was reinforced by the still-living Puritan
doctrine of 'calling': the duty of every person to serve God by
serving the community and conforming to the ethical canons
of moral behaviour.[41] Both placed great emphasis on the duty
of all men to put public welfare above private interest; this
appealed especially to elites whose status encouraged them to
identify with society as a whole. Reciprocally, a republican
form of government would assist men to pursue morally
acceptable conduct.

Republican social theory was linked particularly to two
components: the concept of a simple society, and the rational
ordered universe of enlightened science. Republican citizens
were active, autonomous members of the community who
were committed to its welfare and possessed both rights and
duties. They were sufficiently independent of the coercive
influence of others to be capable of exercising a free and
independent political judgement. The ideal citizen was the
yeoman farmer possessing his land as a freeholder rather than
a tenant. As such he was beholden to no one; he was also
sufficiently educated to be able to generate an informed
political opinion. The concept of the relationship between
citizens and their government was contractual, flowing partly
from John Locke but adapted during the Revolution to being
a contract among citizens to form a government rather than
a contract between government and subjects. In this rationally
ordered universe within which government derived its authority

from contract, it was essential that the citizens should be in certain crucial respects equal. Since colonial America was a socially differentiated society (especially one that had enslaved almost all its black inhabitants) the concept of equality caused particular difficulty. Essentially it meant equality by virtue of creation, equality of moral responsibility and equality of rights such as liberty and equal consideration of legitimate interests. Enjoyment of liberty was of prime importance for, as Jefferson indicated in the Declaration of Independence, it was a fundamental natural right.

Liberty thus meant many things and included the possession of associated rights. It incorporated the residual medieval concept of liberty as privilege, immunity or franchise granted by superior authority and guaranteed by law; thus the heart of the colonies' case against parliamentary taxation was their insistence that they enjoyed the liberty or immunity from it. This form of liberty defined the boundaries separating one powerful social entity from another; it did not protect the powerless from the powerful. Another concept of liberty was the right to security of possession – that is, enjoyment of legal title. At yet another level liberty meant the power which every man enjoys over his own actions, and his right to enjoy the fruits of his own work; this physical liberty, as the British radical writer Richard Price who was much read in America put it, was what gave a man control over his own destiny.[42] Civil liberty was the right of access to the community's network of law and justice, political liberty being the right to participate in the community's political direction, and religious liberty being the right to free religious – and in practice secular – belief and freedom from discrimination on confessional grounds. Liberty and virtue, in the sense of disinterested concern for the public interest as superior to private interest, were reciprocally essential.

Another strain of liberalism flowed from the Hobbesian and especially Lockean notions of a state of nature which preceded the social contract. According to this theory of liberty, man had been free and equal in the prior state of nature. He had formed governments for convenience. In exchange for abandoning certain natural rights he enjoyed the benefits of policing and order but added no fresh rights. The function of government was only to protect its citizens' lives, liberty and property. If it failed in this primary purpose, thus breaking the contract, the people were entitled to withdraw their consent to its authority and form a new government. This notion of the contractual basis of authority underpinned the legal case for repudiating allegiance to George III, and forming new governments; it was articulated in the Declaration of Independence. Liberty in this sense also evolved into the nineteenth-century individualism which permitted the citizen to do anything that did not harm others and was not prohibited by a minimalist government. It was philosophically compatible with the individual acting as entrepreneur in the capitalist market economy which, as Joyce Appleby has shown, was gathering strength in eighteenth-century America as well as England.[43] In this framework the citizen was socially and economically self-responsible and free to strike virtually whatever bargains he wished on the assumption that the public interest was best achieved by the consequences of men pursuing their private interests. Thus the concept of liberty that underpinned the new American governments meant several different and not entirely compatible things. Certainly it did not imply the positivist libertarianism of the twentieth century, but neither did it necessarily suggest the atomistic individualism of the nineteenth.

In many ways these differing conceptions of republicanism and liberty conflicted with one another. Classical republicanism was a public doctrine, stressing the supremacy of the community over its individual members. As such it was compatible with hierarchy and elitism since it was also static. Its ideal citizen, the independent fee-simple yeoman farmer, also represented a form of economic organisation which implied that the United States could only grow through replication rather than development and change. The historical rights doctrine represented by the ancient constitution tradition had similar limitations. Though libertarian theory based on custom and common law was capable of adaptation to changing circumstances, it could be profoundly conservative when its interpretation was entrusted to certain hands, as the English courts constantly demonstrated. Lockean liberalism, with its insistence on a contractual relationship between

citizen and limited government inaugurated for certain specified purposes, was individualistic, materialistic, instrumental
and egalitarian. In these respects it offered a political counterpart to the Smithian economic theory of the market economy
and as such was potentially developmental.

In retrospect it is evident that Lockean liberalism and
capitalist individualism became the dominant political economy of the following century, yet they failed to destroy their
rivals during the formative years of the American Revolution;
in particular the theological moral order remained influential
as a means of regulating private and public behaviour, as did
the more clearly secular principles of classical republicanism.
In reality the American mind, in its moral, scientific and
political dimensions, was diverse and pluralistic. The threads
of American ideology were interwoven so as to form a complex
and unlogical network of public thought that was at certain
points reinforced by elements such as a deep fear of insufficiently controlled government which developed from
colonial experience with British policy during the final years
of empire. This pessimism had a profound effect on American
political thinking during the Revolution.

# 3
# THE COMING OF THE
# REVOLUTION

The nature and pace of American development changed spectacularly after 1763. Long-term demographic and economic growth continued, but there was considerable short-term disruption. Development, mobility and change were themselves disturbing, and their effects were aggravated by the emergence of major problems which previously had been only latent. Almost every colony was affected. Economic difficulties developed, and a number of dysfunctional processes disturbed the prevailing social order; in some colonies the supremacy of local elites was questioned. Externally, American relations with Britain, previously harmonious on the whole, degenerated into bitter conflict. This imperial crisis aggravated domestic tensions as well as leading to war. In so doing it triggered a drastic transformation of American society and politics.

## I

In spite of the restoration of peace, the period between the Great War for Empire of 1756–63 (known as the Seven Years War in Britain and the French and Indian War in the United States) and the outbreak of the War of Independence in 1775 was frequently turbulent. One consequence of colonial engagement in overseas trade was American susceptibility to the rhythms of an economic cycle which brought recession during the early and late 1760s only moderated by recovery between 1765 and 1767 and again between 1770 and 1773. Apart from coastal South Carolina, whose rice and indigo exports were little affected, and rural New York and Pennsylvania, where

European demand for wheat and flour mitigated its effects until the end of the decade, most areas suffered. For a time British purchases of war supplies caused a boom, but once the fighting ended the supply of commercial credit shrank, leading to a recession in Boston, New York and Philadelphia which did not reach its nadir until 1768.[1] Massachusetts suffered from steady prices for its limited exports of livestock, lumber and fish at a time when the cost of imported wheat and flour was rising. In the Chesapeake area of the upper South the availability of British credit had tempted planters into excessive purchasing, often of luxury goods. When merchants began calling in their loans, especially during the early 1770s, their actions caused serious difficulties. Rich planters could ride out the storm, but smaller men could not. Increasing numbers were brought to court: the number of actions for recovery of debt in Prince George's County, Maryland, rose from 50 in 1769 to almost 120 in 1774.[2]

These difficulties were compounded by increases in the ratio of population to land and the rising price of both land and slaves in long-established counties. By mid-century, availability of land, particularly good land, was diminishing in many areas. Ordinary New England farms had shrunk to a point where they were seldom more than 100 acres in extent. In Connecticut the amount of land available per family had diminished from 404 acres in 1700 to 106 in 1770; in Suffolk County, Massachusetts, it contracted to only 43 acres by the 1780s, and in many instances the quality of soil was poor.[3] Further south, rising population, the vagaries of the tobacco market and the beginnings of soil exhaustion were having significant effects. In Prince George's County, as elsewhere, population was increasing rapidly, thus reducing the amount of land available and contributing to a rise in its price that was three times faster than that of tobacco. For those possessing extensive land and many slaves, high tobacco prices were beneficial. Others found their position deteriorating, and many younger sons were obliged to become tenants. The proportion and size of landholdings diminished for ordinary men. In four Maryland counties only 37 per cent owned land in 1771, and in All Hallows Parish the average labourer had less than the 50 acres he required for a viable family farm; by

1782 the acreage per worker contracted to only 49 in the prime tobacco growing area of the southern part of the state.[4]

Such reductions in opportunity were unlikely to lead to hunger but did require substantial adjustments if people were to accommodate to new circumstances. In practice this meant constant out-migration to new lands in the West or North, or sometimes to the cities (though they too had problems) or worse, to a peripatetic existence. Even the rich were not immune. The confidence of the Tidewater elite was unsettled by the growing practice whereby locally-based Scottish merchants threatened their economic supremacy by trading directly with planters in the interior rather than through old-established plantations. The effects of this competition were only partly reduced by the decision of many Chesapeake planters to shift from tobacco to wheat as a cash crop during the closing years of the colonial period. It brought profits but also changes, for wheat was in many ways unsuited to cultivation by slave labour and required entry to a different market-system based on milling in towns like Norfolk and Baltimore rather than direct dispatch from plantation wharves to Britain. Moreover, it undermined the self-esteem of men whose public reputation was partly based on their skill in the difficult art of producing tobacco in perfect condition. There was also disagreement among the greater planters between those who favoured western development and those who more cautiously did not. Fresh settlement in the West itself threatened the supremacy of coastal society.[5]

Urban America was undergoing stressful change at the same time. Post-war depression severely affected the three northern ports. Boston was least damaged but the limited character of its hinterland held back its growth. New York and Philadelphia expanded rapidly, spurred on by the mixed blessing of the arrival of large numbers of British, Scotch-Irish and German immigrants. New opportunities for creating wealth undoubtedly existed, but at some cost. Smaller towns began competing with larger rivals, as Salem did with Boston, Providence with Newport in Rhode Island, and Baltimore with Philadelphia. More important was a long-range trend towards greater concentration of wealth. On the eve of the Revolution the top 10 per cent of wealth-holders increased their holdings to 56 per cent in the colonies as a whole and 69 per cent in the South, but wage rates for the less affluent often failed to keep pace with rising prices. At the lower end of the social hierarchy, unemployment and insecurity among dockworkers, seamen and other unskilled and even skilled workers increased and the numbers of poor expanded greatly to a point where poverty became the norm for many people. In New York the rate of poverty increased from about 9 per 1000 to between 26 and 36 per 1000, and Boston and Philadelphia suffered similarly.[6]

Other disharmonies were more obviously political in character. At colony level there was a growing degree of political immobility. Plural officeholding was becoming more common in higher offices, and those excluded from office resented the power of their more successful rivals. The Otis family's displeasure at the influence of Thomas Hutchinson (who was president of the council, lieutenant governor and chief justice) and his family was notorious in Massachusetts. Elsewhere there was growing resentment at the presence of British placemen who blocked advancement for men such as Henry Laurens in South Carolina. James Kirby Martin has argued that there was also tension between politicians holding lower offices in the lower houses of the assemblies and county and local offices and those who held higher, generally appointive, offices which clustered round the governors.[7] Virginia escaped many of the problems that beset its neighbours, but not all. Political disagreements such as that over the pistole fee that Governor Botetourt attempted to levy on land patents in 1753, and the so-called Parsons Cause, a dispute over whether clergy of the established church should be paid in cash or tobacco, were unsettling. The scandal of Treasurer John Robinson, who on his death in 1766 was discovered to have paid large sums of retired paper money to cronies among the leading gentry instead of burning it as required by law, raised important questions as to the probity and disinterested trustworthiness of the elites.[8]

The middle colonies were similarly unsettled. Pennsylvania politics were especially turbulent. Rivalries inherent in the province's economic, social, ethnic and religious diversity were compounded by the policies of the proprietor. Many mid-century disputes revolved around the increasing activities of the Penn family and their supporters. Efforts to resolve the problem by securing a royal charter had an increasingly destabilising effect on local politics, especially when worsening relations with Britain from 1765 onwards made such a proposal seem increasingly unwise. Factionalism also characterised the politics of New York, dominated as they were by the great Hudson Valley patroons. There were other problems besides, including notably a quarrel between the governor and Assembly over the tenure of judges and the inviolability of jury decisions, efforts to establish the Anglican church, Presbyterian demands for incorporation of their own churches, and the attempt to organise King's College (now Columbia University) as an episcopal seminary.[9] The type of factionalism so evident in both colonies may have been an inevitable feature of pluralist societies, but it was often debilitating, and both provinces were disturbed by the expansion of their principal towns, and the development of commercial economies and the increasing self-interestedness of their attendant values.

Virtually every colony also suffered outbreaks of violence during the generation preceding the Revolutionary War. Some were essentially ritualistic assertions of the integrity of the crowd and served primarily as safety valves: this was clearly the case with the Pope's Day battles between North End and South End gangs that took place in Boston every fifth of November. Others were manifestations of popular belief in an unwritten yet imperative code of principles that supplemented formal law. Their purpose was often to enforce customary morality, as in the case of attacks on Boston brothels, or to defend public welfare, as when mobs forced closure of a smallpox hospital in Marblehead in 1773–4, isolation of those who had been vaccinated in Norfolk in 1768, and the protection of land titles in New Jersey and the Carolinas.[10] Actions such as these complemented rather than defied normal authority and posed little or no threat to the status quo. Some violence was directed against external targets, as in the case of frontier wars against the native Indians. Occasionally it even needed British assistance; thus Virginia and South Carolina both needed help to suppress the

Cherokee Indians in 1760, and three years later British troops were required in order to suppress Pontiac's rebellion in the northwest.

Other violence was more alarming to the elites if only because it demonstrated the limits of their supremacy. Several land riots took place in New Jersey and especially New York. From 1750 onwards the Hudson Valley landowners found their privileges and practices being challenged by their inferiors; there was particular resentment at their ostentatious behaviour during a period in which growth was temporarily slowing down. The crisis came to a head in 1766 with the so-called Tenants Revolt. When tenants on the Philipse estate bought land from Indians and refused to pay rent to landlords who had nominally been granted the land, they were taken to court and ordered to be evicted. Other tenants joined them in an anti-rent movement which led to violence that had to be suppressed by British troops. The experience was disturbing, but the riots need to be carefully interpreted. They were not so much a form of class conflict as a dispute between different groups each anxious to secure property at a time when patroons were attempting to increase profits by asserting their right to receive feudal dues such as quit rents.[11]

Two other outbursts were more serious. One flowed from the impact of Pontiac's Rebellion on western Pennsylvania, an area which had filled rapidly but was still exposed to Indian attack. Faced with continual raids during the winter of 1763–4, settlers had massacred peaceable Indians at Conestoga, and resented the protection given to refugees by the provincial government; their anger was compounded by the pacifist reputation of the powerful Quaker group. In February 1764 about 200 armed men, known as the Paxton Boys, marched on Philadelphia demanding both aid against the Indians and improved western representation in the assembly. Their challenge was parried with minor concessions, but it introduced yet another complication to provincial politics and raised questions concerning the sectional balance of power and the supremacy of the existing elite. But the greatest threat to the status quo was the Regulator Movement that began in North Carolina in 1768 and spread to South Carolina before being defeated at the Battle of the Alamance in 1771. Since the participants were mostly small to middling backcountry planters with a smattering of well-to-do ones, the movement expressed elements of western resentment of eastern control and their rhetoric had undertones of class conflict, but its character was more subtle than this suggests. The Regulators protested against what they claimed were excessive taxes, but also expressed resentment at the corruption and embezzlement practised by public officials in their rapidly developing area; they also deplored the arrival of lawyers and merchants. But though their stated purpose was only to restore the status quo, their actions challenged the right of old-established gentry to rule the newer areas on the grounds that they were failing to provide the necessary conditions of law and order which would enable hardworking settlers to flourish and develop their landholdings.[12]

Arguably more important than the violence was the emergence of a popular religious and intellectual culture that challenged the hegemony of the elite. Theological speculation was directed primarily at spiritual concerns, but had profound secular implications, especially in new communities which needed firm ideological principles to sustain them. The consequences were compounded by the organisational weaknesses of all churches, which made it very difficult for them to impose solutions in cases of internal dispute. The most potent of colonial belief-systems, Calvinist protestantism, exercised great influence when revived during the Great Awakening of the 1730s and 1740s. Its doctrine of the inescapable depravity of human nature had been used in seventeenth-century Massachusetts to justify the supremacy of government as a means of curbing mankind's corruption, but the 'new light' Calvinism that emerged a century later was corrosive of traditional forms of authority in spite of the wishes of conservatives. It also possessed a much stronger millenarian content than previously: a millenarianism that could be directed towards secular as well as spiritual purposes. By insisting on individual experience, responsibility and redemption it postulated an intellectual and spiritual equality of all men that threatened the traditions and practices of established civil and ecclesiastical authority. By implying that the elite were morally no better than their social inferiors it raised the self-esteem of the lower orders, who became increasingly reluctant to submit unquestioningly to a hierarchical social order whose hegemony derived in part from the purported moral superiority of the elite.[13] The radical implications of this doctrine were not fully worked out before the Revolution, nor were they accepted by all those who were influenced by the Awakening, but the attitudes it engendered continued to ferment.

The immediate effects of the Great Awakening were to intensify ecclesiastical factionalism. The fragmentation of religious sects continued, even in New England where religion was central to communal cohesion. Previously dominant churches were challenged by dissenters. Some ministers, notably Jonathan Mayhew and Charles Chauncy in Boston, continued to fly the flag of rational Christianity, but many congregations divided over the issue. The effect of this, when coupled to growing commercialisation, became clearly visible in Connecticut. By 1765 the established Congregational Church was no longer an agency of social control or a symbol of communal coherence, but was only the religion of the majority. The religious heterogeneity of the middle colonies was further intensified, though the inherent equalitarianism of the Quakers' doctrine of the inner light was muted by their quietist political stance. In Virginia the backcountry was being occupied by men whose values and outlook were also shaped by the Great Awakening, and many people abandoned the established church in favour of the new sects. The Baptists in particular gathered substantial numbers. Without being radical democrats in a political sense, their strong commitment to equal fellowship which admitted even slaves to membership of individual congregations, their location of authority in individual churches, their salvationism and their concern for the restoration of virtue in the community also posed threats to the elite's customary supremacy. They did not challenge order as such, quite the reverse, but offered an alternative model to traditional prescriptive hierarchy; their ultimate authority was not secular but that of God discovered by personal experience. Their challenge was further strengthened by the expansion of Methodism, which similarly emphasised the oral culture of the people and individual interpretation of scripture rather than written culture and biblical interpretation by authority.[14]

These developments were accompanied during the 1760s by a significant increase in aspirations among the middling and lower orders of white society. Their interests were developing beyond the specific concerns of particular groups such as the wartime fear of impressment among sailors and dockworkers. Growing awareness of the extent to which the elite needed their support during the struggle with Britain, coupled to relatively high levels of education encouraged them to articulate claims that went beyond the customary enforcement of traditional values and the regulation of market prices for food in time of shortage. Instead, urban artisans and mechanics (often men of modest wealth), and even unskilled labourers began to claim the right to express broad political opinions; as the Anglican minister Jacob Duché sourly remarked in 1772, 'the poorest laborer upon the shore of the Delaware thinks himself entitled to deliver his sentiments in matters of religion and politics with as much freedom as the gentleman and the scholar'.[15]

Yet no true sense of class solidarity emerged. In Boston the lower orders were generally quiescent in relation to their social superiors, though not in relation to the town's deteriorating relations with Britain. New York artisans were as divided as others in relation to the factional politics of that province. Many were economic clients of conservative merchants, landlords and lawyers, and the system of open voting exposed them to pressure from above. Neither was there any sense of unity between urban workers and their counterparts among the rural poor and tenant farmers of the Hudson Valley and Chesapeake. Only in Philadelphia did a sense of artisan unity develop with some success, especially over non-importation and closure of the port of Boston in 1774. But the idea of equality, previously more nominal than substantive, began to take hold as an ambition, and rhetoric sometimes became stridently egalitarian. One writer expressed the logic of the position succinctly by declaring that: 'As all Men sprang from the same common Parent they were all originally equal, and all equally free.'[16] Many artisans and small farmers began to believe that the rich had interests different from their own, and came to challenge the implicit confidence of the elite that they alone possessed the capacity and right to govern. In its crudest form their belief consisted of a jealous conviction that the rich were exploiting the privileges of public authority to their own private advantage, yet they had no wish to attack property as such, for many artisans in the towns and small farmers in rural areas were themselves modest property-owners and consequently recognised the legitimacy of property rights. Also, in the South the aspirations of poorer whites were modified by their acceptance of the need to maintain racial solidarity in face of the enslaved labour force of blacks.

Nevertheless, elites found their position less secure than they wished. One behavioural mode, in which they aped idealised English models, was dangerous since it relied on English society living up to expectations they imposed upon it; implicitly it depended on continued Anglo-American harmony.[17] Further, the market-oriented values of an increasingly commercial economy were at odds with the more traditional principles of hierarchy. Social complexity, political factionalism and expansion made the problem especially acute in the middle colonies. More fundamentally, perhaps, the social and economic gap between elites and other whites was insufficient to justify claims to prescriptive authority comparable to that of the English aristocracy. Thus traditional social relationships between men of different social status which were based on trust, reciprocity of obligations and respect were beginning to disintegrate during the years before independence.

The American colonies were going through a tense and stressful period on the eve of the Revolution. The nature of the unease varied from colony to colony, and perhaps only Connecticut and South Carolina remained largely undisturbed. However, the intensity of the unease should not be exaggerated. Whether caused by the effects of the economic cycle, a credit crisis in the early 1770s, or shrinking availability of land, growing concentration of wealth in cities coupled to rising poverty, economic dislocation in the upper South caused by the transfer from tobacco to wheat production or the ramifications of the Great Awakening, it was insufficient by itself to challenge immediately the integrity of colonial society. Moreover, the evidence suggests that although the new communities in the Virginia and Carolina backcountry started as relatively egalitarian frontier communities, they increasingly aspired to imitate the older Tidewater societies once they became more stable and coherent as communities. They worked to create a prosperous commercial market-oriented and competitive economy, and wished to exploit dependent people whose enslavement brought great profit to their white owners. In time they wished to construct additional hierarchical societies in which economic rewards and political power would go to the 'best' people who would control the new communities along traditional lines.[18] The process was complete in the older-established counties of the Shenandoah Valley, but was far from complete in Lunenburg County, in Virginia's southside, or the newly settled areas of the Carolina backcountry.

It is possible, perhaps probable, that all these problems could have been resolved within the existing Anglo-American community had not other events intervened. What the tensions did was to create an unstable context within which the imperial dispute would take place. Conversely, the deterioration of relations with Britain heightened American sensitivities over a range of political, ideological, cultural and economic issues, and aggravated tensions already present in colonial society.

## II

Within twenty years thirteen loyal colonies became one independent republic. Their separation from Britain had been anticipated for many years on both sides of the Atlantic, but at mid-century disunion was still presumed to be several generations in the future. Most people in Britain – and some in America – believed the colonies were still immature and thus needed British protection; they concluded that American best interests lay in remaining within the empire, and regarded the possibility of imminent independence as absurd. Later events demonstrated their mistake, and in retrospect it is evident that the seeds of independence, sown at the moment of settlement, were rapidly growing seedlings by 1750. Yet the process was far from a straightforward linear progression. Alternative paths of development presented themselves at several points, and the timing of separation was unanticipated. Rapid development and rising maturity placed the colonial connection with Britain under increasing strain, especially in the 1760s, but neither economic nor political self-interest were sufficient to outweigh conclusively the advantages flowing from membership of the empire and the psychological bonds of affection. Almost all Americans came to consider independence as a desirable goal only when their dispute with Britain reached crisis point in the mid-1770s. Until that time their actions consisted far more of *ad hoc* responses to unfolding British policy than purposive intentions of their own.

In particular, continental unity was much more a product than a precursor of the Revolution. Before the eve of the imperial crisis the colonies were still only thirteen links in a chain of settlements stretching from Newfoundland and Nova Scotia in modern Canada, through the West Indies to the mainland of central America. Each had formal political ties with Britain but none with its sister colonies. Many customary features of nationhood were missing: the army, customs service and post office were British, and there was no single established church, legal system or monetary system, neither was there a continental elite. The highest level of community for pre-Revolutionary Americans was not the continent but the empire. Commonality consisted largely of shared experience as subordinate members of a wider imperial society. American acceptance of this situation is demonstrated by their frequent protestations of loyalty to the crown, and more substantively by military contributions to Britain's North American campaigns during the eighteenth-century wars; colonial troops participated in central American campaigns and the capture of Louisburg in 1745 and Québec in 1759. At most there was some regional unity, but it was defined more by differences from other regions than by internal cohesion.

Feuding among neighbouring colonies was almost constant. Much revolved around political boundaries, but some was more serious and led to violence. New York and New Hampshire each laid claim to the area that became the separate state of Vermont during the Revolution. Virginia and Maryland quarrelled bitterly over control of the Potomac river, and rivalry between Virginians and Pennsylvanians around Pittsburg threatened to get out of hand. Most serious of all was rivalry between Connecticut and Pennsylvania. A Connecticut group, organised as the Susquehanna Company, claimed that their colony's charter extended from sea to sea and thus included part of Pennsylvania. From 1754 onwards they settled in the Wyoming Valley of interior Pennsylvania, but ignored Pennsylvania law; by 1771 there were 3000 settlers. After attempts to drive them out failed they organised themselves as part of Connecticut, and in 1774 they sent representatives to its assembly.[19] There was also much jostling between companies speculating in land west of the Appalachians, and especially among speculators and settlers from those provinces that possessed no western land and the governments of those that did. Andrew Burnaby, an English clergyman who visited America in 1759, judged that the colonies were so different from each other that 'were they left to themselves, there would soon be civil war, from one end of the continent to the other'.[20]

By contrast several features of mid-century America were conducive to unity. The topography of North America emphasised the geographic coherence of the thirteen colonies in relation to the British settlements in Canada (which faced the northern Atlantic rather than southwards), the Spanish empire west and south of the Mississippi, and both the British and French colonies in the Caribbean. Cultural dependence on Britain and shared Protestantism bound the colonies to each other, and there were increasing numbers of intercolonial connections and associations. Sects such as the Quakers and Presbyterians held regional meetings, and the evangelical Great Awakening extended across almost every colony. The American Philosophical Society had members in every colony except North Carolina, scientists observed the transit of Venus in virtually every centre from Philadelphia to Providence, and the *Pennsylvania Journal* had numerous subscribers throughout the middle colonies and Chesapeake and a few in every other colony. How far this had already led to

cultural convergence, and whether it was leading inexorably
to national unity is debatable, but there were other influences
at work. Gradual improvement of roads supplemented sea
communications, and intercolonial commerce increased considerably; between 1734 and 1772 the number of ships trading
between major colonial ports quadrupled. This increase had
significant political consequences during a period in which the
number of American newspapers published rose from 9 to 38.
By 1775 not only was there six times more news of other
provinces' affairs in each colony's newspapers, but according
to Richard L. Merritt the papers contained far more of what
he calls 'symbols of American community' such as the words
'American', 'continental', and 'united colonies' than symbols
implying membership of the empire. Especially after 1763 the
newspapers increasingly implied the existence of an American
political community possessing interests different from those
of Britain.[21]

By the 1760s a potential framework for union was slowly
but uncertainly emerging. It was still tenuous and lacked
formal institutions. Such formal precedents as existed were
not encouraging. The British government had attempted to
force several colonies into a Dominion of New England in the
1680s but was thwarted. The Albany Congress had drafted a
plan of union under the supervision of Benjamin Franklin in
1754, but only the New England colonies, New York, Pennsylvania and Maryland had attended, and it came to nothing.
After 1763 British policy drastically changed the context of
colonial politics. It encouraged incipient American nationalism and propelled the colonies towards voluntary union.

## III

British victory in the great War for Empire precipitated the
Anglo-American crisis by creating a major problem of imperial
reorganisation. General James Wolfe's capture of Québec in
1759 led to withdrawal of France from what became modern
Canada and the Mississippi Valley, and Spain from Florida.
British acquisition of these vast territories required that the
newly extended North American empire should be placed on

a regular and systematic footing; in particular it was necessary to establish British government in Canada and reorganise defence of the new territory against Indian risings and attacks and the possibility of French or Spanish revanchism. In anticipation of a continuing struggle against France and in the interest of economic development it was also thought necessary to strengthen imperial authority in America. Logic as well as policy suggested the desirability of stronger central direction, and the subordination of local colonial interests to the greater good of the empire as a whole. Necessarily, it was assumed, overall command and responsibility for formulating general policy would rest with the British government in London. Previous attempts to assert British authority, particularly between 1748 and 1756, had led to few results before being interrupted by war. This time the government felt that reform was essential, even if it took time to formulate and implement a coherent policy.[22]

From 1763 onwards a sequence of unstable British administrations attempted with diminishing success to deal with the colonial problem. Frequent changes of leadership prevented articulation of a consistent long-term policy, and the greater political stability achieved under the premiership of Lord North after 1770 failed to improve matters. With the possible exception of Charles Townshend, Chancellor of the Exchequer from 1766 until his death the following year, no British minister had any deliberate wish to restrict or diminish American domestic liberty or impose authoritarian administration on the colonies. But each was obliged to take careful account of British opinion inside and out of parliament, notably the common belief that Americans were neither contributing sufficiently towards the cost of their own defence nor carrying their fair share of the burden of imperial affairs. Widespread horror at the increase of the national debt to £130 million, much of which was due in British eyes to recent campaigns in America, also had to be reckoned with. Inescapably British policies impinged on the inhabitants of the thirteen seaboard colonies, and especially those who had commercial interests and ambitions west of the Appalachians. Government intentions (though not perhaps the unintentional consequences likely to flow from official policies) were increasingly misunderstood by the colonists. As time passed, Americans of all shades of opinion except those most clearly identified with British authority became persuaded that ministerial intentions threatened their personal liberty, political autonomy and economic development.

The first phase of the crisis lasted intermittently for ten years. It began with formation of a new ministry by George Grenville in 1763. A Proclamation in October of that year dealt with the new territories by establishing temporary governments in Québec and East and West Florida, and prohibiting for the time being the granting of new lands and the establishment of fresh settlements west of a line drawn along the Appalachian watershed. Twenty battalions of British troops were posted permanently to the Americas for the first time. Most were sent to the frontier, where they could defend the recently extended empire and manage Indian affairs; whether they were intended to maintain British authority in the colonies is uncertain. There is no positive evidence to support such a judgement though it was clearly intended that the Americans should pay their costs.[23] Responsibility for relations with the indigenous Indians was assigned to civilian superintendents. This attempt to devise a policy that would both protect the interests of Indians and satisfy Euro-American land speculators and settlers was expensive and proved to be unenforceable. A second element in Grenville's programme consisted of strengthening trade legislation, improving the efficiency of collecting customs duties and raising revenue for colonial defence. The Sugar, Plantation or Revenue Act of 1764 did this by reorganising the system of levying duties on American imports and in particular halving the molasses duty to 3 pence (3d.) per gallon and tightening customs procedures; raising revenue was only a secondary objective. The Currency Act of the same year extended to other colonies the prohibition on issuing paper money previously imposed on New England in 1751. It aroused considerable opposition since the colonies were habitually short of specie. It also threatened to inhibit commercial activity at a period of post-war economic difficulty.

A third piece of legislation provoked great fury. Grenville's Stamp Act, foreshadowed in 1763 and enacted in 1765, was explicitly intended to raise revenue to finance American defence by imposing duties on a wide range of legal and other documents, newspapers and other items. A few minor precedents apart, the principle of a direct internal tax was new, and raised a host of questions about the extent of parliamentary power in America and the claim of colonial legislatures to the exclusive right to impose taxes within their respective limits. Several colonies had already protested against the Sugar Act on constitutional and commercial grounds, but the American position was ambivalent, as James Otis of Massachusetts demonstrated. He argued hard in *The Rights of the British Colonies Asserted and Proved* that there was no distinction between an internal tax and an external tax on trade, and insisted that both could be imposed only by colonial assemblies – but inconsistently went on to argue on both sides of the proposition that parliamentary power was absolute.[24]

Opposition to the Stamp Act became vehement and sometimes violent. Americans resented Grenville's refusal to respond to their petitions while the bill was passing through parliament, and their opposition intensified once its text became known. Virginia's House of Burgesses gave the lead by adopting five resolutions proposed by Patrick Henry, a young backcountry lawyer. They declared that the colonies enjoyed all the rights possessed by British subjects in England, and especially insisted that the House alone had the right to raise taxation in Virginia. A fifth resolution, which was rescinded, warned that any outside attempt to impose taxation was unconstitutional and would destroy British as well as American liberty. In Boston the response led to violence. The stamp distributor was compelled to resign his post and opposition came to a climax with the systematic destruction of Lieutenant Govenor Thomas Hutchinson's house. By November only the Georgia distributor had not been coerced into resigning.

Four other developments emphasised the scale of colonial resistance and set precedents for the future. The rise of the Sons of Liberty, first in New York then elsewhere, created a framework for collaborative action. Membership of the Sons and other groups was socially widened as new men were brought in. Members of the upper ranks of colonial society served on committees in some areas such as Newport R.I., Virginia, and North Carolina, but in New York many members came from the middle ranks and John Lamb and Isaac Sears were self-made men; in Charleston the Sons of Liberty were mostly artisans of some substance, and considerable efforts were made to widen the social base by holding mass meetings and involving the 'body of the people'.[25] Delegates from nine colonies held the extra-legal Stamp Act Congress in New York and passed a series of collective resolutions, and merchants began a non-importation movement as an instrument with which to apply pressure on Britain. Well before the end of the year the Act had been effectively nullified. But its repeal in 1766 resulted from a change of government made for domestic reasons and pressure from British merchants, not from colonial action. The new administration led by the Marquess of Rockingham reasserted parliament's right to legislate for the colonies in all cases whatsoever by passing a Declaratory Act to that effect, though Americans were carefully permitted to interpret it as excluding taxation.[26]

Repeal of the Stamp Act appeared to end the crisis. Its resolution was superficially confirmed by colonial acquiescence in the accompanying Revenue Act which was a tax-raising measure as well as a regulatory one – one which brought in more revenue through improved methods of collection in spite of lowering the molasses duty still further to one penny per gallon. Yet first impressions were misleading. Hostility to the Stamp Act had been unexpectedly extensive and deep, and acceptance of the 1766 Revenue Act was grudging; the colonists had also denied the validity of any form of British taxation which might be imposed on them even though Benjamin Franklin, Pennsylvania's agent in London, and others had attempted to distinguish between external taxation on trade, which was acceptable, and internal taxation, which was not.[27] Moreover, the Act had extended parliamentary authority and challenged the principles of government as understood by the colonists. Perhaps politically more important, it threatened to neutralise one of the most effective instruments available to colonial assemblies by challenging their exclusive right to authorise taxation and, by extension, to control expenditure.

Within eighteen months the dispute flared up again. Local disputes over issues such as quartering British troops, the effect of the Currency Act, and compensation for damage caused during the Stamp Act riots in Massachusetts rumbled on continuously. In England the newly appointed Chancellor of the Exchequer, Charles Townshend, decided to reassert the authority of parliament and raise a revenue. In 1767 an act was passed suspending the New York legislature until it agreed to implement the Quartering Act, and at the same time Townshend carefully skirted American objections to taxation when imposing duties on tea, glass, paper, printer's colours and red and white lead. The proceeds were assigned partly to defence, as in previous legislation, but primarily – and far more importantly – to supporting royal government in the colonies by paying judges' and officials' salaries, thus giving them a substantial measure of freedom from the assemblies upon whom they had previously depended for their pay.[28] Finally, machinery for enforcing the duties was created by establishing a Board of Customs Commissioners whose head-quarters were provocatively located in Boston, and a year later erecting Vice-Admiralty courts, three of which were placed in Boston, New York and Philadelphia.

Colonial reaction took some time to develop. In October the Boston Town Meeting organised a non-importation policy in New England with the reluctant support of merchants, and protested against what it insisted was the introduction of arbitrary government. Two months later John Dickinson, a Philadelphia lawyer who was already active in provincial politics and would later play a prominent role in continental affairs, formulated the American position in his *Letters from a Farmer in Pennsylvania*, which was quickly reprinted in other colonies and also in England. He conceded that parliament could regulate trade and acknowledged that the process might bring in some incidental revenue, but denied that any duty could be imposed which had the prime object of producing tax, and raised the temperature further by warning of the possibility of an extension of authoritarian government to America.[29] Besides petitioning the crown, Boston radicals led by Samuel Adams (one of the few men to have wanted independence before the final crisis) persuaded the Massachusetts assembly to send a Circular Letter to all other legislatures in February 1768 in order to encourage concerted action. It argued that parliament derived its authority from the constitution and could not overstep its limits, and insisted that the Townshend duties infringed American rights since the colonists were represented not in parliament but only in their own assemblies. The Circular Letter was well received, and other lower houses petitioned the king. Conversely the Earl of Hillsborough, the Secretary of State for American Affairs, exacerbated tension greatly by instructing Governor Francis Bernard to order the Massachusetts legislature to rescind its letter, and dispatching his own circular letter to all other governors requiring them to dissolve any legislature which considered the Massachusetts circular. Members of the Massachusetts legislature were applauded when they refused to obey, and following the Boston example the colonies organised a series of non-importation and non-consumption agreements; the efforts of customs men to collect the duties were resisted to considerable effect. The October arrival of two British regiments to aid the civil authorities in Boston reinforced the Americans' worst fears as to the government's real intentions. By early 1769 it was apparent that collecting the duties would be difficult. On 5 March 1770 those on glass, china, paper and other minor items, which had brought in trifling sums, were repealed as a symbolic gesture. The threepenny tax on tea, which had been lucrative, was retained; by continuing it the government maintained the central principle that parliament was entitled to levy duties.[30]

On the evening of the same day in Boston the dispute took a further dramatic turn. Violence between British troops and civilians had become common, and in January a man had been killed by soldiers at Golden Hill in New York City, and a customs man had killed a boy in Boston. But when frightened British soldiers killed five men in King Street it was termed a Massacre. The event quickly entered colonial demonology and fears of British intentions were greatly heightened.

For three more years the crisis simmered with occasional flare-ups. Anglo-American trade resumed at a high level. Repeal of all but the duty on tea divided the conservative merchants from more radical agitators, thus destroying the solidarity of the non-importation policy, which collapsed. But appearances were again deceptive. Several legislatures engaged in niggling disputes with their royal governors. In North Carolina the legislature defied the governor by adding to every pertinent statute a clause permitting the courts to attach property owned by non-residents (in practice British merchants) against debts they owed to residents. Governor Sir James Wright of Georgia infuriated his legislators in 1771 by dissolving the house early and vetoing the next choice of speaker. What happened in South Carolina was more ominous. In common with many other Americans, South Carolinians were increasingly if erroneously persuaded that Britain was pursuing a concerted programme to suppress their liberty and establish an authoritarian regime. They were also convinced that the recent expulsion of John Wilkes from the House of Commons was evidence that the government was pursuing a similar strategy in England and that it was linked to events in America as part of a single crisis. In 1769 the house of assembly donated £1500 to the Wilkite cause. A furious row with successive governors broke out which virtually prevented the conduct of normal business until it was overtaken by events in 1774. Continuing resentment over the manner by which British officials attempted to implement customs regulations alienated powerful men such as Henry Laurens of South Carolina, John Hancock of Massachusetts and John Brown of Rhode Island. One consequence was that customs men and naval officers found it almost impossible to secure convictions in local courts, even if the evidence was incontrovertible. In 1772 a number of Rhode Islanders burned to the waterline the *Gaspee*, a naval vessel which had run aground, but escaped prosecution since no witnesses would testify against them.

Over the same period individuals such as Samuel and John Adams in Massachusetts, Alexander McDougall in New York, Samuel Chase in Maryland and Patrick Henry in Virginia were constructing political careers based on sustained opposition to Britain.[31] During the same year as the *Gaspee* incident an event of even greater significance took place in Massachusetts. Rumours were confirmed that Thomas Hutchinson, who had been appointed governor in 1770, and five senior judges were being paid out of customs revenue. This gave Samuel Adams the opportunity to organise opposition by constructing a colony-wide network through encouraging each town to appoint a committee of correspondence. A year later, from March 1773 onwards, the provincial assemblies established their own committees of correspondence at the instigation of the Virginia House of Burgesses, which had become greatly alarmed by British actions in New England.

A secondary controversy ran simultaneously with these political issues. For many years non-Anglicans, especially in New England where the Church of England was increasingly fashionable, although Congregationalists and others remained in a substantial majority, were alarmed by the prospect that a bishop might be appointed for the colonies. Their concern lay not with the spiritual welfare and discipline of Anglicans but with the potential consequences of such a development for America as a whole. They feared that arrival of a bishop would herald a sustained campaign to bring new members into the Church at the expense of their own congregations. More particularly they also feared that establishment of a bishopric would bring in its train the apparatus of ecclesiastical authority over non-members that English dissenters found so offensive. Worse, they were afraid that an Anglican hierarchy would be closely tied to royal authority in the colonies and provide powerful support for it. Ironically this prospect was no more welcome among many Anglican gentry of the South since it threatened to reduce their effective power over local parish clergy. The proposal caused particular alarm in New England during the 1760s but the storm appeared to have blown over before its revival after 1770 caused alarm to Virginians.[32] As with other irritants it was quickly subsumed into the general dispute. Whether justified or not, fears aroused by these incidents heightened colonial suspicions as to the direction of British policy.

IV

On 16 December 1773 the Boston Tea Party initiated a final pre-war phase of the Anglo-American dispute. The affair was provoked by Lord North's decision to ease the East India Company's acute financial crisis by permitting it to sell tea in America through its own agents rather than by the less profitable public auction procedure. He also insisted on retaining the threepenny tax in order to reassert the principle of parliamentary authority as well as to provide revenue to pay colonial officials. The financial threat to colonial merchants engaged in selling smuggled tea was considerable and the political implications were highly alarming in light of events over the previous decade. Deepening suspicions of the British ministry's ultimate purposes determined radical leaders in the major ports of New York, Philadelphia, Charleston and Boston to resist the landing of tea. In these ports the tea was not landed or in the case of Charleston not distributed. At Boston, where the Patriots had been constantly at odds with Governor Hutchinson, the crisis exploded. Townsmen and local committees of correspondence agreed that the tea should be neither landed nor sold. Once three teaships arrived a temporary impasse was reached. On one side customs officials insisted that the duty must be paid and the governor refused to allow the ships to depart; on the other, Patriots prevented the cargo from being landed. When a group of masked men cut through the deadlock by throwing 90,000 pounds of tea into the harbour, both Britain and the Patriots realised that a trial of strength had begun.

Declining to act on executive authority alone, Lord North proposed and parliament quickly approved in March and May 1774 a series of four Coercive Acts. Collectively they were designed to strengthen British authority in Massachusetts and secure colonial dependence on the Crown and Parliament. The Boston Port Act closed the town's port until compensation was paid for the destroyed tea and other riot damage. The Massachusetts Government Act amended the colony's charter by substituting a royally appointed council for one elected by the lower house, thus extending substantially royal authority to appoint judges, local officials and select jurymen, and subordinating town meetings to the governor's control. A third act directed specifically against Massachusetts was the Administration of Justice Act which permitted trials of revenue officials for capital offences committed in the course of duty to be held outside the province if the governor thought it desirable; its purpose was to circumvent the notorious bias of local juries against royal officials in customs and government cases.[33] During the ensuing summer the customs house was moved to Plymouth and the capital to Salem, both by administrative action. The fourth act, the Quartering Act, was directed towards all the colonies and authorised the governor or commander-in-chief to billet troops in unoccupied private buildings without obtaining the consent of local justices. When taken together the four statutes were labelled 'Intolerable Acts' by the colonists.

American determination to resist the new policy was intensified by the arrival in May of General Thomas Gage, the commander-in-chief in America, as military governor of Massachusetts, and three more regiments of soldiers. News of a fifth act further outraged American opinion during the summer. The Quebec Act extended the boundaries of that province south of the Great Lakes to the junction of the Ohio and Mississippi rivers, confirmed continuance of the French civil code, established an executive system of government in Canada and permitted the Roman Catholic Church to remain established there. Though not formally one of the Coercive or Intolerable Acts it seemed cognate in character and raised additional fears over the thrust of British policy.

Just as the British government had interpreted the Tea Party as a challenge that could not be ignored, so the colonists saw the Intolerable Acts as requiring vigorous response. As David Ramsay of South Carolina argued, they seemed to be 'a complete system of tyranny' and every colony could see that policies presently directed at Massachusetts could be quickly directed elsewhere.[34] Yet not every action by the Bostonians attracted general support. Resistance to the landing of tea was almost universal – at Annapolis, Maryland, the tea ship *Peggy Stewart* was burnt along with its cargo in October – and there was strong sympathy for Boston when news of the closure of its port spread to other colonies. But there was little enthusiasm for reviving economic coercion as a political instrument since the previous non-importation agreements had disintegrated, and the Boston radicals' Solemn League and Covenant which proposed a far-reaching boycott of British goods was felt to be premature and divisive. It met with little support elsewhere – even among other Bostonians.[35] An alternative strategy, proposed first by the Providence, Rhode Island, town meeting, then in Connecticut, New York, Philadelphia and Virginia, and accepted by the Boston radicals and Massachusetts legislature at what proved to be its final meeting as a colonial institution on 17 June (it was dissolved by the new governor, Thomas Gage), was to call a congress of all the colonies. The previous year such a proposal had been regarded as dangerously provocative. In the changed circumstances of 1774 it was considered to be restrained and its purpose far from radical.[36] In New York and Pennsylvania in particular, conservative Patriots saw it as an opportunity to out-manoeuvre their more radical and socially inferior rivals, and in each case managed to secure the election of moderate delegates. However Virginia's call went beyond earlier suggestions for colony-wide congresses by recommending that the proposed body should meet annually to discuss 'those general measures which the united efforts of America may from time to time require'.[37]

Only in retrospect can the First Continental Congress, which met in Philadelphia from 5 September to 26 October 1774, be seen as the first stage of independent American government. Initially its purpose was to organise protest, and formally its business was conducted within the frame of a continuing Anglo-American empire. The outcome of the crisis remained unclear to participants on both sides of the struggle. Of the 56 members, Pennsylvania and Rhode Island alone were represented by delegates chosen by their full legislatures, and Massachusetts by its lower house. Elsewhere delegates were nominated by extra-legal bodies: provincial congresses, conventions and mass meetings and in Connecticut by the Committee of Correspondence. Only Georgia failed to send any.[38] Among its members were a few radicals such as Samuel and John Adams of Massachusetts, Thomas Mifflin of Pennsylvania, Patrick Henry and Richard Henry Lee of Virginia and Christopher Gadsden of South Carolina. Most, like Joseph Galloway of Pennsylvania, and John Jay and James Duane of New York, were moderates.

The importance of the issues raised by the prospect of the

Congress can be measured by the debate in the press. Three pamphlets stand out by advancing the colonial argument. Dickinson argued in *An Essay on the Constitutional Power of Great Britain over the Colonies in America* that parliament's right to regulate trade derived not from any supreme authority over the colonies, but from its position as representative of the mother country and thus its ability to be the best judge in commercial matters. Furthermore, he declared, regulations must be to the benefit of the colonies as well as Britain. Thomas Jefferson, whom illness prevented from representing Virginia, presented advice which was published as *A Summary View of the Rights of British America*. He argued that the colonies had a natural right to free trade and criticised George III, whom he insisted was no more than a chief magistrate who could execute the powers of each state within its own boundaries, but could not impose the authority of one (i.e. Britain) on the others (i.e. the colonies). A third writer, James Wilson of Pennsylvania, went further in *Considerations on the Authority of Parliament*. In it he denied all parliamentary authority over American affairs, including control over commerce, and argued that colonial allegiance was solely to the king.

The outcome of Congress's deliberations was a series of statements justifying the colonists' position. During its meeting Congress approved the Suffolk Resolves, brought from Boston where they had originated. Their preamble, which declared that George III was only sovereign by virtue of compact, was inflammatory, and the substance went on to propose civil disobedience to Gage's administration and recommend commercial resistance and military training. At first sight Congress's action was radical, but in reality its purpose was to bring Massachusetts under collective continental control rather than incite it to fresh action.[39]

More importantly, it was the first colonial meeting other than the Albany Congress of 20 years earlier to have had a plan of continental union placed before it. Joseph Galloway's Plan of Union proposed an all-colony Grand Council which would have a president appointed by the crown and would function as an inferior branch of the British parliament. Debate was close. A procedural vote to postpone consideration effectively killed the proposal, but this was passed by only six colonies to five. As Jack Rakove has pointed out, Galloway had conceded too much by creating a royal official with powers greater than those of existing governors and allowing parliament a veto over colonial legislation; delegates were convinced that the problem lay in excessive claims to authority by ministers and parliament, not the inadequacy of colonial legislatures.[40] Instead, Congress issued a Declaration of Colonial Rights and Grievances, which asserted the exclusive right of colonial assemblies to legislate and impose taxes. Though repudiating parliamentary claims to authority and listing 13 acts since 1763 which violated American rights, the Declaration allowed parliament to regulate American trade by consent but denied its right to appoint colonial councils or to station soldiers in any colony without its legislature's approval.

Even more crucial was approval of the Association. As a non-importation, non-consumption and non-exporting agreement, it was intended as a peaceful means of persuading the British government to redress American grievances. Non-importation would begin on 1 December 1774, non-consumption on 1 March and non-exportation, the most drastic, on 1 September 1775. It also set out detailed regulations for enforcement and called for election of committees of inspection. Debates were vigorous, but there was broad agreement on the two central issues. Only Galloway opposed non-exportation; everyone condemned the principle of parliamentary supremacy.[41] The First Continental Congress ended by publishing a series of addresses to the king, and the peoples of America, Britain and Canada, and agreeing to meet again on 10 May 1775.

During the winter 1774–5 Britain and the colonies drifted towards war. General Gage, both commander-in-chief and governor of Massachusetts, organised defences against a possible uprising by fortifying Boston and demanding 20,000 additional troops from Britain. By supplying only 4000 the British government aggravated American fears, without sending sufficient troops to be effective. In England, George III and Lord North ignored American petitions. In February 1775 the government reasserted parliamentary supremacy, rejected Lord Chatham's conciliatory proposals, and enacted a transparent scheme which was intended to give the colonies the illusion of exclusive control over taxation while enabling parliament to retain the substance. Parliament passed two more bills, first to restrain New England trade and then to extend the restriction to all other colonies except New York, Georgia and North Carolina, which it believed would be more loyal. In March the government also drafted a declaration that Massachusetts was in rebellion.

Across the Atlantic the colonists began to organise systematic opposition. Throughout the colonies, town and county committees and congresses were quickly established to enforce the Continental Congress's Association. Their actions were frequently coercive, but their increasing effectiveness had a potent and crucial role in continuing the task of politicising the population that had begun during the Stamp Act crisis. In South Carolina enforcement was controlled from the provincial congress and in Maryland and Virginia, which had already begun the process during the summer of 1774, county committees enforced it with a zeal far greater than that displayed in supporting the earlier non-importation agreement. North Carolina was divided and Georgia took no action. Unsurprisingly in view of the heterogeneous social structure of the middle colonies there was much opposition to the Association in New York and Pennsylvania, though it was rigorously enforced in New York City. Moreover, political activity was marked by an important extension of political participation. In Maryland the Congress was taken over by popular leaders, and in Virginia mass meetings elected many men who had not previously held office to the county committees. In Philadelphia new men of lower social status were constantly being brought into active politics, and the Committee of Inspection and Observation was dominated by radicals who were predominantly artisans and less affluent than previous committees had been. In Pennsylvania as a whole, the beginnings emerged of what became the important alliance between Philadelphia and the backcountry farmers. At the assembly elections in October Galloway and his allies were replaced by Dickinson, Charles Thomson and other new men. Moreover, throughout the colonies the Association ceased to be a semi-voluntary policy acceded to by consent, however reluctant. It represented the compulsory, if extra-legal, authority of the majority.

In some colonies the preparations were more explicit. At the heart of the storm, New Englanders resisted implementation of the Intolerable Acts, hunted 'tories' and began to collect arms and train their militia for action. Early in October 1774 delegates elected to the meeting of the Massachusetts legislature which had been cancelled by Gage resolved themselves into a Provincial Congress. From then onwards it was the Congress rather than the governor which exercised effective authority in the province. Many other colonies, particularly Virginia, began preparing for war but ironically the Massachusetts Provincial Congresses were deadlocked over the question of establishing an army during the winter of 1774–5. And even during the last months of peace virtually all Americans continued to hope that a solution could be found within the framework of a continuing Anglo-American connection.

Fighting began in April 1775. Prodded by the British government to be more active, General Gage dispatched an expedition to capture colonial military supplies stored at Concord, a few miles west of Boston. Early on the morning of 19 April this foray encountered about 70 American minutemen drawn up on Lexington green. Sweeping them aside and killing 8, the British troops continued onwards. They were repulsed by American militia at Concord and were forced to retreat under continual fire. The British lost 273 casualties and achieved nothing. Nearly 4000 American militiamen participated in the fighting and began a war.

Necessarily the confrontation with Britain came to occupy front stage for the next eight years. It can be argued that independence was an almost entirely autonomous process because American society was stable, orderly and harmonious and therefore its dispute was wholly external. Yet it is clear that, if only temporarily, the colonies were disturbed. The dispute with Britain went to the heart of this in two respects. Firstly because the disagreement impinged on the core of their political system and secondly because once the dispute reached its military stage, the struggle against Britain affected every section of American society. The colonists were not united against Britain, but without the support (active in most instances) of the majority of the population, the scale of unity and ultimately victory, could not have been achieved. This fact alone had major political consequences. Similarly, the character of the derangement of American society on the eve of independence – especially the paradox that while the elite were attempting to move it towards a European social model, the lower orders were becoming more self-aware and moving towards a more democratic model – would influence greatly the terms on which the new republic would be constructed.

# 4
# ACHIEVING INDEPENDENCE

It took eight years to conclude the Revolutionary War. Colonial objectives were initially defensive and limited in scope. In the early stages Americans fought to protect their liberty and preserve their autonomy; beyond this few possessed a clear sense of constructive purpose. For eighteen months they struggled to contain the British by force while debating what their ultimate goal should be. During the summer of 1776 they defined their objective as total separation and declared independence. Yet declaring independence was not the same as achieving it. George III's government regarded their actions as no more than rebellion and remained determined to crush it. Congress still faced innumerable challenging problems with no certainty of success. On several occasions Britain appeared on the verge of success, notably as early as 1776 and again in 1779–80, for American forces were weak and British military and naval power enormous by comparison.

I

The first phase of the war was short. News of Lexington spread so rapidly that everywhere north of Maryland had heard within a week, South Carolina had heard by 10 May, and an account was printed in Savannah, Georgia, by the end of the month. For the time being conduct of operations remained in New England hands. Leadership in Massachusetts devolved on Dr Joseph Warren, president of its Provincial Congress. Within a short time Massachusetts had supplied 13,000, Connecticut 6000, Rhode Island 1500 and New Hampshire 2000 men to participate in the beseiging of

General Gage in Boston, but there was no unified command.[1] Other colonies began organising for war but most were too busy with their own problems to send assistance to New England. Further west, on the shore of Lake Champlain, a group of Vermonters and New Yorkers captured Fort Ticonderoga on 10 May. The men gathering round Boston were enthusiastic but poorly trained and badly armed. They were put to the test on 17 June when Gage made an ill-considered attack on American emplacements across the Charles River. His victory at Bunker Hill (more correctly, Breed's Hill) was Pyrrhic. He lost over 1000 men, compared to total American casualties of 400 (including Warren), and was compelled to fall back into the town. Elsewhere fighting was sporadic and local for the next twelve months. Governor Dunmore seized the Virginia powder stock at Williamsburg, but was compelled to retreat to a British warship. British naval vessels attacked Falmouth (now Portland, Maine), Norfolk, and Charleston, and in January 1776 a Loyalist force was defeated in a ferocious battle at Moore's Creek Bridge in North Carolina.

By fortunate chance the First Continental Congress had resolved in October to meet a second time on 10 May. Out of 65 members of the Second Continental Congress 50 had served in 1774, including the Adams cousins of Massachusetts, John Dickinson of Pennsylvania and Richard Henry Lee of Virginia, thus giving an important measure of continuity between the two bodies. Among the newcomers were John Hancock of Massachusetts, Benjamin Franklin (recently returned from England), James Wilson of Pennsylvania and, after six weeks, Thomas Jefferson of Virginia; representation of all thirteen colonies was completed when a delegate from Georgia arrived. Their instructions directed them to seek redress of American grievances and restoration of harmony with Great Britain, but this proved unrealistic. Events forced a drastic change in Congress's functions compared with those of its predecessor. The First Continental Congress had been a protest body summoned to express and coordinate colonial opposition to the Intolerable Acts. It had issued several addresses but lacked the capacity to take positive action by itself. Delegates created a potentially powerful coercive instrument in devising the Association but of necessity execution had to be left to local congresses and committees. Under the new circumstances, the Second Continental Congress (the term 'Second' becomes redundant) immediately became a deliberative and administrative body which accepted active responsibility for the conduct of common affairs.

For many months Congress was ambivalent. A handful of members including the Adams cousins believed separation was essential; John Dickinson and others were convinced that it was not. Many were undecided. For several weeks delegates debated in secret and acted only when compelled by events. On the one hand Congress resolved to promote reconciliation; on the other it resolved that 'these colonies be immediately put into a state of defence.[2] In spite of this hesitation, many decisions implicitly pointed towards independence. They advised the New York Provincial Congress to raise militia and prepare to defend the city. They began to organise military supplies, and voted to issue $2,000,000 in paper money. Denomination of the issue in Spanish dollars (which circulated widely in the Americas) was an indication of future developments in American currency, although pounds sterling continued as a common unit of money throughout the Revolution. In mid-June Congress voted to raise troops in Pennsylvania, Maryland and Virginia for service outside Boston, formed the Continental army and issued a set of military regulations. George Washington of Virginia was elected commander-in-chief on the nomination of John Adams and assumed command of the New England troops at Cambridge, Massachusetts, on 3 July. His selection was partly based on his military reputation as an experienced militia officer and partly shaped by political considerations, for it was a device for binding the largest, richest, and most influential colony to what was still primarily a New England war. Appointment of four major-generals was influenced by similar geographical considerations, though seven out of eight brigadiers came from New England since that was where the fighting was taking place, and most of the troops came from that region. Later in the year Congress established a navy.

In raising money and establishing armed forces Congress exercised powers customarily the preserve of sovereign governments, but its members remained uncertain over their ultimate objective. On 6 July they issued a Declaration of the Causes and Necessity of Taking up Arms, drafted by Dickinson and Jefferson; two days later they adopted the so-called Olive Branch Petition, written solely by Dickinson, which to John Adams's fury protested vehement loyalty to the king and a desire for reconciliation. The same month Congress formally rejected Lord North's conciliatory proposals, but remained careful not to move too fast. On 21 July it put off consideration of a plan for confederation proposed by Benjamin Franklin and a proposal from Richard Henry Lee that unless British restraining acts were repealed royal custom houses should be closed and American ports opened to all except British ships. Congress was also reluctant to accede to requests from Massachusetts, New Hampshire and South Carolina for guidance on the organisation of government. Nevertheless the sinews of reconciliation were weakening.

In contrast, the drift towards independence continually gathered pace. Most conventions in the states continued to instruct their delegates to seek reconciliation, but British policy made the prospect less and less probable. George III and his government had already decided that forcing the colonies into submission was the only alternative to permitting them to secede. They denied that the First Continental Congress had represented 'the true sense of the respectable part of their constituents', and remained convinced there was a large reservoir of Loyalists in America who formed the majority of Americans and whose support could be tapped in the campaign to suppress the rebels – opinions they obstinately maintained until the bitter end.[3] Throughout 1775 reinforcements were gathered, and since the number of British regiments was insufficient 17,000 German mercenaries were hired in the spring of 1776. No notice was taken of the petitions. Instead, on 23 August the king issued a Proclamation declaring the colonies to be in rebellion, and in December the American Prohibitory Act forbade commerce with the colonies until they submitted to British authority, made their ships forfeit to the crown as if they belonged to an enemy, and declared their crews liable to impressment. Appointment of peace commissioners was authorised, although they were only permitted to receive submissions and grant pardons, not to negotiate terms. Effectively it was a declaration of war and, paradoxically, a powerful propellant to American independence. But on 17 March 1776 the British, whose position had been rendered untenable by the arrival of guns from Ticonderoga, abandoned Boston. For a time there was no British army in the thirteen colonies, yet American celebration was premature. General William Howe, who succeeded Gage as commander in October, had retired to Halifax, Nova Scotia, only to prepare a massive counter-attack aimed at establishing a base in New York from which reconquest of the colonies could be launched.

During the winter and spring of 1775–6 one major issue was resolved. Thomas Jefferson and other members of Congress initially hoped that Québec would complete the American union. They were disappointed. In spite of indications of popular support Anglophone merchants in Montréal (many of whom had migrated from the thirteen colonies) decided their best interests lay with Britain. They feared that joining the United States would deprive them of vital British credit, supplies and markets, and expose them to damaging American competition. For their part, the French elite consisting of seigneurs and the Roman Catholic Church had benefited from the Quebec Act since it confirmed their legal position and privileges. The habitants (or smaller farmers) who disliked the Church and resented the confirmation of seigneurial rights, were more sympathic towards Congress but they too preferred to remain neutral.[4] Two attempts to draw Québec into union failed. A military expedition under General Richard Montgomery took Montréal in 1775 but could not capture Québec City and was obliged to settle down to a seige. In the spring a civilian delegation consisting of Benjamin Franklin, Samuel Chase and Charles Carroll of Carrollton (a Roman Catholic) were unable to persuade the Québecois to rebel, and the army withdrew. One important consequence was exclusion from the United States of the largest and most distinctive ethnic, religious and linguistic community in North America that was geographically sharply defined.

Other British colonies also remained loyal. East and West Florida, acquired in 1763, were only lightly held and even more lightly settled. They were easily retained until returned to Spain in 1783. Bermuda rejected an invitation to join the Revolution since, like the West Indian islands, it was constantly exposed to foreign attack and thus dependent on British protection. To the northeast, Newfoundland and Nova Scotia had many New Englanders among their 17,000 population but were unmoved by issues such as restrictions on western settlement and imperial taxation. Both benefited from commercial protection and their geographical position linked them more closely to the British Isles than to the thirteen colonies. Political neutrality and the profits from providing war supplies were more appealing than rebellion.[5]

During the early months of 1776 the political tide began moving more purposefully. Royal authority virtually collapsed throughout the colonies. Governors, from William Tryon of New York to Sir James Wright of Georgia, had fled or been neutralised; Sir Robert Eden of Maryland and others would depart later. On the patriot side Congress was by no means the only body to be exercising *de facto* power. In place of royal governments, congresses and county committees administered local affairs and organised military resistance. Since the previous summer increasing numbers of people had come round to the view that independence should be actively pursued. The Adams cousins and Richard Henry Lee devoted much time and skill to persuading their colleagues of its necessity. British actions, both civil and military, continually reinforced their arguments, and in January Thomas Paine published *Common Sense* in which he attacked the king directly and flatly declared that: 'Everything that is right or natural pleads for separation'.[6] Paine's vivid rhetoric was potent and persuasive, and 120,000 copies were sold within 3 months. Though not decisive in itself, its success demonstrated that public enthusiasm in all ranks of society strongly favoured change; what had previously been unthinkable was now a popular cause. Shortly after publication of Paine's tract, Congress responded to the British Prohibitory Act, news of which arrived in February, by authorising the arming of American vessels so that they could capture British merchant shipping. It also sent Silas Deane to France to obtain supplies and sound out the government's views on the situation. On

6 April, after much hesitation, it opened American ports to ships of all countries except Britain.

Even so, opinion was divided, particularly in the middle colonies, and there was strong opposition to the possibility of independence throughout the winter of 1775–6. Pennsylvania and New Jersey instructed their delegates to vote against it, and there was similar resistance to it in Maryland and among some Virginians such as Carter Braxton. New York was so divided among radical and moderate Patriots, Loyalists and trimmers, that a royal Assembly as well as the Provincial Congress attempted to exercise authority until it expired in April; on 14 February the two bodies met simultaneously in the same building.

A further stage in the process of separation opened on 12 April. On that day the North Carolina Provincial Congress became the first to pass a resolution explicitly empowering its delegates at the Continental Congress to vote for independence. Massachusetts, South Carolina and Georgia had earlier given their representatives instructions which implied consent to independence. On 4 May the Rhode Island legislature, not wishing its officials to take the customary oath of allegiance to the crown when entering office, repealed legislation imposing the oath, expunged all references to the king from its charter and laws, and authorised its delegates to cooperate with the other colonies in defending American rights. In effect it had unilaterally asserted independence. Another critical point was passed on 15 May when the newly elected Virginia Convention instructed its delegates to propose that Congress should declare independence, form alliances and construct a confederation, providing only that each colony should retain control of its own affairs and government.[7]

By then the gathering momentum was virtually unstoppable and Congress had moved ahead of many states. A majority of delegates realised that a decision was imperative for pragmatic as well as other reasons. With the war entering its second year Congress was increasingly aware that securing loans and military supplies, making foreign agreements and regularising the legal status of American forces (who as rebels were legally guilty of treason or piracy under British law) would be easier if it could secure recognition as a sovereign power. There were also ill-founded rumours that Britain was about to negotiate a partition of North America in treaties with France and Spain. At John Adams's instigation and with Lee's approval the Continental Congress working as a Committee of the Whole adopted a resolution on 10 May: 'That it be recommended to the respective assemblies and conventions of the United Colonies, where no government sufficient to the exigencies of their affairs have been hitherto established, to adopt such government as shall, in the opinion of the representatives of the people, best conduce to the happiness and safety of their constituents in particular and America in general.' Such directions were all but equivalent to a declaration of independence, but five days later, on the same day as the Virginia resolution, the point was reinforced by inserting a preamble. Referring to the British crown, it argued that 'the exercise of every kind of authority under the said crown should be totally suppressed, and all the powers of government exerted under the authority of the people of the colonies'.[8] Hardly surprisingly, this preamble encountered considerable resistance among those moderates who still hoped for reconciliation.

The final phase began on 7 June when Lee, acting on the direction of the Virginia Convention, proposed a resolution 'that these United Colonies are, and of right ought to be, free and independent States'.[9] Four days later a committee consisting of Jefferson, John Adams, Franklin, Roger Sherman and Robert R. Livingston was appointed to draft a declaration of independence. Conservatives succeeded in delaying consideration of Lee's resolution until 1 July to give themselves time to marshal opposition. Carter Braxton of Virginia was far from alone in doubting whether the time was ripe for such a move. Edward Rutledge of South Carolina tried to drum up support for delaying tactics, and insisted later that his delegation only assented to the motion for the sake of unanimity on the crucial day. The greatest resistance came from the middle colonies. New York, New Jersey and Delaware continued to hesitate, and until the end of the month the Pennsylvania and Maryland delegates were formally committed to vote against independence. Maryland came round to supporting independence in the nick of time, but as late as 1 July Pennsylvania

and South Carolina voted against independence in the
Committee of the Whole, and Delaware was divided. Even on
the following day, when Congress took the crucial decision,
the Pennsylvania delegation was able to support the main
independence resolution by a margin of three votes to two
only because John Dickinson, who continued to hope that the
crisis could be settled within the imperial connection, and
Robert Morris deliberately absented themselves. South Carolina changed its vote, and arrival of an extra delegate permitted Delaware to come off the fence.

On 2 July, therefore, Congress had resolved on independence. Two days later, on 4 July, Congress approved the
Declaration of Independence, although New York was unable
to vote until its delegation received positive instructions from
a newly elected Provincial Congress on 9 July. Ten days later
Congress ordered the document to be engrossed on parchment
and signed; only then could it be described as 'The unanimous
Declaration of the thirteen United States of America'. By then
it was clear that, as Abraham Clark of New Jersey put it, the
United States 'must now be a free independent state, or a
Conquered Country'.[10]

The Declaration of Independence comprised three parts.
First came a philosophical preamble, then a long list of the
alleged crimes of George III, and lastly a restatement of the
resolution: 'That these United Colonies are, and of right
ought to be Free and Independent States.' The legal core of
the document lay in the list of grievances which provided legal
justification for the withdrawal of allegiance from the crown.
Previously the colonies had complained against the king's
ministers and parliament's claims to exercise domestic
authority over fellow subjects, but accepted the obligation of
allegiance to the crown; now this was repudiated. The preamble, technically the least important section of the document, raised the discourse to a significantly higher level. Its
affirmation of the 'self-evident truths' that all men are created
equal, that they possess unalienable rights – among them
being the right to life, liberty and the pursuit of happiness –
and that governments are instituted in order to secure those
rights and depend on the consent of the governed, formed
an ideological agenda for the new nation. The document's

author, Thomas Jefferson, always denied these were new principles and insisted they were already in general currency. There is considerable evidence to support his opinion.[11] In this respect the Declaration was also persuasive propaganda intended to sustain American morale when read at the drumhead, and to convince outsiders of the legitimacy of the American cause.

Its issuance marked a further stage in the politicisation of the American people. During the previous year a great debate had taken place in Congress and country alike. Gradually the advocates of independence had become more numerous. Yet the change was not merely the product of a small group of ideologues and radicals as Loyalists and later critics argued. The sense of outrage which had met the Stamp Act and been heightened by the Townshend Duties and Intolerable Acts had reached all ranks of white society, hence the willingness of New England farmers to prepare for armed resistance. Lexington had strengthened this feeling and the combination of fighting and the apparent intransigence of the British government increasingly convinced most Americans that no amicable solution was possible: independence was the only alternative to conquest. Nevertheless, many men, like Dickinson, James Duane of New York, and Edward Rutledge only reluctantly accepted Congress's decision. The Declaration of Independence was kept open for signature for several months as a device for encouraging members of Congress to commit themselves and their states publicly. Many signers had not been present on 4 July, and Matthew Thornton, the last to sign, did not do so until November. Service in Congress, the Continental army and the expanding ranks of state politics strengthened commitment to the cause.

The remainder of 1776 demonstrated the precariousness of American independence. As yet the war was no more than a colonial rebellion, and while Congress was making its grandiose claim in Philadelphia, less than 100 miles away General William Howe and his brother Admiral Lord Howe were deploying 32,000 troops and 72 warships off New York in preparation for a major assault. Between August and November, General Howe drove Washington's much smaller army out of Long Island, across Manhattan Island and into New

Jersey. He captured 2800 American troops, including two generals, and occupied the city of New York, which remained in British hands throughout the war. Had he displayed greater energy he might have captured the entire army and possibly terminated the rebellion without further ado. His brother's simultaneous efforts to negotiate a settlement foundered since he could offer only pardons and was not empowered to negotiate with Congress. Had he possessed appropriate authority he might have been able to exploit the pessimism among moderates such as Philip Schuyler and Charles Carroll of Carrollton to reopen divisions in Congress. By the end of the year the British army dominated the corridor between New York and southeast Pennsylvania but was unable to take Philadelphia. On the credit side, Washington kept the remnants of his army intact and was gaining valuable experience from his own mistakes. Furthermore, in New Jersey he inflicted sharp reverses on the British at Trenton in December and at Princeton in January 1777. As the new year began there was military stalemate. Britain had failed to crush the rebellion and had no clear strategy – but the United States had failed to establish its independence.

## II

In spite of its claims Congress did not represent a fully united nation. Numerous individuals rejected independence as a solution to the dispute with Britain, and many families and communities were divided over its wisdom. Men like Joseph Galloway of Pennsylvania and Daniel Dulany of Maryland were highly active in the dispute with Britain before 1776 but then chose loyalty to the crown. Benjamin Franklin's son William became an exile. Inhabitants of Barnstable, Massachusetts, were divided. At a town meeting, 30 voters supported independence but 35 opposed it, and 65 abstained.[12] Throughout the war large numbers of Loyalists (or tories as they were frequently called) supported the British, served in the British army and caused considerable difficulties for Congress. They were people whose political views were conservative and who had particular need for a British presence in America. For them the empire remained the only community superior to the individual colonies, and allegiance to the crown a higher duty than local interests. By the end of 1783 between 60,000 and 100,000 had left the United States rather than come to terms with the republican regime. Some went to England, some to the West Indies, most migrated to modern Canada. Only a few returned.

Loyalism was endemic throughout the states. John Adams is often misquoted as stating that one-third of the population were Loyalists and a further third were indifferent to the outcome of the war. This estimate may be too high, but at the other end of the scale, Paul H. Smith's estimate of 19.8 per cent of white Americans seems cautious. In good measure any assessment depends on whether a high level of public commitment – such as serving in the British army or civil office – is required, or whether general sympathy is deemed sufficient. Without doubt 19,000 men served in 42 Loyalist units of the British army.[13] They played an important part in southern campaigns throughout the war, especially in the often brutal guerrilla warfare that plagued the backcountry during 1780–1, and were used as occupation troops in the middle states. Others probably served in regular units.[14] A broadband estimate of 20–30 per cent makes clear that the Revolution was an internal civil war as well as a rebellion against the metropolitan government. In spite of their geographic diffusion Loyalists posed a serious potential threat to the new regime. The difficulty of maintaining popular support for a long war was aggravated by Loyalist disaffection and military activity, but Congress was obliged to leave to the states the problem of dealing with them. In November 1776 it had considered sending Continental troops to assist in suppression of loyalism in Delaware without being invited by the state authorities, but some members argued that this would exceed its powers.

The geographical distribution of tories was very uneven. In a few small areas they comprised a majority; in every state as a whole they were a dispersed minority. New England's Loyalists formed scarcely one-tenth of its population. Most were concentrated in and around commercial centres such as Boston and Newport; a few were scattered in inland areas. A very different situation obtained in the South, where between one-quarter and one-third of the population supported the crown. Even here, though, there was considerable variation. Around the Chesapeake loyalism posed a considerable threat to government on Maryland's eastern shore, but in Virginia there were few tories. In the lower South loyalism enjoyed support along the seacoast, especially in Charleston, but was strongest among the recently settled Scots in the backcountry. For long periods neither Loyalists nor Patriots could establish firm control in these areas, and civil authority and public order sometimes broke down.

In parts of the middle colonies loyalism was so extensive that tories formed almost half the population. Around New York City they probably formed a majority even before the area was occupied by the British. Queen's County was a particular Loyalist stronghold in which 27 per cent of the male population were declared royalists compared with 60 per cent who attempted to remain neutral and a mere 12 per cent who publicly renounced their allegiance to the crown. In most parts of New Jersey many people attempted to remain neutral, and support for provincial committees of correspondence was often no more than half-hearted. As one of the major campaigning areas the state suffered severely from the fluctuations and uncertainties of war. When General Howe campaigned in the state during the winter of 1776–7 about 2700 residents were encouraged, persuaded or coerced into taking an oath of allegiance to the crown.[15] Pennsylvania also remained divided. Influential leaders of the Philadelphia community welcomed the British army on its arrival in September 1777. Galloway became Superintendent of Police and Trade during the British occupation and unsuccessfully attempted to make the city a focus for Loyalist expansion; when the army evacuated in June 1778 he departed with it and later fled to Britain. Besides the convinced Loyalists, the position in Pennsylvania was complicated by the presence of pacifist Quakers and German pietists in rural areas just outside Philadelphia. The Quaker refusal to take up arms and their sense of a moral duty to obey existing lawful authority, whatever that might be, unintentionally provided valuable support to the British and Loyalist cause.

Loyalists were drawn from all ranks of society. Categorising them simply as members of the rich elite is insufficient in all but a few small areas. Ownership of great estates or mercantile wealth provides no adequate guide to political allegiance, as a roll-call of the Browns of Providence, Robert Morris of Philadelphia, George Washington and many others illustrates. For every great Hudson Valley family such as the Robinsons and Philipses who became Loyalists, another joined the Revolution. In the south some elite families welcomed the British or, as in Charleston, were prepared to change allegiance, but in Virginia the great planters overwhelmingly supported and led the Revolutionary cause. Some tories, especially in Massachusetts, were lawyers but the correlation between profession and loyalism is too weak to form a clear pattern. Besides those who came from the highest ranks of pre-Revolutionary society, many more came from its lower ranks. In Massachusetts, where the 1778 Act of Banishment identified proscribed Loyalists by occupation, only about one-third were merchants, professionals or 'gentlemen'. A second third were loosely identified as farmers, but the remainder were small shopkeepers, artisans and labourers.[16] In other states an even higher proportion came from outside the upper ranks of society. This was especially true in the lower South where loyalism was strong in backcountry areas largely populated by yeoman farmers, And ironically, in view of Revolutionary rhetoric, more blacks fought for the British in return for promises of freedom than supported the American cause.

Many Loyalists possessed strong links with Britain even though they were native-born Americans. Some, like William Bull of South Carolina and John Wentworth of New Hampshire, were governors, royal officials or persons directly associated with British colonial administration such as the Sewalls, Olivers and Hutchinsons of Massachusetts. Among those who held high colonial office and whose later careers are known, 55 per cent became Loyalists and 22.5 per cent were neutral or in some instances had personal reasons for not continuing in office.[17] Others were merchants possessing strong commercial links with the British market, representing British firms in the transatlantic trade or, like the Scottish merchants in

Virginia, were British expatriates. Notable supporters of the crown, including the newly arrived Scots of the Carolina backcountry and Mohawk Valley in western New York, had particular reasons for their stance. The Carolinians had only recently settled in the area and resented the threat to their position posed by the older established patriot elite on the seaboard; they were also predominantly Gaelic-speaking. For their part the upstate New York Scots deferred to their landlord Sir John Johnson, who was a staunch Loyalist. In general those who were born in Britain were as likely to support the Revolution as oppose it – as James Wilson and John Witherspoon, both of whom signed the Declaration of Independence, demonstrate. Membership of the Church of England offers some guide to political opinion. Many New England Anglicans were Loyalists in a region in which the Patriot cause was particularly associated with Congregation-alism and Presbyterianism, as were clergy throughout the states, from Samuel Seabury of Connecticut to Jonathan Boucher of Maryland. But the correlation cannot be carried too far, even though individual Anglicans everywhere became Loyalists. In many parts of the South, where Anglicanism was legally established, especially Virginia, both lay and ordained members of the Church strongly supported independence.

The key to loyalism lay in three elements: minority status, political conservatism and commitment to the imperial com-munity. Tories were diverse and numerous in the country at large but conscious minorities everywhere.[18] They included Anglicans in New England, Scots in New York and North Carolina, some Germans and those Dutch in New York and French Huguenots who obstinately adhered to traditional practices and felt vulnerable to the pressures of predominantly Anglo-American and Anglophone society. Among them some groups such as orthodox Pennsylvania Quakers and Menno-nites were not actively pro-British though their behaviour assisted the crown, and orthodox (but not Anglophone) Dutch in New York. Roman Catholics and Jews were exceptions, perhaps because they were accustomed to being small perpetual minorities and had adapted themselves to their predicament. Many concentrations of Loyalists were in peripheral areas such as Maryland's eastern shore or the southern frontier.

Some needed military protection against the threat of Indian attack.

Loyalists were also politically conservative and feared the majoritarian tendencies of the Revolution. They shared the Patriots' sense of the great possibilities inherent in the American continent, but not their interpretation of the concept of liberty and sense of how that greatness could be achieved. Individual enjoyment of certain rights was only possible within an established and accepted structure of law and authority. Order was an essential ingredient of a free society, and a social hierarchy which acknowledged differences of wealth, status and education was necessary if stability was to be maintained. They were reluctant to trust the popular will, and believed that the disinterested paternalism of the elite could curb its fickleness – in the interest of the masses as well as individuals and the community as a whole. By comparison with the Patriots, Loyalists lacked confidence. They preferred the status quo, resisted change and were more aware of the possible dangers of the future than its potential.[19] The final element that marked out Loyalists was their distinctive sense of community. Unlike the Revolutionaries, who were constructing a new continental community as well as consolidating their control over local communities, Loyalists regarded the empire as the ultimate community to which they belonged. Within this single Anglo-American community royal government was necessary to protect minorities and prevent American society from degenerating into anarchy; the colonists, they thought, had to be protected from themselves.

## III

Congress had begun to prepare for a long haul well before July 1776. The Declaration of Independence was intended to be accompanied by a formal confederation, but drafting the Articles of Confederation took far longer than expected; until 1781, therefore, the growth of central government was organic and largely shaped by the imperatives of war. During this crucial opening phase, relatively little thought was given to the allocation of power between central authority and local

bodies such as the states, nor was there an established pool
of politicians possessing experience of national as well as local
administration.[20] The primary task facing Congress was to
organise itself as a governing body. Its membership consisted
of delegates appointed by provincial congresses and then state
legislatures; at no time was there any element of direct
popular election. In spite of the disparity of population, territory and wealth between large states such as Virginia and
small ones like Rhode Island and Georgia, each state possessed
only one vote, though it was allowed to determine the size of
its delegation. This equality of representation was the only
practical arrangement at a time when the states were still the
prime units of political activity; no alternative was practical.
The number of members present fluctuated. Turnover was
high, partly because many prominent members were
appointed or elected to other posts – as Franklin and John
Adams represented the United States in Europe and Patrick
Henry and William Livingston were elected governors of
Virginia and New Jersey respectively – and perhaps also
because the work was exceptionally arduous. Almost until the
end of the war Congress functioned as an executive as well as
a legislature: it implemented policy as well as formulated it.
Above all it exercised close supervision over military affairs,
in good measure in order to enforce the principle of civil
supremacy over military commanders – a task made easier by
Washington's acceptance of the principle and his willingness
to defer to Congressional authority.[21]

Gradually Congress devised a new if never wholly efficient
system of administration. It operated through committees of
its own members established to deal with particular subjects.
The Secret Committee of September 1775 arranged for imports of munitions and other military supplies, and the
Committee of Secret Correspondence, established in November, dealt with overseas representatives. Other committees
were founded in 1776 to deal with military and naval matters
and oversee the accounts. But the committees only handled
details; policy formulation remained the responsibility of
Congress itself, and since it was closely concerned with the
organisation, pay and supply of the army from 1775 to 1781
the burden was great. At first it in effect used state officials as

agents. It implemented policy through state conventions and committees which were called upon to raise troops, requisition supplies and do other necessary things to put the country on a war footing, or through its own state delegates, as when the New Jersey delegates were instructed to arrange for a supply of gunpowder, and James Wilson was asked to enquire about possible sources of clothing in Philadelphia. From 1777 onwards it created small executive boards consisting in the main of professional appointees. Further down the line it was obliged to pay purchasing agents for military supplies by commission rather than by salary – a practice frequently criticised for its openness to corruption and exploitation.[22]

One particular problem nearly brought Congress down. Prosecution of a long and large-scale war against a powerful enemy was extremely expensive, especially for a Congress which was still only a rebel organisation and for states which were in the process of establishing their own entities. E. James Ferguson estimates that the war cost between $158,000,000 and $168,000,000, of which the states contributed about half.[23] The American economy was insufficiently developed for sophisticated financial techniques to be available. There were no banks and no existing national currency, and since much individual and state wealth was locked in land or other fixed property it was difficult to realise. There was also a continual shortage of specie and other circulating medium. Alexander Hamilton calculated much later that total money stock (specie and paper, of which only one fourth was specie) in the colonies on the eve of the Revolution was 30,000,000 Spanish milled dollars, the equivalent of £6,750,000 sterling.[24] This may have been adequate for peacetime commerce, but not for war; in 1775 all the hard money in circulation would have been insufficient to meet a year's expenses for the Continental army.

Financing it imposed an acute burden on Congress which bore the major responsibility and lacked much of the power customarily possessed by established governments. Unlike the states Congress enjoyed no authority to impose taxes, and in any case lacked the manpower and administrative structure capable of raising revenue. Neither did it possess bullion

reserves or established credit among financiers. In their place
it was obliged to rely on emissions of paper money and credits
and loans which in effect were a form of borrowing on the
future. Congress correctly believed that the only alternative to
printing money was abandonment of the war. At first it did
well. By the end of 1776 Congress had emitted $25,000,000,
but the increase in economic activity stimulated by warfare
meant that its real value declined little. This financial success
was short-lived. Financing and supplying the war was
achieved only by continual improvisation. By spring 1778
expenditures were about one million dollars every week, and
accelerating emissions of currency ($226,200,00 by 1779)
brought matching depreciation.[25] This decline in value was
effectively a tax on the holders of money.

All efforts to stem inflation by regulating prices and wages
failed. Four New England states meeting at Providence from
December 1776 to January 1777 agreed to enact controls, and
Congress tepidly recommended the other states to follow suit.
The delegates' dilemma was compounded by disagreement
over whether such joint action by a group of states infringed
the powers of Congress.[26] The middle states attempted to
impose restraint but the southern states did not, and there was
bitter resistance from merchants who argued that regulation
was incompatible with their liberty to dispose of their property as they wished. In Philadelphia the more prosperous
artisans also challenged the traditional community concept of
a 'fair price', arguing that the broader public interest was
better served by the free competition of an unregulated
market. In October 1779 resentment among the poorer and
middling citizens of Philadelphia provoked the militia to
march on the home of James Wilson, who was held responsible, demanding the regulation of prices and restoration of
community values. What became known as the Fort Wilson
riot was unsuccessful.[27] In the absence of adequate public
support and suitable enforcement machinery none of the price
controls were effective, and renewed legislation in several
states in 1779–80 also failed.

When Congress revalued its currency in March 1780 it did
so at a ratio of 40 to 1 of specie, a rate almost twice the current
market value. Bills of credit, which were legal tender, met a

similar fate. By April 1781 their value in coin had shrunk to about 150 to 1. This paper money provided the sinews of war during the first five years of the Revolution. No other form of income – loan certificates, state credits and foreign aid – was any more than secondary in importance, and even when combined they were insufficient to meet Congressional needs.[28] Instead the army was sustained by certificates of dubious value which were issued by Quartermaster and Commissary officers in exchange for impressed goods and services. Their nominal value is uncertain though they were used in large numbers, but in real terms they were frequently valueless before 1780 when the system changed.

Congress attempted to solve its problems by leaning on the states. Its decision illustrated with sharp clarity the weakness of Congress as a government and demonstrated the extent to which it depended on them. By this time Congress's credit was so low that it was often obliged to rely on the private commercial credit of officials such as the Philadelphia merchant Robert Morris, who had been the dominant member of the Secret Committee and was virtual controller of overseas purchasing. Substantial action to put national finances on a sound footing did not take place until the states ratified the Articles of Confederation in 1781 and Congress appointed Morris as Superintendent of Finance.

From the beginning the states assisted in financing the war. By 1780 they had collectively raised over $85,000,000, but it was still insufficient. In that year Congress, which was virtually bankrupt, began requisitioning supplies from the states which, since they had no money, they were obliged to collect or seize directly from their citizens. It also imposed on them responsibility for paying their own soldiers and compensating the troops for their losses incurred by being paid previously in depreciated currency. Finally, it required them to share in guaranteeing a new federal currency and ordering them to raise taxes to redeem the old currency; it was to be replaced by a new currency underwritten by Congress but issued and redeemed by the states. The states made great efforts to comply, and seem to have eased the most critical situation, but the plan failed, and hence the severity of the depreciation by April 1781. Similarly the states supported

Congress in its impressment of goods and services throughout the remainder of the war, offering only certificates in payment. By this time the Continental currency had expired and with it state legal tender laws – to the relief of almost everyone – leaving loan certificates as more reliable forms of debt that would later form the basis of the public debt.

A second problem was the development of diplomatic policy. Congress had long recognised the need for foreign help and was already receiving secret assistance from France, but was reluctant to offer a military alliance in exchange since it was determined to avoid entanglement in European affairs. A model treaty of amity and commerce was prepared for presentation to France and Spain. Benjamin Franklin and Arthur Lee were appointed commissioners to join Silas Deane of Connecticut who was already purchasing supplies in France. By the end of 1776, however, the military position was so bad that Congress was prepared to offer American cooperation to France and Spain if they wished to conquer British possessions in Florida and the West Indies as well as a military alliance.[29]

# IV

Necessarily Congress's central concern was with the conduct of the war. The tides of battle turned one way then the other during the summer and autumn of 1777. After a slow start and considerable manoeuvring Howe defeated Washington at Brandywine and entered Philadelphia in September. His capture of the seat of Congress was anything but a decisive victory, since as had happened the previous year he was still unable to destroy the Continental army. Washington was able to retire to extremely arduous quarters at Valley Forge (a few miles outside the city) for the winter of 1777–8, and Congress had already retired to York, Pennsylvania. Washington's survival intact was of great strategic significance, for even if he could not defeat Howe the existence of the Continental army posed a continual threat to the British position and prevented them from imposing their authority on the region. More positively encouraging for Washington and Congress was Britain's failure to isolate New England (which it always considered the most incendiary seat of rebellion) from the rest of the country. Their strategy called for one column commanded by General John Burgoyne to move south from Canada and a second to march east along the Mohawk river, effecting a junction near Albany, New York, in the Hudson Valley. Unfortunately, the government's instructions left vague the plan's key element, cooperation with Howe's army based in New York City. In consequence Howe felt entitled to give precedence to his attack on Philadelphia. Like the New Jersey campaign, Burgoyne's march from Canada was delayed. He failed to reach Albany, and in October he was halted, defeated and forced to surrender at Saratoga.

Victory turned the tide in favour of the United States for the time being. According to Jonathan R. Dull the French government had for some time considered that spring 1778 would be an appropriate moment at which to enter the war openly as part of its strategy against Britain.[30] Moreover, Franklin and his fellow commissioners had been successful in sustaining French interest in America, and in February 1778 they signed two treaties: a treaty of amity and commerce by which France recognised the United States, and an alliance by which France agreed not to make a separate peace if she entered war with Britain. Anglo-French hostilities were inevitable but did not commence until June; Spain entered the war in 1779 in the vain hope of recovering Gibraltar. In the meantime the British government sent a commission under the leadership of the Earl of Carlisle to the United States in the hope of diverting it from the alliance with France. Carlisle was instructed to offer almost every concession Congress had requested in 1775 coupled with an Act of Parliament withdrawing its claim to raise taxes in the colonies. It was too late. Congress ratified the treaties with France and refused to negotiate except on condition of an immediate British military withdrawal. French participation transformed what had been a colonial rebellion into a world war but had little immediate effect in America. Campaigning during the remainder of 1778 was indecisive. Sir Henry Clinton, who replaced Howe as British commander, abandoned Philadelphia in June in order to concentrate his army in New York but Washington was unable to press home the advantage by defeating him. The first fruits of the French alliance, a joint attempt to recapture Newport, Rhode Island, failed.

On both sides the problems were largely those of organisation and logistics during the middle years of the war. French assistance was as yet of marginal utility, and exhaustion and declining morale put the Continental army at greater risk than their British opponents. Congress was publicly accused of ineptitude and racked by severe factionalism, notably over the formulation of possible terms for a peace treaty, which aroused vehement sectional rivalry, and especially over accusations that Deane had profited personally while purchasing supplies and negotiating loans in France. War weariness set in because no end to the war was visible, and there were grain shortages.

In so far as the war began moving to its resolution the initiative was seized by the British. At the end of 1778 they decided on a major shift in strategy. It was intended to establish a secure base in an area presumed to be inhabited by large numbers of Loyalists and led to a transfer of troops to the South. For more than a year the move was successful. Savannah, Georgia, was captured at the end of December and the balance of campaigning favoured the British. The war swung even more firmly in their favour for much of the following year. In May 1780 the American army suffered its worst disaster of the war when General Benjamin Lincoln surrendered with almost 5000 troops at Charleston. South Carolina was brought largely under British control, numerous Loyalists joined them and many Patriots, believing the war was lost, took an oath of allegiance to the crown. In August the American army under General Horatio Gates, the victor at Saratoga, lost another major battle at Camden, South Carolina. Elsewhere the Continental army suffered considerable shocks to its confidence with mutinies at its Morristown, New Jersey, winter quarters (which were worse than those at Valley Forge two years earlier) in May 1780 and two mutinies in Pennsylvania regiments in 1781. Perhaps psychologically more damaging was the defection to Britain of Benedict Arnold, probably the most talented American general, in September 1780. But crucially, Washington once more kept his army intact and prevented Clinton from gaining control of the area between New York and Philadelphia.

British success in the south proved deceptive. Arnold's raids through Virginia as a British general during the winter of 1780–1 did considerable physical damage and humiliated Thomas Jefferson, the incumbent governor, but had modest strategic importance. It was clear that holding coastal cities in the South was no more sufficient a means of suppressing rebellion than occupying Boston, Philadelphia, Newport and New York was in the North. Drawing what seemed to be the obvious strategic conclusion, Lord Cornwallis, commanding the British army in the South, marched inland in hopes of attracting Loyalist support, suppressing Patriot resistance and capturing the Continental army. Fighting and manoeuvring were often confused and always complex, and Cornwallis found himself unable to control more than small areas for any length of time. American victories in South Carolina, by Patriot militia over Loyalists at King's Mountain in October 1780, and part of Nathanael Greene's Continentals under Daniel Morgan at Cowpens in January 1781, could not be nullified by a series of modest British successes. None was decisive.

Hoping to effect a junction with British troops from New York, Cornwallis moved to the coast at Yorktown, Virginia, in the summer of 1781. His decision lost him what little strategic initiative he had previously enjoyed and from that point his army was doomed. American and French forces kept one step ahead of British movements. The French navy blockaded his position near the entrance to Chesapeake Bay and prevented Admiral Graves from relieving him. A force of 9000 American and 7800 French troops commanded by Washington and the Comte de Rochambeau marched from New York to place him under seige while Greene brought the lower South under control and a small force kept watch on Sir Henry Clinton in New York City. On 17 October Graves sailed again from New York with a large relieving force, but he was too late. Cornwallis had opened negotiations the same day and on 19 October he surrendered.

Washington's success at Yorktown was unquestionably a major victory since it brought the war to an effective end by persuading Britain to discontinue offensive operations. Yet the government's reasons should not be misunderstood. Their decision was made primarily on political grounds, for in military terms Cornwallis's surrender was not decisive. Washington and his French allies had not established firm control throughout the entire theatre of operations. Even after losing two large armies, British forces still controlled strategically important areas and had more troops immediately available with more in reserve in the British Isles. Indeed minor actions took place for some time in many parts of the continent, and vigorous fighting between Britain and her European enemies continued in other parts of the world. The decisive factor which determined the outcome of the Anglo-American conflict was that the British were the first to weary of the war, perhaps because they had less to lose. During 1780–1 the British public became increasingly sceptical about the value of continuing what had begun as a popular war but had been transformed into a costly and risky global war in which Britain was isolated in the face of France, Spain (since 1779) and Holland (since 1780). News of Yorktown precipitated a major crisis when it reached London. Backbench members of parliament turned against Lord North and in spite of the king's wish to continue the war he was forced to resign in March 1782.[31]

North was succeeded as prime minister first by the Marquess of Rockingham and when he died by the Earl of Shelburne, both of whom were committed to ending the war. Negotiating terms for an Anglo-American peace settlement proved more difficult than might have been expected, in good measure because the issues to be resolved extended far beyond the boundaries of the United States. Preliminary articles of peace by which Britain acknowledged American independence and accepted a western boundary along the Mississippi river and south of the Great Lakes were agreed in November 1782. The extent of territory acquired by the United States was substantial and represented a considerable success by American negotiators. Even so Britain did not formally terminate hostilities until February 1783 and the definitive peace treaty was not signed until 3 September of that year.

## V

The Revolutionary war was a social process as well as a conflict between soldiers and diplomats. Like other revolutionary wars the two armies struggled less with each other than for the support and control of the civil population, especially in areas like New Jersey and the Carolina backcountry where sympathies were divided. Once General Howe had failed to nip the rebellion in the bud during 1776, the British were unsuccessful in gaining local support, in part because they could not decide whether severity or conciliation was the more prudent policy. Both armies frequently behaved badly towards civilians, but the British army was notably worse. Its German mercenaries in particular were accustomed to the often brutal behaviour common in European warfare, and applied the same criteria of conduct in America. In New Jersey they annoyed Loyalists by the formal lenity with which they treated rebels – and their troops' behaviour alienated their political supporters by treating them badly. Nor were the British more successful in exploiting potential support when they shifted their strategy to the South in the (correct) belief that it contained a pool of loyalism. The war was at its most savage in the backcountry, where it was even more difficult than usual to distinguish between Patriot and Loyalist, and British generals found it militarily impossible to provide adequate protection for their supporters.

The Continental army was doubly more successful. In the narrow – if crucial – military sense it was victorious, and in a broader sense it was more successful in attracting the support of local populations and politicising them for the future. The war was not a conflict between two established nations, but between an established imperial power and insurgents who were still in the process of creating a nation. The army created an image of unified purpose and political respectability as well as military strength. Its constant need for men and supplies continued the politicisation of the population that had begun with the Stamp Act crisis and accelerated with committees of safety set up to enforce the Association in 1774–5 and the provincial and county congresses. In particular, the movement of British troops coupled with the Patriot obligation of universal militia service compelled communities and individuals to make choices – that is, to commit themselves to the cause of independence.[32] Warfare had profoundly important consequences. Independence was not achieved solely by politicians, officers and diplomats drawn from a social elite. It was the achievement of a broad spectrum of American society. The war experience contributed towards converting a protest movement and rebellion into a nascent national community.

Filling the ranks was a constant problem. In the summer of 1776 Congress voted to raise 88 battalions to serve for the duration of the war but never succeeded in raising the requisite number of men; Washington's own army in the Middle Department reached no more than 18,472 men fit for duty in October 1778, and its strength was frequently much lower. It became necessary to offer bounties to recruits and then to introduce a form of draft by requiring townships to provide a specified number of men. Shortage of sufficient whites encouraged many states to recruit blacks for both Continental army and militia service. Rhode Island voted to raise two regiments of blacks, including slaves whose owners would be compensated for the loss of their property; Maryland was the only southern state to include slaves though Virginia permitted free blacks to enlist. John Laurens and his father Henry, who served a term as President of Congress, saw the disparity between the defence of liberty for whites and the enslavement of blacks but were unable to persuade fellow South Carolinians to arm any slaves. In the absence of a professional American army the Continental army had to be constructed from the ill-trained and frequently unmilitary militia supplemented by large numbers of men who had received no military training whatsoever. In addition the states raised their own militia for short-term local service. Many of those who served longest were poorer and socially more marginal than average, but since between 150,000 and 200,00 men served for six months or more, a very high proportion of the available population of service-aged men participated in active service. Thus in Virginia about half the white males over the age of 16 saw active duty, as did about three-fourths of the eligible males aged between 16 and 50 in the small Massachusetts town of Chebacco.[33] Furthermore, about 24,000 men suffered service-related deaths. At least 8000 were killed in action, 8000 died of disease on active service and 8000 died as prisoners of war. These casualties gave a death rate relative to population second only to the later Civil War. It is also estimated that in addition 24,000 men were seriously injured, crippled or permanently affected by disease.[34] After due allowance is made for evasion of service, the mercenary pursuit of enlistment bounties and desertion, the successful prosecution of the war depended on the mass of the Patriot community as well as their political and military leaders. This was especially true of the ocean war, for the great profits of privateering were overmatched by the hazards of being captured by the British, imprisoned and possibly tried for treason. Evidence that Lord Rawdon's units in the final Carolina campaign were full of deserters from the Continental army is more than matched by the determination displayed by American sailors during years of captivity in England when very few took the oath of allegiance in order to secure release.[35]

Nor was this all. The Continental army perpetually lacked sufficient 'gentlemen' of high social status to meet its need for field and company officers, and the problem was even more acute in militia units. Officers possessed on average more property than other ranks but the social gap between them and their subordinates was far narrower than in European armies; as far as the Massachusetts militia and others were concerned there was no clearcut occupational difference between officers and their men. Officers below field rank were elected by their subordinates, and although generals such as Washington and Philip Schuyler came from the elite, others such as Henry Knox and Nathanael Greene came from a modest social background. Within the army the lack of clear distinction had important consequences. Flogging was used as a form of punishment but on a very much smaller scale than in the British army where hundreds of lashes were a common penalty even for minor offences. Discipline had to rest to a much higher degree on persuasion and consent to the exercise of authority than in other armies; even deserters had to be treated with comparative leniency because of the constant shortage of available soldiers. The ramifications of this were far-reaching. Commissions gave many men access to higher social status than they would otherwise have gained – but observation by social inferiors of the limitations of their commanders raised doubts as to the fitness of men to possess civil as well as military authority simply by virtue of high social standing.[36]

The Revolution as a major war had substantial economic impact. For some the effect was devastating. Boston, New York City and Philadelphia were all occupied at one time or another and their populations fell considerably: New York's dropped by 5000 at one point. Many coastal communities like Falmouth and Norfolk were bombarded. New York, Charleston and Newport were severely damaged and although the first two recovered, the third, which was also cut off from its traditional trade with the West Indies, did not.[37] Other towns as well as rural areas such as New Jersey and parts of the South suffered from the campaigning that took place in their territory. Production of tobacco, the Chesapeake's major staple crop, was reduced to no more than a third of pre-war levels and much was destroyed by British raids or at sea. The New England fisheries were temporarily destroyed, and the British discovered that by blockading Charleston they could also frustrate the export of grain from the interior as well as inhibit the coastal rice trade. The import-export trade was disrupted since two-fifths of colonial exports and virtually all imports had gone through Britain or British colonies. Congress's decision to open American ports to all but British vessels in April 1776 was a milestone in the movement towards economic independence but the war masked the effect of emancipation from British regulation and even at its wartime high point in 1782 trade was less than it had been before the war. By 1778 real prices had risen by seven or eight times since the beginning of the decade. Those who suffered included smaller farmers who had difficulty paying debts and taxes, labourers and artisans whose wages did not keep up with inflation, and ironically soldiers who were paid often late in depreciated currency, or in certificates that lost their value or had to be sold at a discount. Overall, Alice Hanson Jones's estimate that American private real wealth per capita declined at 0.5 per cent per annum between 1774 and 1805 implies a very substantial drop during the war, especially in light of the prosperity of the 1790s.[38] The economic stress was so severe that even a normally prosperous state like Connecticut, which was seldom affected by warfare, found its economy near to collapse and its treasury virtually bankrupt as the war reached its nadir in 1780.

On the other side of the balance sheet certain individuals and groups benefited considerably. Some did so from the misfortunes of others. Massachusetts outports like Salem benefited at Boston's expense, as did Providence from the destruction of Newport. Many profited greatly from supplying the army – or the British who normally paid in specie. Farmers outside the immediate war zones did especially well, particularly those in New England and the middle states, and even in the South before the war turned in its direction. Similarly industrialists prospered through supplying iron and other military necessities such as shipping. Privateering was a risky but potentially very profitable operation. Stephen Higginson of Boston is said to have made $70,000 and the town of Providence $300,000 from it during the course of the war.[39] Others who benefited were traders – often with government appointments they could exploit to personal advantage as did Jeremiah Wadsworth and especially Robert Morris, who reckoned to make 500–700 per cent profit on supplies he negotiated for the government during the war. Ironically some at least of this trade was financed by the specie with which the British had purchased goods at a time when American currency was depreciating rapidly. If inflation had disastrous effects for some, the economic activity generated by the war stimulated the development of local industry and domestic production, and probably encouraged the commercialisation of local agriculture.

# 5

# FRAMING NEW GOVERNMENTS

Victory in the War of Independence was only part of the Revolution. Though literally essential it was primarily an enabling act which permitted the simultaneous and more fundamental civil process of founding a republican regime. Few Americans anticipated the need to establish new governments until the exigencies of war made it imperative, for unlike twentieth-century nationalists the revolutionaries of 1776 had not spent decades preparing for the establishment of an independent regime. But once the necessity became evident, many immediately appreciated the exceptional chance that presented itself; as John Adams declared: 'When, before the present epocha [sic], had three millions of people full power and a fair opportunity to form and establish the wisest and happiest government that human wisdom can contrive?'[1] Transformation of the colonies from being subordinate members of a monarchic empire directed from the centre into an independent self-governing nation required considerable and quick thought. It was a complex task which had to be undertaken at two levels: individually by each of the thirteen states, and collectively as a single nation. Each government faced three tasks. It would have to conform to a set of political values acceptable to its constituents, be compatible with the social structure of each state, and be sufficiently effective to prosecute the war, impose its authority on those who rejected its claim to legitimacy and implement whatever policies it chose to formulate.

Founding new governments took until 1781 to complete. The process began in an unstructured fashion in 1774 with the first provincial and continental congresses, and became formalised in 1776. Most states completed it the same year,

and all had done so by 1780. Constructing a central government raised far more difficult questions. It took five years to
draft a national constitution. In the meantime Congress
operated on its own authority with considerable success.

I

By 1776 the problem of government was acute. Except in
Pennsylvania, where the old Assembly fought a vain rear-
guard action in defence of its authority, there were no
institutions that could claim legitimacy as of legal right.
Provincial congresses and committees implementing the
Association exercised *de facto* power but by definition were
extra-legal. What happened in Massachusetts illustrates the
situation. Royal authority began to evaporate during the crisis
over the Intolerable Acts. Ironically the governor, General
Gage, contributed to the transfer of power by summoning the
legislature to meet at Salem in October 1774 and then
changing his mind. Elections were held, the members met and
resolved themselves into a provincial congress and adjourned
to Cambridge; thereafter a series of congresses effectively
controlled the province. Gage's authority – still the only legal
authority – shrank geographically until it was confined to the
area controlled by the British army; in practice it was restricted to Boston. Militia officers holding royal commissions
had already been required to submit to election by their men,
and local tax collectors were required to deposit moneys with
provincial receivers instead of royal treasurers and all law
courts were closed. Other states followed similar paths especially as their committees of safety enforced the Association;
though they lacked formal authority the new bodies often
applied coercive power. The Maryland Convention of November 1774 raised taxes and a militia, and fixed profit levels and
interest margins; other committees and local conventions
regulated prices and encouraged manufactures. In response
to an urgent need for civil institutions such as law courts
which had been closed by the crisis, embryonic governments
began developing even before the war.[2]
The meeting of the second Continental Congress in May

1775 took the process a substantial stage further. It raised the questions of whether new governments should be constructed in the colonies and if so, whether Congress should coordinate the process or leave each colony/state to its own devices. A few individuals inside and out of Congress discussed the possibility of drafting a uniform model constitution during 1775–6. Among them Richard Henry Lee was sympathetic, but John Adams's view that each state should be entitled to draft its own constitution prevailed, and there was a general feeling that the states were sufficiently diverse as to make a single constitution unsuitable. The first state to address the problem was Massachusetts. Its delegate, John Adams, who had been convinced from the start of fighting that independence was the only proper objective, was already convinced of the need to establish new governments. Congress as a body was less certain, and replying in June to a request for guidance from Massachusetts it simply recommended that the state should ignore the royal governor, and elect a new government until the king appointed a new man willing to abide by the terms of the charter, thus implying the possibility of reconciliation.[3] The significance of this recommendation went beyond uncertainty as to the future: it was also an acknowledgement that each province would have to make its own governmental arrangements.

Five months later New Hampshire was the next state to seek advice on administering justice and regulating its domestic affairs. Its royal governor, John Wentworth, had abandoned the province during the summer of 1775, leaving it without an executive or legislature. When its delegates sought advice in October, Congress dithered. On 3 November it gave a carefully evasive answer which recommended the state's Provincial Convention to call 'a full and free representation of the People' and suggested that the representatives 'if they think it necessary, establish a form of Government, as in their judgement will best produce the happiness of the People'.[4] There was no mention of royal authority. Since the chairman of the committee which drew up the advice was John Rutledge it was not surprising that it gave his own state of South Carolina identical advice the following day. A month later Congress recommended that since in its eyes Governor

Dunmore had exceeded the legitimate limits of authority by declaring martial law, Virginia also should hold fresh elections and reorganise its government.

In spite of the British government's steady tightening of the political screw, the pace at which the states formed new governments accelerated only slowly. New Hampshire's fifth Provincial Congress scarcely exploited the full implications of the Continental Congress's advice, but at the same time as conducting the business of a wartime legislature it appointed a committee to draft a constitution. The procedure through which it was approved and implemented in January 1776 was that of normal legislation, and the frame of government at best so sketchy and incomplete that it advanced little beyond the procedures of the colonial regime. It formed itself into a lower house which was authorised to elect an upper house and which in turn was to appoint a President. The document anticipated the possibility of returning to membership of the British empire; since this did not take place, the rudimentary first constitution was replaced in 1784 after a draft had been rejected in 1777. South Carolina's Provincial Congress wrote a more substantial, if temporary, document on 26 March 1776 but also implemented it through the customary legislative procedure, and in May Rhode Island translated its royal charter into a republican constitution simply by expunging all references to a king.[5]

John Adams and his allies gave the process of forming new governments as well as claiming independence a massive boost when they persuaded the Continental Congress to pass the two resolutions of 10 and 15 May. The first recommended the colonies to adopt new governments if no satisfactory authority existed, and the second spelled out some implications of the first by adding a preamble urging that all forms of authority under the crown should be suppressed. The advice was taken. Led by Virginia on 29 June, New Jersey, Delaware, Pennsylvania, Connecticut (which adapted its royal charter as had Rhode Island), Maryland, and North Carolina formed new constitutions by the end of 1776. Georgia delayed until the following year, as did New York because at the moment its convention met the British army was preparing for its successful campaign to recapture the city. Only Massachusetts took longer, not completing its process of constructing a new frame of government until 1780.

Available precedents were unsatisfactory. British constitutional principles were uncodified and unwritten; their most authoritative contemporary commentator, Sir William Blackstone, insisted there was no distinction between the constitution and the current system of laws. At their heart lay the proposition that parliament was sovereign. Its will was supreme and its powers extended to anything that was not naturally impossible; it could even change the constitution.[6] For their part, the colonists had recently repudiated such a doctrine. In most colonies the nearest thing to a constitution was the royal commission and instructions issued to governors at the time of their appointment. Neither were the charters possessed by Massachusetts, Rhode Island and Connecticut entirely suitable as models. Like the governors' commissions their authority was derived from royal grants of privilege, and though the colonists interpreted them as irrevocable statements of principle the Government of Massachusetts Act of 1774 demonstrated that in British eyes colonial charters were still subject to parliamentary authority and could be remodelled at will.

Rejecting these unsatisfactory precedents the states developed an alternative model. It was based on the republican theory of society, citizenship and authority which was sufficiently flexible (and at times variable and even inconsistent) to be acceptable to a broad range of citizens and adaptable to diverse social situations. Before 1776 its anti-monarchical elements had been abhorred by all but a handful of colonists; once allegiance to the crown was repudiated it became the only acceptable system of political values for all but the disaffected Loyalists.[7] It provided philosophical underpinning for an independent society and offered legitimacy for government and authority.

Almost the only thing on which Americans were agreed was that republicanism was more than government without a king. As colonists they had already rejected principles such as the divine right of kings and absolute monarchy (including 'enlightened' despotism), no matter whether they were prudentially justifiable in particular circumstances. Instead they had proudly believed that monarchic government as practised by Britain was fully compatible with the essential principles of good government, and gone further to argue that in the House of Commons the British constitution possessed its own republican component to match and balance the monarchic and aristocratic elements represented by the crown and House of Lords. This was no longer sufficient. The reigning orthodoxy of prescriptive authority within an organic and deferential society seemed inappropriate for an independent society in the new world, and had little attraction for most Americans.

Application of republican principles rested on the central proposition of popular sovereignty. In the words of the Virginia Declaration of Rights: 'All power is vested in, and consequently derived from, the people; ... magistrates are their trustees and servants, and at all times amenable to them'. Quite what was meant by the term 'the people' was ambiguous. All active members of the political community agreed that it referred to the individual states as political entities, but elites were far from willing to construe it as meaning every individual citizen regardless of social status; it was not intended to imply numerical majoritarianism. In practice the elites were able to interpret the term for the time being as permitting them to continue exercising local authority, provided they did so in the interests of the entire community, and not merely their own. Thus even Charles Pinckney, a rich South Carolinian conservative, could insist that 'All power of rights belongs to the people, it flows immediately from them, and is delegated to their officers for the public good,'[8] a view that was shared throughout the states. As the Worcester, Massachusetts, convention put it in 1774, it was necessary to construct a form of government (which they mistakenly believed had existed at some undefined period in the past) whereby: 'The most dignified servants were, as they ever ought to be, dependent on the people for their existence as such.'[9] Since this was not held necessarily to imply majoritarianism, its prime ingredient was more ideological than institutional. The machinery devised to implement these propositions was that of the written constitutions within whose terms would be set out the general principles of government, the structure of its machinery, and the extent and limits of its lawful authority. However, what was understood by a constitution during the early years was so general that there was considerable diversity in the nature of the various state constitutions and especially in the manner in which they were drafted. In eighteenth-century enlightened fashion the states experimented collectively and individually until they devised a satisfactory system.

## II

The distinction between legislation and constitution-making was at first blurred in spite of the developing principle that a constitution was superior to the operation of government. For a time there was relatively little distinction between fundamental and statute law, and the states stood halfway between traditional English parliamentary practice and future American constitutionalism. The Connecticut and Rhode Island legislatures, having made only minor alterations to their colonial charters, did not write fresh constitutions until 1818 and 1842 respectively. Of the earliest states to draft constitutions – South Carolina, Virginia and New Jersey as well as New Hampshire – ignored the Continental Congress's 3 November 1775 recommendation to 'Call a full and free representation of the People'. Instead in each case a constitution was drafted by a committee of the Provincial Congress, which brought it into immediate effect, thus treating it as if it was an item of normal legislative business. North Carolina, Georgia and New York did much the same, and in each instance the procedure was made possible by the fact that the Provincial Congress represented the dominant Patriot faction in the state. The essentially legislative nature of the process was clearest in Virginia, where the members of the state's Congress were little different from those of the old colonial assembly, but it was also true even in New York, where occupation of the city and lower counties by the British had the double consequence of eliminating the influence both of the radical artisans and the most Loyalist section of the entire country. State legislatures that went on to function under the constitutions also acted as their principal interpreters, to a point where they frequently violated the constitutions even where there were nominally procedural safeguards. The South

Carolina legislature's actions were especially flagrant, but the New Jersey legislature amended its constitution in 1777, and North Carolina passed an emergency act in 1780 abrogating the governor's constitutional power over the military. The amending process varied from state to state. States such as Maryland and Georgia allowed their legislature to participate, and others made provision for a revisory convention, though the procedure was not fully worked out; fewer than half the states had a fixed amending procedure by 1780.

Following the Continental Congress's resolution of 10 May 1776 recommending the states to form new governments, four of them took the separation of constitution-making from law-making a stage further by entrusting the task to a specially elected convention. The first was Pennsylvania, which called a special convention under pressure from radical elements in the militia and the city of Philadelphia and with the support of county committees of inspection. The 96 delegates drafted a constitution and declared it in effect on 28 September. They made no attempt to secure the approval of the citizens of their state, even though the document was radical and more democratic than any other Revolutionary frame of government, and under the exigencies of the war the convention administered the business of the state. Delaware, still little more than a dependency of its larger parent and neighbour, did similarly but unusually dissolved itself rather than continuing as a legislature. So did Maryland, though only after some difficulty. Like its northern neighbour, Maryland was a heterogeneous state which had been divided over the question of independence, but whereas the Pennsylvania Patriots had been able to divide and out-manoeuvre the Loyalists, in Maryland the Whig gentry had had considerable difficulties with them and had been obliged to negotiate with their fellow citizens for support, especially among the inhabitants of what in 1776 were the western parts of the state. Under pressure, the gentlemen agreed that a special constitutional convention should be elected, but it would also transact regular business. Even though the elite retained control of the process, debates were long-drawn out, and it was only on 8 November that the Convention approved and implemented the constitution.

Not until Massachusetts completed its exceptionally long

process of drafting a constitution was the transition from royal, customary and essentially prescriptive and superior authority to popular sovereignty completed and the separation between fundamental and statute law fully established. The process did much to illuminate the relationship between people and government in republican ideology. For a time at the beginning of the war the state's General Court (or legislature) operated as an interim government based on the charter of 1691. By June 1776, having already set up a constitution-drafting committee, it asked the state's townships to approve a procedure by which the house and council would draft a constitution, circulate it for comment, and then take a final vote. Although a majority of the towns approved the suggestion, 23 out of 97 respondents objected. Some complained that the current General Court was unequally constituted and demanded a wider franchise before it moved to drafting a constitution. Other criticisms were more fundamental. Pittsfield had argued in May that since George III had broken his contract of government, the colonies had reverted to a state of nature; it was therefore necessary to devise a fundamental constitution as an essential prerequisite of legislation. Since the legislature was the servant of the people, and the constitution ought to be superior to it, it was unfitted to compose a constitution; furthermore, a constitution required the approval of a majority to come into effect. Lexington also insisted that a constitution should be ratified by the towns, while Concord proposed for the first time a special constitutional convention.[10]

The General Court was reluctant to implement all the recommendations, but invited the electorate to choose representatives at the May 1777 election who collectively would act both as a legislature and as a constitutional convention on the understanding that the consequent draft constitution would be sent to the towns for ratification. The Court appointed a drafting committee in June but it did not report until February 1778. When the draft was sent to the towns it became entangled in the political rivalries of the state, notably between eastern commercial and western agrarian interests, and was rejected by 9972 votes to 2083. Many towns gave detailed reasons, but most criticism centred on the electoral process, including in particular the distribution of seats in the proposed legislature. A group of towns in Essex County produced an extended conservative critique, known as the *Essex Result*, which greatly influenced the debates that were to follow.

The position in the spring of 1778 was thoroughly unsatisfactory. The state had moved a considerable distance towards separation of constitutional law from legislation by introducing the process of ratification, yet rejection of the draft left it without a proper system of government two years after it had become *de facto* independent. After some hesitation, the General Court made a further attempt to resolve the problem by asking the towns whether they wished to authorise the election of a convention 'for the sole Purpose of forming a new Constitution.[11] On receiving an affirmative reply, it held special elections. It extended the franchise to all adult men on the grounds that the formation of a constitution was so fundamental an act of citizenship that all men were entitled to participate even if they were normally ineligible to vote. The convention – the first in any state whose sole function was to draft a constitution – met at Cambridge on 1 September 1779. By 2 March of the following year it had drafted a document which was printed and distributed to the towns for their consideration. Once more the towns were invited to vote individually, but their returns were so confused as to require constructive interpretation in light of the requirement for a two-thirds majority for ratification. The methods chosen were carefully designed to produce an affirmative result – by dubious calculation if necessary. In June the Convention declared that the Constitution had been approved, and on 25 October 1780 it came into effect.[12] The first round of state constitution-making was complete, and a model procedure for future use had been devised.

## III

One of the most difficult tasks facing the framers was to bring the high ideological principles articulated with particular clarity in the Declaration of Independence together with the actuality of a socially hierarchical society. Equalitarianism was a central ingredient of American rhetoric, and Jefferson stated bluntly that 'all men are created equal'. Defining the term 'equality' caused great difficulties since the social perspectives varied considerably. Many members of the elite accepted views articulated by the Virginia planter Richard Bland that '*rights* imply *equality*', and by Thomas Shippen, a member of one of Philadelphia's most prominent families, that '*a certain degree of equality* is essential to human bliss', but they continued to insist on the importance of hierarchical stratification and the subordination of the lower orders to their social superiors.[13] They interpreted the proposition that 'all men are by nature born equally free', as George Mason put it in the Virginia Declaration of Rights, to mean only that men should be independent from the control of others and that all were entitled to equal liberty. Like the more conservative Loyalists the Patriot elites were convinced of the need for stable, orderly government, and the protection of property. They denied that the lower orders – those who worked with their hands – should be permitted to share in the administration of public affairs, and feared that if they were so permitted they would immediately launch raids on the property of the rich. Jeremy Belknap, a New Hampshire divine, declared: 'Let us state as a principle that government originates from the people; but let the people be taught ... that they are not able to govern themselves.'[14] At the other end of the social hierarchy were men who demanded a 'well-regulated Democracy', insisting that the people knew their own best interests and were best able to rule themselves.[15]

Each state worked out its own equation between equality and hierarchy when constructing its new government. The struggle for independence demonstrated that the elites were in significant respects dependent on their social inferiors, and could not coerce or browbeat the majority of their white fellow-citizens. Successful political resistance before 1775 had depended in part on the willingness of the lower orders to support the elites. Moreover, there were indications that the urban artisans, mechanics and labourers were self-motivating, independent in their behaviour, and calculating in their violence. In Pennsylvania much of the impetus towards independence came from artisans who applied sustained pressure on reluctant merchant elites; even in Virginia the gentry needed to attract the support of the lesser farmers and others, first in their campaign of encouragement for Boston, later in support of the independence movement. Elite dependence on popular support had become all the more crucial during the years 1774–6, when the extra-legal authority of county and provincial congresses, committees of correspondence and public safety, and other Patriot organisations including the Continental Congress, was especially tenuous and subject to challenge by Loyalists and other conservatives. When elite leaders realised the critical necessity of attracting local support for the non-importation section of the Continental Association, they encouraged the establishment of town and county enforcement committees, and probably more than 7000 men participated.[16]

Traditional deferential conservatism was discarded along with the crown, but that still left competing alternatives. John Adams argued that a representative assembly should be an exact portrait of the people at large, but he was far from radical on social issues and was vehemently critical of Thomas Paine's equalitarianism. In practice the question was whether the new governments would institutionalise elite trusteeship, or whether they would approximate to popular democracy.

Radicalism achieved its greatest success in Pennsylvania. A strong artisan radicalism developed in the city of Philadelphia as the province moved to war, and for a time acquired a dominant position in state politics. Its most powerful elements were highly skilled mechanics such as David Rittenhouse, who had started as a watchmaker and became a scientist, and Charles Willson Peale, who moved from poverty to become a silversmith, clockmaker and later a portrait painter. It also included professionals such as Thomas Young, a physician, James Cannon, a college teacher and ideologue who worked closely with Thomas Paine, Timothy Matlack, a disowned Quaker, and for a time Benjamin Rush, a Presbyterian doctor with a practice among the poor. Its heart lay in the militia, and in particular in the Committee of Privates which extended political activity sufficiently beyond the ranks of master craftsmen and the higher echelons of artisans to include the lesser mechanics and labourers. Richard A. Ryerson points out that although the leaders were a relatively small band of shipwrights, brewers, blacksmiths and others who were richer than their constituents, they understood the need to gain the support of those beneath them in order to deploy the weight of numbers against those above them; Pennsylvanians were entering an age of mass politics.[17] The ideology of this committee was partly secular, and drew heavily from Paine, but it was also shaped by the millenarianism and spiritual equalitarianism that flowed from the Great Awakening. At its most radical it argued that a very high concentration of property in the hands of a few individuals was destructive of the common happiness of mankind, and that the state possessed the right to discourage the possession of such large amounts of property. These were men who believed that the elite were taking a dangerously aristocratic view of government by claiming the right to govern. Radicals were determined to challenge this position.

Their opportunity was created by divisions among the elite. Pennsylvania had long been the most heterogeneous of the provinces, and possessed no single dominant group once the majority of Quakers had withdrawn from politics in 1754. By tradition its provincial politics had been dominated by English and Welsh Quakers and Anglicans, but on the eve of independence their supremacy was challenged by other groups, including in particular the Scotch-Irish Presbyterians. Simultaneously, there were social and economic divisions between the inhabitants of the city of Philadelphia, and those of its immediate hinterland, and the further interior. Within the city were a further variety of interest groups and divisions such as the importing and wholesale merchants, the retailers, and the artisans, mechanics and labourers. In politics all these rivalries were also complicated by disagreements over the position and role of the proprietor and his representatives. As the province moved through the pre-Revolutionary crisis, those who formed the social elite were divided among themselves in a society that was difficult to control and whose politics were deeply factionalised. An elite which had already lost much of its coherence was further divided by the issue of relations with Britain to the point at which leading politicians such as

Joseph Galloway became Loyalists. Also many members of the patriot elite were devoting their attention to continental affairs.

Such a fragmented elite was unable to sustain its political supremacy. The fact that Pennsylvania had a legally elected assembly as late as May 1776 did not help them. When the Continental Congress recommended that the states should form new governments if necessary, the Pennsylvania Assembly's more conservative members argued that it was still governing satisfactorily and responsibly, and that the courts were operating and public finances were in order. In good measure at the instigation of the militia rank-and-file Committee of Privates, a public meeting attended by 4000 Philadelphians insisted that a provincial convention should be elected to draft a constitution. A Provincial Conference of Committees of the Province of Pennsylvania arranged the elections and significantly extended the suffrage beyond those who were normally eligible to vote to include all members of the militia, who were also permitted to stand as candidates; conversely they excluded those whose allegiance to the independent regime was suspect.[18]

Membership of the Provincial Convention, which sat from July to September, was very different from that of the old assembly, whose authority faded away. Numerically it was skewed in favour of the western counties, whose delegates were mainly unsophisticated farmers, but it was politically controlled by the Philadelphia delegates, who included radical ideologues such as Matlack, Cannon and Young (all of whom were members of the militia), as well as the more experienced lawyer George Ross and a prosperous and intelligent merchant, George Clymer. Benjamin Franklin was a member, but seems to have taken little part, and outside the Convention was another radical, George Bryan, with Paine probably in the background.[19] Besides their egalitarian strain those who drafted the constitution and later defended it had three characteristics: they tended to be Scotch-Irish Presbyterians, men of moderate economic status, and residents of the northern and western parts of the state. They were determined to exploit the opportunity that presented itself.

The consequent constitution, approved with its attendant

Declaration of Rights on 28 September 1776, was designed to leave the people, by which was meant the individual citizenry, as the active as well as nominal fount of power. As such it was profoundly democratic. Every other element of government was made dependent on the legislature, and the legislature in turn was made dependent on the electorate. Its Declaration of Rights largely copied that of Virginia but put it to egalitarian uses. It united the principles that men were created equal and enjoyed certain rights to the proposition 'that the people of this State have the sole, exclusive and inherent right of governing and regulating the internal policy of the same' and drew the conclusion that the franchise ought to be very wide. All taxpaying freemen over 21 and their adult sons were deemed to be eligible to vote, and even more strikingly were entitled to stand for office; there was to be no religious test other than a belief in God.[20] John Adams's argument that a second, balancing, house was essential was rejected in favour of a single-chamber General Assembly.

Implementation of such a democratic constitution brought about drastic change. The traditional model of an hierarchical society (often at risk in the particular circumstances of Pennsylvania) had broken down. No longer was there a mutual trust, respect and partnership among men of differing social status. The men entering power were not common men, but they came from a lower stratum of society than their predecessors. Perhaps as important, the old Anglican and Quaker control of the colonial assembly was broken: by 1777 the Scotch-Irish Presbyterians and German Reformed Churchmen and Lutherans occupied 90 per cent of the Assembly and six seats on the Supreme Executive Council. Not surprisingly such drastic changes provoked considerable opposition. In March 1779 a Republican Society was founded in Philadelphia with the object of repealing the Constitution on the grounds that it had a general tendency to reproduce the worst features of bad government. The Republicans were mostly conservative and their numbers were dominated by Anglican Whigs from the eastern counties; 35 were merchants and 10 had been staff-officers in the Continental army. For a decade Pennsylvania politics were dominated by the struggle between Constitutionalists and Republicans until the critics succeeded in obtaining a new Convention which drafted a more orthodox and conservative constitution in 1790.[21]

At the other end of the spectrum South Carolina and especially Maryland drafted profoundly conservative constitutions. As the colony with the richest inhabitants, South Carolina had been a harmonious community dominated by a small group of rich coastal planters who controlled provincial politics; the backcountry, occupied by four-fifths of the white population, had been seriously under-represented in the assembly. In spite of a significant number of Loyalists among the leading families, leadership of the resistance to Britain and demands for independence lay in the hands of this elite. They were determined to retain control of the new state if possible – especially those among them who were cautious about independence. In March 1776, before independence had been approved but on the somewhat ambivalent suggestion of the Continental Congress, the Provincial Congress appointed a committee to draft a temporary constitution. The backcountry members had already departed, so the committee consisted of eleven Tidewater gentlemen such as John Rutledge, Charles Cotesworth Pinckney and Henry Laurens. They made no attempt to obtain a 'full and free representation of the people' as the Continental Congress had recommended, but tried to ensure that the conservative political order was sustained. The new constitution made concessions, consisting principally of reapportioning the lower house of legislature so that the backcountry now elected 38 per cent as compared to 6 per cent but in other respects the change was limited.[22] The colonial freehold property franchise of 100 acres or its equivalent was retained, and members of the House were still required to own at least 500 acres and 10 slaves, or other property worth £1000 clear of debt. Unlike Pennsylvania, moreover, the administration of government was insulated to some degree from popular influence by the establishment of an upper house, a privy council and a governor possessing an absolute veto.

Hostility to the new constitution quickly developed. Charleston artisans and backcountry farmers complained there had been insufficient change, and much criticism was directed against what was seen as excessive authority located in the hands of the executive. The Patriot elite had gone too far in attempting to protect their own interests. When the constitution was revised in 1778, the vote was extended to all free whites owning 50 acres, the upper house was made more representative of the entire state, and the governor was stripped of his veto. In the other direction the qualification for membership of the Senate was raised to £2000 and for the governorship to £10,000. The product was an unsatisfactory compromise. Rich conservatives found it too democratic, so that when the British occupied the city from 1780 to 1782 many wealthy Charlestonians welcomed them. Other whites remained dissatisfied on the grounds that the changes did not go far enough, and continued to challenge the influence of the elite; in particular, inhabitants of the backcountry demanded more representation. After a third constitution was drafted in 1790 they met with success.[23]

Of all the states, Maryland produced the most conservative constitution. At first sight this is surprising since it shared some of its northern neighbour's social features. Like Pennsylvania, though less so, it had been heterogeneous before the Revolution and certain elements of its economy were changing rapidly, yet apart from the expanding town of Baltimore it remained overwhelmingly rural. When war came, the state had to deal with an element of loyalism so strong, especially on the Eastern Shore, that for a time it had to divert more men to suppressing domestic dissent than to fighting the British. As in South Carolina and Virginia, leadership during the political dispute with Britain was in the hands of a rich Whig elite, and they were determined to retain control of the independent state. They succeeded, but only at the cost of constant struggle. Men such as Charles Carroll of Carrollton were fully aware when they claimed to be defending American liberty and other rights against the British government that the same arguments could be turned against themselves. The challenge on this front was sometimes explicit: an article in the *Maryland Gazette* on 15 August 1776 insisted that even poor men possessed rights and could be injured by government. It declared that every citizen who supported the state had 'an equal claim to all the privileges, liberties and immunities with every [one] of his fellow countrymen'.[24] The elite's

difficulties were exacerbated during the war since the mobilisation of 18,700 men, including 1700 officers, put great strain
on the gentry and forced them to search outside their own
ranks to fill the vacuum with men whose social status would
not normally have allowed them to occupy prestigious public
office. Their immediate difficulties were compounded when
the freemen of Anne Arundel County, one of the most
important counties, instructed their delegates at the constitutional convention to vote for universal white male franchise
and insisted on annual elections of officers and judges as well
as legislators.[25]

In spite of these vigorous challenges the Maryland elite
successfully maintained their supremacy. What they wanted
was an ordered society controlled and directed by the rich,
and for a time they managed to keep their social inferiors in
check. The Provincial Convention was elected on the old
colonial suffrage but although its members were younger,
more diverse and more representative than their predecessors,
it was dominated by a group of great planters, mainly from
the northern and western Western Shore, who came from
long-established elite families and often had commercial and
cultural interests away from Chesapeake Bay. Among them
were men such as the two Charles Carrolls – of Carrollton and
'Barrister' – William Paca and Matthew Tilghman; they outmanoeuvred the more liberal members and dominated the
committee that drafted both the Constitution and the Declaration of Rights.[26]

Following their own inclinations and influenced by John
Adams's *Thoughts on Government* (a brief pamphlet published
early in 1776 in response to Paine's political proposals) and
the recently approved Virginia constitution, the Maryland
Whigs made limited concessions but ensured their own continued dominance. The voting requirement was eased from
£40 sterling to 50 acres freehold or a visible estate worth £30
current money (worth less than sterling), but delegates were
required to possess property worth £500 current. An electoral
college for electing senators, who had to be worth £1000,
contributed to elitist control, which was further enhanced by
the requirement that the governor should be worth £5000, of
which £1000 should be freehold. The consequence was as the

Whigs wished: of the state's white male freemen, only 70 per cent at most, possibly fewer, were eligible to vote, 20 per cent were qualified to sit in the House, 10 per cent in the Senate, and only 2 per cent for election as governor. The Convention had explicitly connected the possession of property with attachment to the interests of the community, and thus with regard to the right to vote, in the Declaration of Rights, and as far as officeholding was concerned the new constitution was more restrictive than its predecessor.[27]

Pennsylvania and Maryland represented the democratic and conservative ends of the political spectrum, with the other states at various points in between. New Jersey was closer to the Pennsylvania model, though it established a two-house legislature and significant property qualifications, while Georgia (still an undeveloped society in 1776) adopted a very democratic constitution with a modest property qualification for voting and a higher requirement for membership of the single-chamber Assembly. It included a provision that most county officials be subject to annual election.[28] North Carolina represented an individualistic amalgam of democratic and conservative elements. The province had been seriously disrupted by the Regulator movement before the Revolution, and its consequences impinged on the process of constitution-making. A strong yeoman farmer interest in the interior challenged a divided elite with some success. Citizens of Orange and Mecklenburg Counties, in the Piedmont, demanded a democratic constitution, but the balance of power in the drafting committee was probably held by conservatives, and its work was heavily influenced by Adams's *Thoughts on Government*. Its product, which was quickly approved by the Congress, made a number of reforms earlier demanded by the Regulators, extended the franchise and redressed the balance of representation between the Tidewater and the Piedmont somewhat. Nevertheless, officeholders were required to possess 100 acres for members of the lower and 300 acres for members of the upper house of a two-chamber legislature, and the governor was required to be worth £1000 freehold. Implicitly the new constitution was expected to promote a stable property-based social hierarchy. Perhaps the state's smaller farmers appreciated the sanctity of property and accepted a system intended to protect it; perhaps as men of limited education they were willing to defer to the leadership of their more sophisticated social superiors.[29]

New York underwent an unusual process. Extra-legal committees, particularly in the city, were in the lead in destroying royal authority and encouraging the departure of rich Loyalists such as Frederick Philipse, James DeLancey and Sir John Johnson at the beginning of the Revolution. The Committee of Mechanics demanded in the spring of 1776 that the people should retain the power to change the constitution and, by changing deputies, to ensure that the government always stemmed from the people's voluntary choice.[30] Their interpretation of the term 'the people' was implicitly an egalitarian one in which individuals were entitled to equal freedom from the domination of others, and an equal share in government and liberty. Unfortunately for them, the British occupied the city and five most southerly counties from August 1776 until November 1783 so they were deprived of their main source of support. Dismissing the mechanics' complaint that their proposal was improper, the Provincial Congress that approved the Declaration of Independence on 9 July appointed a committee to draft a constitution. It was dominated by conservatives like John Jay, Gouverneur Morris and Robert R. Livingston, yet included more populist whigs such as Robert Yates and John Morin Scott. The disturbances of war prevented it from submitting a draft until March 1777, and it was only in April that the document was approved.

Not surprisingly, the New York constitution was somewhat conservative, though there were signs of compromise and concession. The suffrage requirement was reduced to £20 freeholders and extended to tenants for the first time, but was designed to exclude rootless men such as seamen, farm labourers and the urban poor. A proposal to introduce the secret ballot was rejected though an experimental ballot was included. In a series of attempts to ensure conservative control, election of senators was confined to those owning £100 freehold, and although the governor was very unusually made subject to popular election the same qualification was required of those who elected him. He was given a three-year term in order that he might be insulated from popular influence, and a complex Council of Revision was devised which was given authority to alter bills proposed by the lower house and the right to impose a veto which could be over-ridden only by a two-thirds vote in each house.[31] A Council of Appointment was established with the intention of keeping offices in suitably conservative hands. The extent of conservative influence was further demonstraed by explicit confirmation of royal land grants. But there were also more popular elements such as an elective senate and governorship, annual elections for the lower house, an increase in representatives from 31 to 70 and provision for redistribution by census. Both conservatives and radicals would have preferred more extreme provisions, but each settled for a middle-of-the road document.[32] When it came into effect, the first election inaugurated the shrewd yet populist politician George Clinton into a long period of office.

## IV

The constitutions and declarations of rights set out the general terms on which the principle of the sovereignty of the people could be applied to the operation of government. Republican theory instructed citizens to place the public welfare above private interest, but experience dictated the need for formal machinery to protect them against those who violated its principles – especially those who held the instruments of government at their command. Besides being concerned over social relationships, those who framed them were especially concerned (as they had been before the war) over one central conflict of interest which, they believed, infected virtually every aspect of political action: the disposition of power, and its apparently natural tendency to overwhelm the more tender liberty of the citizen.[33] Both power and liberty were desirable within limits, yet each could get out of hand. In the circumstances of 1776 Americans were especially sensitive to both possibilities: to the need for effective government made obvious by the imperatives of the war with Britain, and to the dangers of excessive authority, as demonstrated in their eyes by the tyrannous behaviour of the British government which, they had convinced themselves, was conspiring to destroy their liberty.

The first element in establishing an acceptable equation between the conflicting interests was the written constitutions themselves. They not only set out the powers of the governments operating beneath them, they also set out the limits. This was especially evident in the case of those states that attached declarations of rights to their constitutions. Thus the Virginia Declaration, written by George Mason and used as a model by other states, set out a number of grand principles: – the equality of men and their rights, popular sovereignty, the duty of government to promote 'the greatest degree of happiness and safety', and the right of the people to alter government should reform be thought useful. Thereafter, the Declaration continued by listing a number of procedural safeguards such as the right to a fair trial and elections, prohibition of suspending laws and general warrants, and an affirmation that 'freedom of the press is one of the great bulwarks of liberty, and can never be restrained but by despotic governments'. In formulating the structures of government they carefully devised a system that would make government as responsive to the will of the people as possible short of substituting direct decision-making by the entire community for the system of representative government. All assembly representatives were subject to annual election, and in some states governors and members of the upper houses were prohibited from being continuously re-elected as the price for longer terms in office.

The second component in the structures of limited but effective government was the separation of powers. Virginia was the first state to spell out explicitly the proposition that 'the legislative, executive, and judiciary departments shall be separate and distinct', but all other states attempted to follow suit to a greater or lesser degree. There was little doubt, however, that the legislature was the dominant element in the triarchy. Apart from New York and Massachusetts, where they were directly elected, all governors were appointed by their legislatures and were subject to annual re-election. None were formally confined only to executing laws enacted by the legislatures, but they were not allowed to become the potentially powerful and uncontrollable figures they had seemed to be in some colonies before the Revolution. Apart from their obligation to act as military commanders-in-chief of their state militia they were given few independent powers and were deprived of the prerogative powers enjoyed by their colonial predecessors, including in particular the right to a conclusive veto over legislation proposed by the assemblies. Even in Massachusetts, which went furthest along the route to a strong governor, his veto could be over-ridden by a two-thirds majority of the legislature. All except New Hampshire established an advisory executive council, but none developed any significant power or exercised any effective control over the governor. Effective executive leadership was difficult, as able men like John Rutledge of South Carolina and Patrick Henry, Thomas Jefferson and Thomas Nelson of Virginia discovered to their discomfort. At one point Rutledge vetoed a draft revision of the constitution; it did no good because the legislature ignored him and brought it into effect. The embryonic system assumed that policy would be formulated totally by the legislatures in spite of an inherent factionalism consequent on the representation of differing interest groups and the absence of organised parties or other forms of legislative discipline. Nevertheless the state constitutions contained many seeds of future powerful executive leadership. The judiciary, which was to assume major importance in nineteenth-century American constitutionalism, was scarcely developed and barely mentioned in some states. Apart from South Carolina, judges were appointed during good behaviour for clearly fixed terms, thus giving them a substantial degree of independence. They had not as yet acquired the authority to invalidate unconstitutional legislation; this was left to the governor's delaying veto or to councils of constitutional revision.

Great debate took place over the composition of the legislature. Among the radicals, Thomas Paine had briefly sketched the ideas on the structure of government in *Common Sense*. He denied that the English division beween king, lords and commons was an appropriate model for the United States, arguing that the first two elements represented the remains of monarchic and aristocratic tyrannies respectively. Only the commons contained any acceptably republican elements, and in consequence he recommended for the states a unicameral legislature.[35] The Pennsylvania Convention, dominated by Philadelphia radicals in the absence of the customary members of a temporarily divided conservative elite and influenced by intellectuals such as Paine's friend James Cannon, followed his recommendation. It established a single-chamber Assembly which was to possess all necessary legislative powers, but was prohibited from altering the Constitution itself. The Assembly's constant dependence on the people was to be ensured by annual elections, with the proviso that no member should serve more than four years in seven. To reinforce this subordination, all debates were to be held in public, proceedings were to be printed and, apart from emergency legislation, all bills were to be published with arguments in their favour and were not to be finally approved until the people had considered them. The executive power, in itself very limited, was located in the hands of an annually elected Supreme Executive Council which with the Assembly would appoint a President every year. Even judges were to be elected, though for the longer term of seven years. As a final safeguard a septennial Council of Censors was established whose duty was to ensure that the provisions of the Constitution were being observed. The President (as the governor of Pennsylvania was titled) was dependent on it. Only the minor states of Georgia and Vermont followed this example, but Paine's proposal had been sufficiently radical as to provoke great opposition elsewhere, even before the Pennsylvania Convention met.

Far more influential, at least on this matter, was the more conservative John Adams. He had begun discussing the structure of independent government in Congress long before the end of 1775 and expressed his views in *Thoughts on Government*; later he became the principal draughtsman of the Massachusetts Constitution of 1780. In opposition to Paine he insisted on the necessity of a balanced form of government. In a republic, he argued, the representative assembly 'should be in miniature an exact portrait of the people at large. It should think, feel, reason, and act like them'; it followed that there should be equal representation.[36] Unlike Paine, however, he believed that a single-house legislature would be dangerous. Its judgement would be poor and often hasty. It would tend to be self-interested, and it was unfitted to exercise executive power. His solution was the election of a second chamber which would act as a mediating agency between the assembly and the executive. Virginia and the other states followed Adams's advice with modifications. They constructed two-house legislatures and with few exceptions insisted on annual elections. The great change from colonial practice that would prove significant for the future was that apart from Maryland, whose initial Senate was virtually self-perpetuating, they insisted on the upper house being subject to election by the community.

Construction of legislatures posed other problems in devising an acceptable form of representation. On the whole communities remained the units of representation in the legislatures, brigaded differently in each house. In the southern states the communal locus was in the counties, and in New England in particular in the towns. Only limited effort was made to relate the districting to population. The outcome in the South was constant rivalry between the older established seacoast counties and the rapidly populating backcountry areas. In New England, over-representation of rural townships compared with the commercial centres of Newport and especially Providence caused continual difficulty in Rhode Island. In Massachusetts tension between the heavily populated commercial towns and counties of the eastern part of the state and the numerous small townships of the west bedevilled the General Court's efforts to provide the state with a constitution.

More serious was the problem of establishing an acceptable balance between the interests of the propertied elite and the remainder of an often articulate and demanding population. Conservatives conceded that men were born equally free and equally possessed of natural rights including liberty, but were reluctant to concede the principle of majoritarianism. Instead they hoped to devise an institutional protection for the interests of a propertied elite. Bicameral legislatures provided an acceptable solution to the problem. Implicitly the two houses would give expression to the great political interests: the 'democracy' or mass of the people, and the 'aristocracy' or educated and wealthy elite. As the *Essex Result* of 1778 suggested, the lower house would represent the numerical majority and the political honesty of the people, and the upper house would represent the wisdom and firmness of character possessed by the elite.[37] All states also attempted to ensure that the electorate was capable of exercising independent judgement and was free from the influence of others by insisting on a property qualification for the franchise. This had the added advantage of ensuring that the voter had a stake in society and thus a commitment to its interests.

The extent of the requirements varied from state to state. In rural areas it was generally 50 acres, though Virginia reduced the amount to 25 acres, or an estate worth 40 shillings per year. Urban electors were required to own property of comparable value. Ironically the Massachusetts Convention, elected on a universal male franchise, increased the qualification required for voting. Only Pennsylvania approached such universality in its franchise, for it extended the vote to all adult male taxpayers and their sons. Beyond the electorates for the lower house the required qualifications rose sharply for candidates for all offices, and electors for the upper houses. Not all constitutions imposed qualifications on their governors since they were usually elected by the legislature, but at the conservative end of the spectrum South Carolina required extremely high property qualifications for senators and their governor. In all, seven states required electors and candidates for the upper house to be worth more than those for the lower house.

Only Pennsylvania also challenged the principle that the new governments should contain both a mixture of estates and a balance of powers. Yet it proved impossible to implement this principle fully. In spite of the widespread admiration for the British constitution, (or more accurately, what were considered its 'true' principles) a balance of social estates could not be erected in America since it lacked the strongly differentiated social structure upon which British practice depended; notwithstanding the views expressed in the *Essex Result* no state possessed any counterpart to monarchy and prescriptive aristocracy. Attempts were made to link membership of the upper houses with the possession of substantial property, both to protect property owners against an assumed threat from the majority and on the assumption that the rich were also 'the men of the most wisdom, experience and virtue' as the Maryland constitution put it. But only in Maryland, where it was effectively self-perpetuating, did the senate begin to approach the position of an independent aristocratic estate. Everywhere else senators as well as representatives were responsible to an electorate, though in five states they were elected for more than the usual single-year term.

The implications were slowly worked out during the first decade of independence. The potential dangers of executive power had been long understood, and their reality was being confirmed by contemporary experience with Britain. Dangers inherent in legislative authority became evident (at least in the eyes of less radical politicians) in the supposedly danger-ous behaviour of untrammelled legislatures first in Pennsyl-vania, later in Rhode Island. Discussing the Virginia legisla-ture, which in spite of the rhetoric of separation of powers contained in the Declaration of Rights was the dominant branch of government, Jefferson remarked that '173 despots would surely be as oppressive as one'. As Gordon Wood has argued, all legislators and governors had been made respon-sible to the people, and thus the principle of balance could no longer be one of estates. Instead it had become a balance of functions among the elements of the constitutional structure: between executive, judiciary and legislature, and within the legislature between upper and lower houses, each of which was directly if differently dependent on the people.[38]

Other features reinforced the dependence of the new state governments on the will of their communities. Pennsylvania, North Carolina and Massachusetts explicitly guaranteed the right of the electorate to instruct their representatives, and the practice was not uncommon elsewhere. Legislatures were required to conduct their debates in public, and freedom of the press ensured that they were reported. Even the nature of constitutions was changing, to the advantage of the commun-ity. British and colonial constitutionalism had consisted of established prescriptive axioms which were applied rather than altered by courts and governments. Elites could justify their policies and conduct as implementing constant principles and so could demand their inferiors' obedience to their own self-interested interpretation of them. From 1776 onwards state constitutions sustained similar fundamental principles by reference to popular sovereignty; they were no longer unchallengeable prescriptions whose authority could be exploited by elites to their own advantage. Though superior to the governments that operated under their regulations, they had been demoted to amendable grants of the people's ultimate authority.[39]

Critics of the new constitutions and the governments that were elected under them frequently complained that they were dangerously democratic and unconducive to good government. Without doubt the concept of the sovereignty of the people and the pervasiveness of representation was politically more advanced than the old colonial regime, let alone eighteenth-century England. Yet conservative elements remained important and influential. The doctrine of majoritarian individualism for white males had been implied but not conceded, except perhaps in Pennsylvania. Property qualifications restricted the electorate and eligibility for office. The balance of functions insulated governments to some degree from any idiosyncrasies in the electorate. The experience of Massachusetts and to a lesser extent North Carolina demonstrated that even a broad electorate preferred stable and orderly government that would protect the rights of property as well as the people. The decade that followed independence demonstrated that representative government could be effective, even if it was not always so; it also demonstrated that conservatives could retain considerable influence provided they promoted shrewd policies and made well-timed concessions. Indeed, the evidence shows clearly that the social environment within which each government operated was of fundamental importance to its operational behaviour and political success.

By 1780 the first round of state constitution-making was complete. Even the unrecognised state of Vermont had completed the task. The principle had been established that the people was the constituent power and ultimate location of sovereignty. Hesitantly the states had moved from the pseudo-parliamentary principle that constitutional authority and legislative power could be united in the same body and were therefore to some degree intertwined, to one in which the two were clearly distinguished from one another. By attaching declarations of rights to their constitutions, six states also affirmed that there were certain rights which, according to the anonymous author of *Four Letters on Interesting Subjects* (published in Philadelphia in 1776) 'man never mean, nor ever ought, to lose, should be *guaranteed* not *granted*, by the Constitution'.[40] Also, Massachusetts had by trial and error constructed a procedure whereby the will of the people could be tapped, a constitution could be drafted in a convention elected solely for that purpose, and the approval of the electorate sought for its ratification. The system was not immediately accepted as the only permissible mode of constructing a constitutional system, still less did it guarantee equality, good government, or the protection of liberty, but it did become a model which was first emulated by the federal convention of 1787 and later copied by other states.

## V

Creation of a national union began simultaneously with the formation of state governments. It was a slower and more hesitant process that was bedevilled by major disagreements over the extent of the new central government's powers. Emergence of a vigorous united nation was not the only possible consequence of independence. Pre-Revolutionary American society contained a number of unifying elements – but also possessed centrifugal forces militating against unity. Before 1774 the only general associations were individual colonies at one end of the hierarchy and the empire at the other. What the Revolution made necessary was a new layer of community where previously none had existed. The war, with its need for an army and centralised direction, did much to promote unity but was not sufficient by itself. Congress conducted national affairs without any formal authority for six years, but this arrangement was no more than a short-term expedient. A formal system of national government was essential for the long-term future.

The first national constitution was the Articles of Confederation. Six drafts were prepared for Congress in 1775 and 1776 but a definitive version, significantly different from its predecessors, was not approved by the states and put into effect until March 1781. Benjamin Franklin offered a hasty plan on 21 July 1775 which circulated widely but was not formally considered because Congress adjourned twelve days later. Silas Deane produced one draft the same year and a second in March 1776, and three variants of a draft by John Dickinson of Pennsylvania were debated between June and August 1776. A final draft was prepared in 1777.[41]

Under the particular circumstances of the first year of warfare, the most pressing concern was preservation of intercolonial unity, especially since rivalries between Connecticut and Pennsylvanian settlers in the Wyoming Valley were worsening and there were overt regional animosities among the troops outside Boston.

Other issues were inescapable. The central problem was the old one of the disposition of powers between different levels of authority, for the colonies had rebelled against Britain in order to control their own internal affairs. They had been equally represented in both the First and Second Continental Congresses since there had been no practical alternative, and the smaller ones in particular were determined to maintain the principle of state equality as a means of sustaining their influence and identity. Franklin's plan divided both representation and taxation by population, thus giving greater influence to the most populous states, notably Virginia, Pennsylvania and Massachusetts, which together contained almost half the nation's population. Deane attempted to compromise by permitting representation by population in most instances but recommending that the states should count equally when determining major issues of policy such as war and peace. Both also proposed that each state should control its own domestic affairs, yet allowed Congress to make general ordinances, control major aspects of resistance, settle disputes between colonies and set up new colonies. Such systems would have produced a substantial transfer of power from the states to the central government. However, the full implications of a permanent constitution were scarcely appreciated, and Congress continued to exercise *de facto* power as best it could.

Congress's decision to declare independence was intended to be accompanied by a plan of confederation. Nevertheless most men were too absorbed in the process of constructing state constitutions to pay great attention to the matter. Those who gave the matter some thought agreed broadly with Carter Braxton when he stated that Congress should have authority 'to adjust disputes between Colonies, regulate the affairs of trade, war, peace, alliances &c. but they should by no means have authority to interfere with the internal police [i.e. affairs] or domestic concerns of any Colony'.[42]

A drafting committee was set up on 12 June 1776 with John Dickinson in effective control. By nature conservative and doubtful about the timing of independence, he did not believe the states would conduct their affairs wholly in the national interest, but considered it essential to place the interests of the union above those of the individual states. At first sight Article Three of his draft Articles of Confederation favoured the states by allowing them to retain their existing laws, rights and customs and granting them 'the sole and exclusive Regulation and Government of its own internal police', but it immediately withdrew the benefit by declaring that state laws should not interfere with the Articles and implicitly assigning all other powers to Congress.[43] As a clause which did not appear in the final draft made clear, the states might have been permitted to enjoy their current laws, but they were not necessarily to be allowed to control their own affairs in the future. Dickinson proposed to impose by national authority what in effect was religious toleration on each state as a means of defusing one of the most dangerous sources of potential strife. This implied that the confederation was to be superior to the states, and though it was denied a direct power of taxation, Dickinson's scheme laid the foundations for executive departments. What his draft did was to impose restrictions on the states and grant extensive powers to Congress.[44]

When the revised draft came before Congress there were three major issues of concern: representation, taxation, and control of the West. In spite of protests by the more populous states, voting in Congress was permitted to remain on the basis of equality among the states, and in spite of protests by the slave states, expenses were to be apportioned according to total population, but all exclusive powers over western lands were removed from Congress. Implicitly Congress was proposing to divide government powers: the authorities of Congress and the states were clearly separated and distinguished from each other, though the matter of sovereignty was never deliberately raised. Even so, formidable obstacles to ratification remained. Each delegate was obliged to consider the impact of the draft on the interests of his own state, and on some issues there was strong disagreement. In particular Virginia insisted on retaining its land claims, and conversely Pennsylvania, a landless state, demanded that Congress should control the western lands. In any case it was an open question whether the states would ratify the Articles in their current form.

Pressing war business prevented Congress from considering the draft Articles again until 1777. It was clear that the central issues were unresolved. Members could not agree whether the New England states had impinged on the powers of Congress when they had considered acting jointly to regulate prices in 1776. John Adams, and James Wilson and Benjamin Rush of Pennsylvania, who advocated strong central government, insisted that the subject impinged on continental affairs and usurped the functions of Congress. The action was condoned, but the issue refused to go away. When Congress considered a proposal that it should authorise local committees to apprehend suspected deserters until such time as the states could act, Thomas Burke of North Carolina persuaded his colleagues that Congress possessed no authority to exercise coercive power within a state. Burke, a new member, was determined to reassert the principle of state sovereignty.[45] He went on to persuade Congress to adopt an amendment which became Article Two, reversing the thrust of Dickinson's centralisation by declaring that: 'Each state retains its sovereignty, freedom and independence, and every power, jurisdiction and right, which is not by this confederation expressly delegated to the United States, in Congress assembled.' Although Article Thirteen of the draft required the states to abide by the decisions of Congress on questions submitted to them by the Confederation, and although Congress was necessarily acquiring increasing executive authority, Burke's amendment significantly altered the nature of the union by explicitly affirming the legal supremacy of the states and by reducing Congress to the status of an agent possessing strictly defined powers.[46] At the same time debate over the allocation of government costs was reopened. In spite of the solid resistance of the New England states, which believed their land more valuable per acre than that of other states, it changed the basis on which the contribution of each state to national expenses was calculated. Instead of basing assessments on population they would be based on the value of lands that had been granted and the buildings and improvements on them.

Congress did not approve a final version until November 1777, and hopes for speedy ratification were disappointed. The landless states were bitterly disappointed by the lack of Congressional authority over the western lands, and jealous of the added financial advantages enjoyed by those states which possessed them. Much of the jealousy was politically calculated, since land speculators based in the landless states found themselves at a disadvantage when dealing with lands located within the claims of rival states. Maryland was the last to hold out, and only ratified in 1781, when the landed states agreed for their own reasons, including in particular the security of their boundaries, to transfer title to the United States. Maryland was also under pressure from the French representative, the Chevalier de la Luzerne, who refused to supply ships in Chesapeake Bay until the Confederation was ratified. The transfer of British military attention to the South was another powerful stimulant towards agreement from 1780 onwards.

The Articles functioned until replaced by a new federal constitution in 1789. Their structure gave expression to a limited conceptualisation of national government. Each state possessed an equal vote in Congress which, unlike most states, continued to have only one house. The central government's powers were severely restricted. In particular Congress lacked an autonomous authority to impose taxes (it had to requisition funds from the states), and regulate commerce; apart from admiralty jurisdiction it lacked its own courts and so its interests and legislation were enforceable only in state courts whose judgements were influenced by local interests. But perhaps the Articles' crucial deficiency was the requirement that consent for amendments should be unanimous, for it gave individual states the right of veto over essential changes. The heart of their weakness lay in the disjunction between the substantive if tenuous growth of the institutions of central government and certain elements in the Articles on the one side, and the affirmation of the supremacy of the states contained in Article Two on the other. But conceding formal equality among the states did no more than acknowledge the reality of their political position. Americans faced a problematical future, for war had been a powerful unifier, and peace diminished one of the most powerful imperatives to union. And many problems remained to be solved.

# 6
# POLITICS IN THE STATES

For most of the Revolutionary era the individual states remained as much the primary stage for political and social activity as their predecessors the colonies had been before 1775. Many of the ideological principles so eloquently articulated in the Declaration of Independence could be implemented only within their domain for they, not Congress, retained responsibility for most of the duties of government. Congress directed the war but initially possessed little further authority. Each state determinedly defended its sovereignty and controlled its own finances, trade and economic policy; it also dealt individually with a host of political and social issues. In spite of the calls of national politics, many able men served as state governors or legislators, among them James Bowdoin and John Hancock in Massachusetts, Jonathan Trumbull in Connecticut, George Clinton in New York, John Dickinson in Pennsylvania and Delaware, Charles Carroll of Carrollton in Maryland, Thomas Jefferson, Patrick Henry and James Madison in Virginia, and John Rutledge in South Carolina. Under the particular circumstances of founding a nation they were obliged to be more activist than colonial administrations had been even, though the state constitutions proclaimed the merits of limited government. Their actions were central to the Revolution, and their record of effective administration far better than contemporary and later critics have allowed.

I

Many problems facing the states flowed directly from the processes of becoming independent. Some states had difficulty asserting their authority throughout their territory, and several faced threats of secession during the war and for some time after. Two New York counties, Gloucester and Cumberland, formed themselves into a separate state of Vermont in 1777 and some of New Hampshire's Connecticut valley towns persistently threatened to join them; the crisis was not resolved until Vermont was admitted as the first additional state in 1791. Berkshire County, the most westerly county in Massachusetts, functioned virtually independently of the rest of the state as well as of Britain for much of the war.[1] In the South, western settlers constantly posed problems for Virginia and North Carolina to the point at which, like Vermont, they were admitted as separate states during the 1790s. Georgia, always a weak state with few settlers in the eighteenth century, was in danger of disintegrating; in 1776–7 it rejected an invitation to incorporate into South Carolina.[2]

The war itself created acute problems. Once the British resumed their efforts to suppress the Revolution during the summer of 1776, the operations of both armies frequently made civil administration very difficult and sometimes impossible. Occupation of New York City deprived the state of its capital and lower counties for the remainder of the war; its government was able to function only with some difficulty from Kingston, almost 100 miles up the Hudson river. Similarly the Pennsylvania government was driven out of Philadelphia for several months in 1777–8. In South Carolina British troops were distributed throughout the state and occupied Charleston, thus preventing the legislature from meeting at all between February 1780 and January 1782. Worse still, the British were able to restore royal government for a time in Georgia, though not regular elections. At the same time much of the southern interior was either under British control or the scene of bitter fighting between Patriots and Loyalists; even where there was no formal campaigning British raiders often marauded and threatened the integrity of the new government, as happened when Benedict Arnold rampaged through Virginia in 1780–1.[3]

Dealing with loyalism was another major test for the new regimes. Both neutralism and loyalism provoked suppressive action throughout the country. In some areas, like most of

Virginia and the Connecticut valley in western Massachusetts, loyalism posed no significant threat but this was
unusual. New York's problems, which stemmed particularly
from the occupation of its lower counties and strong loyalism
in the Mohawk valley, led to a sequence of anti-loyalist
legislation. It ran from the Confiscation Act of 1779 to the
Citation Act of 1782, which suspended suits by residents of
the occupied area against debtors in the free area, and the
Trespass Act of 1783, which permitted refugees to sue anyone
who used their property during the British occupation. Maryland in particular faced great difficulties. An insurrection on
the Eastern Shore had to be suppressed by force in 1777, and
the militia had to be used to collect taxes in 1780. Similar
risings took place in two of Delaware's adjacent three
counties.[4] Every state enacted a series of test laws which
required men to take oaths of allegiance to it and used them
to coerce dissidents into submission. Further legislation was
intended to restrict Loyalist actions deemed inimical to the
new governments by defining treason in such a way as to
coerce those who were reluctant into choosing between the
risks inherent in loyalism and a commitment to the revolution.
Other laws banished or imprisoned Loyalists, taxed their
property and confiscated their estates – especially those like
the DeLanceys and Philipses of New York who overtly joined
the British. In Pennsylvania, however, the Revolutionary
government distinguished between lands held by the Penn
family as proprietors, which it confiscated as punishment for
their loyalism, and those they owned as private persons,
which were eventually returned. Many Loyalists were victims
of mob violence, especially in war zones such as New Jersey
and the Carolina backcountry where the fabric of social
relationships disintegrated for a time. Much concerned for its
own security, one of the new Pennsylvania legislature's first
acts was to banish eleven leading Quakers (including Thomas
Wharton and three members of the Pemberton family) to
Winchester, Virginia, in 1777; all had been influential members
of the Philadelphia mercantile community and prominent
figures in the city. In certain states, including Pennsylvania,
which enacted a treason law directed against Loyalists, it was
sometimes easier to convict tories of lesser offences and then

impose the death penalty. Forty-eight men were hanged in these circumstances. Once the Patriots regained control of South Carolina, the legislature confiscated or amerced the estates of 284 persons. Almost all lived in the low country round Charleston, for it was considered that any attempt to punish backcountry residents would re-ignite dangerous animosities.[5] The extent and success of anti-Loyalist action illustrated not only the endemic fear among Patriots and the threat posed to the new regimes by tories. It demonstrated that individual states enjoyed sufficient popular support to be able to coerce dissident minorities in the absence of the British army. It also proved that the new governments could enforce their will against opposition if need be.

Several states continued to have difficulties deriving from the forms of government they had constructed at the beginning of the Revolution. New Hampshire had drafted its constitution far too rapidly in 1776; its new system of government proved so inefficient that it had to be replaced eight years later.[6] At the democratic end of the political spectrum, much of the domestic politics of Pennsylvania revolved round the political consequences of its 1776 constitution. The conflicts it aroused were not resolved until the state drafted a second constitution in 1790. Those who had drafted and then defended the original constitution had in many cases been economic and social outsiders, and were often of German or Scotch-Irish Presbyterian stock; many were virtually unknown in politics before April of the previous year. Their opponents were Anglican-Quaker Patriots and men of wealth. Here also a change took place, for in the absence of the Loyalist elite, merchants such as Robert Morris, who would shortly become a major national figure, assumed political leadership for the first time. They were conservatives of notably broader horizons than the supporters of the Constitution and deplored what they regarded as its excessive democracy. In March 1779 they formed a Republican Society with the prime object of securing revision of the obnoxious Constitution, whose supporters promptly organised themselves as the Constitutionalists. The simple division was complicated by inflation and speculation by the rich which caused great hardship to the poorer members of the community. Later the same year merchants' resistance to the traditional methods of alleviating distress by regulating prices provoked the attack on James Wilson, a lawyer who defended their interests in the law courts, which became known as the Fort Wilson Riot. It was rooted in a conviction that citizens possessed the right to redress longstanding grievances that the government was unable or unwilling to remedy; in the absence of effective political influence, physical coercion was legitimate. Other issues were linked to changes in the state's power structure in the interest of the new men. They included the abrogation of the College of Philadelphia's charter on the grounds that it was controlled by the anti-Constitutionalists, though a sub-stitute University of the State of Pennsylvania failed to flourish and the charter was restored in 1789. Similarly Constitutionalists resisted the establishment of the Bank of North America until 1782 because it was identified with financial interests and conservative politics. The Constitu-tionalists were also determined to confiscate the Penn family's proprietary (but not private) lands and exclude former Loyal-ists and British sympathisers through the medium of test oaths.

Slowly the Republicans gained control and redressed the political balance. Ironically it was only by coming to terms with the unicameral legislature that they secured revision of the Constitution. By the mid-1780s the Constitutionalists had lost their majority control, and in 1790 a new and more orthodox Constitution was drafted by a state convention and approved by the people.[7]

Not that conservatism guaranteed political harmony. With-out doubt the Maryland Constitution was the most conserva-tive of the thirteen, and as with Pennsylvania its character strongly influenced the course of future politics. In practice all three elements of the state's government were placed in the hands of a small and rich elite. The dangers of such extremism in a heterogeneous state quickly became manifest. Turbulence and resentment against authority became endemic, especially among those who had little property, and politics were bedevilled by constant rivalry between the elite and their challengers.

The consequences were not entirely what conservatives

would have wished. Their more prudent leaders such as
Charles Carroll of Carrollton believed in the wisdom of
concessions in order to avert more dangerous challenges; they
realised that although the carefully constructed constitution
enabled them to control the state's established institutions,
they had no popular mandate and their power-base was
shrinking. A graduated property tax was introduced in place
of the customary poll tax in 1777, and the definition of taxable
property was widened. A proposal to establish a state university out of two private colleges, St John's College, Annapolis,
and Washington College, Chestertown, was withdrawn when
poorer whites objected that their taxes would be used to
support an institution which would benefit only those richer
than themselves. The need for constant vigilance made it
necessary for Carroll to reject a nomination to serve at the
national Constitutional Convention in 1787.[8] His decision
proved worthwhile, for he considerably influenced the format
of a legal tender law permitting the issue of paper money
which was necessary as part of the price to be paid for
retaining elite leadership. His shrewdness paid off by enabling
the rich to retain control which they might otherwise have
lost, but did not last indefinitely. After a quarter of a century
of rivalry, population changes by 1802 forced Maryland to
become the first state to introduce universal white manhood
suffrage.[9]

The South Carolina elite's determined attempts to retain
control were less successful. The first constitution made
concessions to those outside the seaboard elite, but left city
artisans in Charleston and farmers in the rapidly expanding
backcountry dissatisfied. Once roused to action by the struggle against Britain they refused to return to the subordinate
political roles previously deemed appropriate for them by
their social superiors. The claim by the rich to exercise
authority within the community as of right was no longer
tenable, especially since many of them had been only too willing
to welcome the British when they occupied Charleston. In a
divided state the coastal patriot elite won a measure of interior
support by recognising the political and military ambitions
of leading backcountry men. Gradually the inhabitants of
the interior counties built up their influence, especially after

their recovery from the ravages of war. A second, then a third, constitution improved their position by reapportioning the legislature, and the backcountry victory was symbolised in 1790 by the transfer of the state capital from Charleston on the coast to Columbia at the centre of the state.[10]

In Virginia, largest and most influential of all the states, the elite also faced challenges but included in their ranks a group of men, among whom Jefferson was pre-eminent, who were determined to seize the opportunity of independence to introduce reforms. They had led resistance to the British but had also been careful to attract the support of their social inferiors among the white community, if necessary by playing the race card. During the crisis that began in 1774 they brought lesser gentry, many of whom had never held high office, onto local committees of safety but were careful to retain control in their own hands. This policy was extended also to yeomen who insisted on political influence. Nevertheless, loss of the governor's court and the symbols of royal authority, coupled with demands from the new evangelical sects and inhabitants of their recently settled areas in the Southside and Piedmont weakened their control, though it took some time for the effects to be felt.[11]

Jefferson believed he could be more influential in his state than in Congress. He accepted a seat in the Virginia legislature in October 1776 in preference to another term in Congress and pursued a vigorous policy of legal reform. The results were mixed. In 1776 he secured abolition of primogeniture, by which intestate estates were passed to the eldest son, and entail, a legal device by which inheritance of family land could be channelled though several generations. Suppression of these feudal remnants had little substantive effect, since landowners usually avoided them, but their repeal was symbolic of revolutionary change. At the same time, Jefferson was appointed to a committee for revising all the state's laws. Together with George Wythe he reported 126 bills in 1779, and by the end of the war about two-thirds had been enacted. Some were technical and others were concerned with the organisation of representation and local government. An attempt to reform and codify criminal law failed by one vote, and a bill to introduce complete religious freedom had to wait until 1786 for enactment. A bill to create a public education system also failed to be accepted but was indicative of the cast of his mind. Jefferson believed that a republican government required an educated electorate, and accordingly its prime object was to promote good citizenship; it was only secondarily utilitarian in purpose. He proposed that all white children, including girls, should receive three years of free elementary education. Beyond that level there would be grammar schools which would be rigorously selective for those dependent on state support, and at the peak would be a reformed College of William and Mary, to which a final survivor of the selection process would be sent annually at public expense to join those whose families could afford the fees. The bill was never approved.[12]

Conservative leaders in New York, also expecting to command the state through a carefully constructed constitution, were disappointed. They faced continual pressure from below, and from 1777 onwards they began losing control. One loss was Vermont when it organised itself as a separate state. Even though election of the governor and senate was restricted to £100 freeholders new men began appearing in the senate, and George Clinton defeated the conservative and elitist landlord Philip Schuyler for the governorship. His popularity derived from a sound military record and republican reputation; he was also a shrewd politician who appreciated the value of patronage.

The new government's policies demonstrated popular influence. A spate of legislation punished the Loyalists and their sympathisers. Land policy was amended to reduce the special privileges enjoyed by great landowners; primogeniture and entail were abolished in 1780, remaining remnants of feudal legal privileges were abrogated and the state's 1787 bill of rights guaranteed tenants the same rights as landlords. Land was still available in huge tracts to speculators, but it was also available in smaller tracts of 640 acres. A particular problem was dealing with the southern district once the city had been evacuated by the British. Apart from disestablishing the Church of England, radical attempts to control Trinity Church (which was a major landholder), the chamber of commerce and King's College (translated into Columbia

College), met with only limited success. By the middle of the decade New York conservatives were able to regroup, though the terms on which they did so were significant. Their attempt to institutionalise conservative control by balancing property against the people and setting a high property requirement for voting in elections for the governorship and senate, had failed. Like their contemporaries in other states, they could no longer lay claim to the traditional deference of artisans, tenant and yeoman farmers; instead they had to accept new men in the legislature and the actuality of direct popular involvement in formulating policy. The solution was to raise politics to the national level and form a party – but one that would acknowledge the need for a popular base. Conservatism and wealth remained important in New York politics, especially under the brilliant leadership of Alexander Hamilton, but their special privilege in church, senate and council was lost.[13]

Financial problems were a continual scourge for almost every government. They stemmed from three general causes: the difficulty of financing the war and its consequent public debt, the continuing shortage of specie and the question of social equity involved in imposing taxes. At first the states preferred to issue bills of credit, but in spite of popular reluctance they were obliged to resort to taxation from 1777 onwards. Every state except New York, which began in 1778, Delaware, whose taxes were nominal until 1778, and Georgia, which raised one tranche of taxes in 1778 but no more until 1783, began levying taxes in that year and was forced to increase the amounts drastically to keep pace with inflation. Every possible form of taxation was explored: taxes on polls, land, other property, professional services, imports, luxury goods and salt. Each had its disadvantages and was unpopular among some taxpayers; all raised the question of whether taxes should be paid in specie, paper or goods. And in the end, the revenue raised was insufficient. The states were responsible for supplying both men and matériel for the army and met about half the cost of the war. The burden on taxpayers was enormous. In Maryland the average annual cost of the war to each white resident was almost 50 per cent of gross per capita income.[14] They also issued currency, and

during the 1780s several came increasingly to assume responsibility for servicing that part of Congress's debt held by their
own citizens, as they realised they would have to meet the cost
anyway since Congress met its own expenses by imposing
requisitions on them.

The consequences of the inescapable need to finance the
war by issuing paper currency, bills of credit and loans also
came home to roost. An immediate post-war boom in 1783–
4 expanded trade – especially imports – and was quickly
followed by a severe recession in mid-decade. By the end of
the war most states had refused to accept paper in payment
of taxes and ceased to make it legal tender for settlement of
private debts. Virginia, Maryland, Massachusetts and New
Hampshire could not hold this conservative position in face
of the economic crisis. Faced with a shortage of specie, their
own needs, and the demands for financial support from
Congress, seven states resumed issuing paper money in
1785–6. The key to the success of the issues lay, as in colonial
times, in the political and commercial status of those who
controlled it. It met immediate needs and worked well in
South Carolina, where it was accepted at par by merchants
and bankers as well as the state until 1787, and on the whole
in Georgia, Pennsylvania and New York, but was less successful in New Jersey, and North Carolina, where there was
substantial depreciation.[15]

Things were very different in Rhode Island, where the issue
of paper money provoked great scandal. The Constitution
gave its legislature almost complete authority, and inevitably
in such a small and sharply divided state, the issue became
entangled in the seemingly perpetual rivalry between its two
large towns and the small rural townships. Faced with
financial difficulties caused by its substantial contribution to
the national cause at a time when its commerce, and thus its
capacity to raise revenue, was damagingly disrupted, the state
felt obliged to introduce paper money. Over vehement protest
£100,000 was issued in 1786 and declared legal tender for
settlement of private debts as well as payment of taxes. Severe
penalties were specified for creditors who refused to accept the
money, even though its value dropped well below parity with
specie. When John Trevett took John Weeden of Newport to

court for refusing to accept paper money at par, the judges dismissed the case for lack of jurisdiction but expressed the opinion that the law was unconstitutional. The legislature responded by dismissing three of the judges, and continued its efforts to impose paper money on the inhabitants of the state until the legal tender clause was repealed by a fresh legislature in 1789. Meanwhile reports of the scandal circulated throughout the United States. Many critics interpreted the issue of paper money less as an economic question and more as an attack on the integrity of private property since individuals were legally obliged to provide goods and services at less than their true economic worth. Horror felt at Rhode Island's behaviour more than outweighed the success of paper money elsewhere and was often cited as a warning against excessive democracy.[16]

Taxation policy had other wide-reaching implications. It touched on a host of internal debates such as the agrarian-commercial divide in Rhode Island and the dispute over the constitution in Pennsylvania, and was shaped by consideration of the purposes to which the revenues would be applied. Thus in Maryland during the 1780s there was a continual battle between the Intendant of Finance, Daniel of St Thomas Jenifer, who insisted that the state had a duty to sustain and pay for the national debt, and Charles Ridgely, who championed provincial interests and argued that the war debt should be ignored and the state's fiscal policies constrained.[17]

There was also an important question of social equity. In the past colonial tax laws had overburdened the politically impotent to the benefit of the influential and rich (particularly the landed rich) though particular policies varied with shifting political fortunes. Faced with the challenging demands of the war the states faced increasing demands that taxation should be levied in relation to capacity to pay. In effect currency depreciation acted as a tax on money and penalised most those who held most bills — that is the rich merchants and politically more important, the soldiers. Lines were therefore sharply drawn between the poor and those in financial difficulties on one side and the prosperous on the other who preferred collection of taxes in specie, strict enforcement and high poll taxes. Ultimately it came down to a question of whether the new states were to respond to the popular majority or attach more importance to what in conservative eyes was the higher interest of sound finance. In Pennsylvania some men saw willingness to respond to popular pressure as a natural application of Revolutionary principles; Robert Morris, among others, interpreted it as a fatal weakness. In southern states victory went to those who demanded reform, and by the end of the war four out of five had moved some way towards the principle of taxation according to ability to pay.[18]

At the other end of the country, demands for financial reform in Massachusetts were determinedly resisted with disastrous consequences. The legislature elected under the new constitution pursued a relentlessly conservative financial policy designed to pay off the war debt and establish a firm financial base for its overseas commerce. In 1780 and 1781 it imposed heavy taxes, made specie the only form of legal tender, and accelerated the repayment of state debts. Such a policy impinged harshly on the poorer and less prosperous western counties, especially since one-third of new taxes were assigned to polls rather than property. When coupled with post-war recession, the customary shortage of specie in the area, resentment at eastern domination, and the area's democratic sentiments, the effects were felt severely in the western part of the state. Creditors both public and private used the courts to enforce their debts, and required debtors to be sold up to meet their obligations and sometimes to be imprisoned. In the summer of 1786 the western counties held conventions modelled on those of 1774–5 and forcibly closed on a number of courts, thus preventing the execution of judgements against debtors; similar conventions, and attacks on courts took place in Connecticut, New Hampshire and Vermont. Their hopes of influencing the state government were disappointed, and after an interval the dissidents slowly gathered an army of perhaps no more than 2500 men under the leadership of a Revolutionary war captain, Daniel Shays. Their plans to capture the federal arsenal at Springfield were frustrated, and the rebellion was easily suppressed in January and February 1787 though violence spluttered on until June.

The importance of Shays's Rebellion can be interpreted in

several ways. Much of its rhetoric on both sides revolved around class interests, that is, between the poor and rich, and farmers and the moneyed community. It was also a mutiny of traditional agrarianism against the expansion of commercial interests and values; Shays attempted to organise the rising on a basis of communities rather than class solidarity in the three western counties, but failed to attract all their members.[19] The rebellion gave conservatives a terrible fright and had an important effect on national politics, but its real significance was different. It demonstrated three things: firstly, that even a government derived explicitly from the sovereignty of the people could provoke rebellion if it pursued excessively conservative policies in the interest of a particular section of the community; secondly, that the Massachusetts government possessed the capacity to suppress a minor rebellion without national assistance; and lastly, that the structure of its constitution was generally firm and sound.

## II

In disposing of confiscated Loyalist property, the states overlapped the boundaries between the pressures of financing the war, punishing dissenters and pursuing social policy. The effects were extensive but mixed. Confiscation led to some restructuring of ownership, though the extent varied from area to area and was certainly less than it might have been. During the course of the war state governments confiscated land and other property worth millions of pounds from Loyalists and the proprietors. Some properties were substantial in size. Massachusetts auctioned property in 1779 which fetched almost £600,000 in depreciated currency. The Point Judith estate in Rhode Island extended over 1000 acres, and proprietary and other estates in the middle and southern states were even larger. In New York at least one major estate was confiscated in every county. Proprietary land in Pennsylvania was sold for £130,000, and Henry Harford, who inherited the Calvert proprietary estates in Maryland, lost 250,000 acres. But even had it been thought desirable to do otherwise, the imperatives of war finance often made it essential for the state governments to sell to the highest bidder rather than to distribute the property, and a further complication in what was primarily an agrarian society was that much of the property was urban rather than rural. Another consideration was the wish of politically influential men to secure land. On the other side of the ledger, in the case of Massachusetts some of the proceeds were retained for creditors, widows and children. Without doubt some states benefited considerably for the scale was enormous; thus Maryland received £450,000, and New York £3,085,000. New Hampshire, New York, Virginia and the Carolinas and Georgia acquired crown lands, and in North Carolina the Granville estate was also added to the public domain.[20] After the peace treaty had been ratified the United States acquired the huge territory between the Great Lakes and Florida as far west as the Mississippi river; all became open to settlement once Indian titles had been extinguished.

Some distribution did take place. North Carolina sold land at 50 shillings per 100 acres. New York gave land bounties to soldiers. Squatters were given pre-emption rights, and in the Hudson Valley several hundred tenants of Loyalist landlords were able to buy the land they already rented; thus increasing the number of freehold farmers in counties such as Dutchess, where tenantry had been common. Tenants of Patriot land-lords such as the Van Rensselaers, Livingstons and Schuylers were not, of course, given the same opportunity. Significant change took place on tenanted estates elsewhere. Confiscation of the Maryland proprietary estates led to a redistribution of land, a development which was accentuated by the sale of land owned by wealthy loyalists such as the Dulany family. Much of it went to investors, but many tenants were able to buy land at state sales. The process of change was also advanced by the donation of warrants for western lands given to soldiers (many of which were sold) and the decision of a number of tenants to move westwards in the absence of sufficient opportunity in Maryland.

Even so, much of the land was directly or indirectly purchased by men who were already prosperous or could obtain credit. In the West it was especially easy for them to assemble huge speculative tracts; by 1783 Washington held

58,000 acres beyond the Appalachian mountains. This pattern of transfer of confiscated property to other prosperous men is clearer in towns. In major cities such as Boston, New York and Philadelphia the transfer was predominantly from one prosperous conservative group to another. In Baltimore, twenty-four men purchased twenty-five estates at a price of £1500 each, and also the Loyalist-owned Principio Ironworks. Around Norfolk, Virginia, much of the property had been owned by expatriate merchants and was purchased by other merchants, while in Annapolis, Maryland, it went to merchants and lawyers. All in all there seems to have been a rough distinction between the disposal of urban and rural properties, between land held in great patroonships or proprietorships and other lands, and perhaps between the South and the rest of the country. Some of the new owners were undoubtedly former tenants and new farmers, but if others were new people they were also prosperous to a degree and their purchases only confirmed their growing wealth. New men were taking up places vacated by the previous elite. Yet while in New Hampshire up to a tenth of the state's land changed hands, probably only less than 4 per cent of the nation's total real and personal wealth changed hands. Probably three-fourths was transferred to merchants, speculators and professionals.[21]

## III

Termination of royal authority brought opportunities to make changes in the taxation and inheritance of land in the hope of widening landownership, and created considerable potential for social change. One immediate consequence was the abolition of quit rents which had been payable to the crown or proprietor, though since they had been widely evaded their abolition marked no significant modification. Much the same was true of the abolition of primogeniture and entail, which Jefferson had included in his law reform programme for Virginia and had seen as an essential part of his attack on aristocratic privilege in favour of opening up opportunity for small farmers. But the importance of the two devices had become largely symbolic before the Revolution in consequence of the widespread availability of land and the common practice of speculation. By 1786 only Massachusetts and Rhode Island had failed to abolish them.[22]

Independence gave the states opportunities for reform in other areas of social life. In numerous ways the important issues of religious liberty and denominational equality intersected with secular principles and political action. One major change that crossed the boundaries between social and political behaviour and intellectual life was the reordering of the relationship between religion and government. Religion in both its spiritual and ecclesiastical dimensions remained one of the central bonds sustaining the integrity of American society, as the provisions of the state constitutions clearly confirmed, but the first substantial steps were taken towards separating it from secular authority. Belief in a supreme being (in practice usually a Protestant God) was regarded as one of those shared values that gave cohesion to every community. The citizens of Ashfield, Massachusetts, insisted 'we will take the Law of God for the foundation of the forme [sic] of our Government'.[23] Some of the diversity that had characterised colonial religion continued into independence, though with important modifications. All states permitted freedom of worship but since they believed it necessary to confine officeholding to persons who were believed to be committed to the values of the community all except Rhode Island imposed some form of religious test. Almost every state expected its officeholders to be Christians. New Jersey, Georgia and South Carolina continued to require them to be Protestants, and Delaware demanded they be Trinitarian. Maryland, the only state with a substantial and influential Roman Catholic population, extended eligibility to them, thus allowing Charles Carroll of Carrollton, one of the richest men in the country, to hold office for the first time.[24]

A closely related matter was the question of religious establishment. Most states possessing an established church dealt with it in their constitution. New York, New Jersey, Delaware, Maryland, North Carolina and Georgia prohibited any establishment, and South Carolina dealt with the matter by legislation. Pennsylvania confirmed its rejection, and

Rhode Island had no need to act. Virginia was slowest of those that took action during the Revolutionary period, but went furthest. Its Anglican church had been tightly linked to secular authority before the Revolution, especially at parish level, but its position was being challenged by evangelical sects to a point at which it probably had fewer members than the Presbyterian, Methodist and Baptist churches by 1775. Its position was further but unjustifiably weakened by its inescapable association with the royal regime. Virginia's Declaration of Rights asserted the principle of free worship but permitted establishment to continue. Not until 1779 was the compulsory payment of tithes by all citizens discontinued, though Anglican ministers retained their sole right to conduct marriages, and also their glebes and other parochial property. Such a situation was unsatisfactory for all concerned.[25]

James Madison and Thomas Jefferson wished to separate church from state entirely, so that religion would become entirely a private matter and philosophical truth could prevail through the cut and thrust of free debate. Presbyterians joined those led by Patrick Henry who argued for a general assessment which would require all persons to pay a tax for the support of organised religion but would distribute the proceeds among all sects. This principle was unacceptable to evangelicals as well as to Madison and Jefferson, and especially to Baptists; they believed that all forms of state intervention impaired the purity of the relationship between men and God, and that the relationship between the secular state and church would have to be severed if the truth – by which they meant the revealed doctrines of grace – were to prevail. The struggle was long, and only in 1786 was Jefferson's 1779 Act for Establishing Religious Freedom approved by the legislature. It prohibited all forms of state intervention in religious affairs, sang praises to freedom of intellectual speculation in the search for truth, and uniquely its benefits were explicitly intended to be universal in application, rather than confined to Protestants or even Christians. Passage of the act was the result of an unusual combination. The phraseology and philosophy underpinning it were unquestionably Jefferson's, and responsibility for piloting it through the legislature belonged to Madison. But the key to its enactment lay in the

support given by backcountry evangelicals.[26] Once they realised the battle had been lost, the older Anglican elite came to
terms with their rivals.

In New England outside Rhode Island disestablishment
had to wait until long after the Revolution. Though the
Congregational Church was far from unchallenged, it enjoyed
the advantage of being associated with the victorious Patriot
cause. The greatest dispute during the Revolutionary period
took place in Massachusetts and revolved around the terms
of the 1780 Constitution. Article II of the Declaration of
Rights confirmed the right of every citizen to freedom of
worship, but Article III asserted the principles of religious
taxation and compulsory church attendance. A major advance was the concession that taxes were to be allocated
according to membership of every Protestant church, but this
policy required registration and continued to infringe the
Baptists' principled insistence on the need to separate churches from the state for spiritual reasons. It was easy to evade
but offensive to splinter sects and those who did not wish to
declare membership of any church. Of all the provisions of
the Massachusetts Constitution Article III aroused the
greatest criticism, but the urgent need to declare the whole
document ratified ensured that it would be brought into effect
along with other sections.[27] Not surprisingly it was bitterly
resented, and debate over establishment continued unabated
into the nineteenth century, but the Congregational Church's
association with the new republican regime was so close that
it was not disestablished in Connecticut until 1818 and in
Massachusetts until 1833.

A second issue that was treated very differently in each state
was the question of the position of African Americans. One-
fifth of the population had been imported by force to serve as
unskilled labour or was descended from those who had been
brought to America earlier. Some African Americans were
free, though they formed less than 1 per cent of the population, but slavery was legal throughout the colonies. By the
middle of the eighteenth century, however, white American
opinion was beginning to turn against slavery, in keeping with
enlightened opinion in Europe. In the meantime the status of
blacks in Revolutionary America was rich in tragic irony. By

the end of the war, only South Carolina and Georgia had not
recruited African Americans, whether free or slave, into the
army. There was no slave rebellion, but blacks clearly hoped
for freedom – and in the Chesapeake region 3000 to 5000
(about 2 to 3 per cent) of adult African Americans fled to the
British in the hope of obtaining it.[28] The Revolution accelerated the trend towards emancipation but failed to complete
it. Slavery continued to expand in the southern and southwestern states until brought to an end by the Civil War.

The relationship between anti-slavery agitation and the
Revolutionary movement was far from straightforward. The
disjunction between libertarian rhetoric and chattel slavery
was obvious, and the movement to abolish slavery had begun
several decades previously. Under the spur of John Woolman,
a New Jersey Quaker, and Anthony Benezet of Pennsylvania,
the Philadelphia Yearly Meeting of Friends urged its members not to import, buy, sell, or even keep slaves. In 1773 New
England Quakers began freeing their slaves, and in 1776 the
Philadelphia Yearly Meeting agreed to expel slaveowners
from membership. Benezet also crusaded against the slave
trade, and as the Revolutionary crisis heightened awareness
of ideological principles, so the anti-slavery movement gathered
strength in every province from Pennsylvania northwards. In
Massachusetts a group of blacks pointed to the disparity
between slavery and the colonial protests against British
infringement of their own liberty, and petitioned for freedom
in 1773. Both Rhode Island and Connecticut abolished their
own slave trade. The position was clearly influenced by the
structure of each colony. Where Quakerism was strong, as in
Pennsylvania, west New Jersey and Rhode Island, considerable progress was made towards changing public attitudes.
Revolutionary sentiment had similar effects in other parts of
New England. In New York, where toryism was strong and
Quakerism weak, and up to a fifth of the population in the
area around the city was enslaved, anti-slavery was slow to
develop. In the South, where 85 per cent of the slaves lived,
there was little movement.[29]

Building from colonial beginnings, substantial but incomplete progress towards emancipation began during the Revolution. By 1787 every state except Georgia had prohibited

the commercial importation of slaves or, in Pennsylvania and North Carolina, imposed prohibitive duties. Vermont banned slavery in its constitution when it organised itself in 1777, but no other state took such a drastic step. The first state to abolish slavery by statute was Pennsylvania in 1780. Massachusetts took a more complicated path. One criticism of the rejected 1778 draft constitution had been that it condoned slavery, yet the 1779 convention did not discuss and the constitution did not mention the matter. A series of legal cases revolving around the relationship between a black, Quok Walker, and his putative owner, Nathaniel Jennison, led to an unsatisfactory resolution of the problem when the Chief Justice declared in the Supreme Court in 1783 that slavery was incompatible with the new constitution. The legal position remained uncertain, but the practical situation was that slavery had in effect been abolished, and in 1790 the first Federal Census of Massachusetts reported no slaves. New Hampshire had followed a similar path by 1810 without any legislative or legal action. The remaining New England states began the process of gradual emancipation in 1784. In all these states the task was relatively simple, though except in Vermont not easy, since only 2 per cent of the population was enslaved except in southern Rhode Island. By 1790, about 20,000 northern slaves were freed. Elsewhere it was another matter. Since sections of New York and New Jersey had substantial slave populations in which large sums of capital were invested, resistance to emancipation was accordingly more determined. Even here the process of emancipation eventually began in 1799 and 1804 respectively, but it was a deliberately gradual process. In all instances freedom was only made available for future generations so that slavery was not ended in New York until 1827, and 18 men were still semi-enslaved apprentices in New Jersey on the eve of the Civil War.[30]

Movement towards emancipation was very limited in the South. Although they detested slavery, most sophisticated leaders of Virginian society were economically shackled to it; even Jefferson and Washington occasionally if reluctantly bought and sold blacks. Many rich whites in the lower South were actively committed to the institution, and many less affluent whites throughout the South saw slave labour as an instrument for increasing production, exploiting fresh land and enabling them to enjoy the rewards of greater wealth and social advancement. For most southerners, especially perhaps poor whites, slavery was also a method of defining relations between the races and sustaining the myth of the equality of all white men. In 1778 Virginia abolished the commercial importation of blacks for sale, but Jefferson failed to obtain an amendment to introducing gradual emancipation; he also admitted that since most whites believed there were deep natural divisions between the races it was necessary that free blacks should be required to leave the state.

Efforts in Congress to outlaw the slave trade permanently also failed during the life of the Confederation. The demand for labour in the lower South after the war was so great that the trade was reopened for a time. Limited advances took place in the upper South: manumission was made easier in Virginia in 1782, Delaware in 1787 and Maryland in the 1790s, leading to a sixfold increase in the free black population of those states by 1800. Both Maryland and Virginia also discussed gradual emancipation, but in spite of the shrinkage of tobacco as a component of their economies, nothing came of it. For a time some southerners hoped that changes in the structure of their economy would make the region less dependent on its unskilled labour force, and that slavery would therefore decay of its own inutility, just as white indentured servitude had expired by the 1790s.

This hope proved too optimistic. Instead slavery spread further into the Piedmont and the upper South exported surplus slaves to the developing areas of the lower South, where white resistance to concessions was total. At the Constitutional Convention in 1787 the South Carolina and Georgia delegates threatened secession if any attempt were made to interfere with slavery within their states. They conceded that Congress should have authority to close the international slave trade in 1808, but meanwhile imported large numbers of blacks.[31]

Another subordinated group, white women, contributed materially to the attainment of independence but shared very little in the political benefits of the Revolution. Many, especially poor women, performed vital support services such as

nursing the sick for the army. The service of others was less
direct. Their political views were assumed to coincide with
those of their husbands – whether Patriot or Loyalist – and
they were expected either to confine themselves to the traditional domestic sphere or to be supportive of their husbands
in public life. Thus Abigail Adams, a highly able woman, ran
the family farm while her husband John attended Congress
and served overseas. She urged him to 'remember the ladies'
while drafting the new government but to no avail. Nowhere
was there any significant improvement in the legal status of
women, and if anything the ability of married women to control their property diminished as equity courts (which provided some protection) were merged with common law courts
which were bound by customary male-oriented precedents.
They briefly enjoyed the franchise in New Jersey, but according to Mary Beth Norton the effect of the Revolution on
American women was felt in their private lives – familial
organisation, their personal aspirations and their self-
evaluation.[32]

# IV

White men outside the highest ranks of society were more
fortunate. For them, the Revolution brought important
changes in their relationship with their social superiors and
greater participation in public life. These changes were also
partly consequences of other secular developments. The
popuation was increasing and in older communities its density
per square mile was rising; settlement was also extending
westwards and to a lesser extent northwards from existing
communities. Before the war the British government had been
reluctant to create new counties and townships and fresh
offices and political districts to accommodate fresh communities lest they should lose control. When pressing demands
were coupled to natural developments during the Revolution
these demands became irresistible. In many states such as
New Hampshire the exigencies of revolution attracted increased numbers of men into politics, and the size of the
legislature increased accordingly. Reorganisation of counties

and electoral districts had similar effects, as did the concession of representation to western and other more recently settled areas, which seldom had elites comparable to those in the seaboard and urban centres of colonial America: in each case the creation of new counties and townships increased the demand for men to populate new offices. Also, colonial offices to which incumbents had been appointed by the crown frequently became elective or were indirectly elective. Increased frequency of elections, including those for the upper house, in New Hampshire, New Jersey and North Carolina and the governorship in Massachusetts and New York, generated more opportunities for new men to enter political life. Opportunities were widened still further by limitations on the tenure of office in a number of states.[33]

More men became eligible to vote. In part rising prosperity and inflation made it easier to meet the suffrage requirements but six states (Pennsylvania, New Hampshire, Vermont, New Jersey, Georgia and Maryland) deliberately lowered the qualifications, with the effect that the electorate increased to 60–90 per cent depending on state and local area. Removal of many religious restrictions enfranchised almost all Christians and some Jews, and some free blacks were permitted to vote in Pennsylvania, North Carolina, New York, New Jersey, Maryland and Massachusetts. For a number of years several states imposed loyalty oaths designed to exclude tories, but Pennsylvania's Test Oath was repealed in 1786. In New Jersey careless drafting of the constitution extended the franchise to all free inhabitants, thus permitting even women and free blacks to vote for a time. Turnout at elections also increased in most states. This tendency was encouraged by wider use of the secret ballot and increased competition among candidates that rose through the 1780s to a climax during the elections to the constitutional ratifying conventions of 1787–8.[34]

The democratising effects were clearly visible at other levels of state politics. According to Jackson Turner Main's study of six legislatures from New Hampshire to South Carolina, their members after the Revolution were significantly different from those before it. During the late-colonial era, the farmers and artisans who comprised up to three-quarters of the voters overwhelmingly selected their representatives from among those tenth of white males who were either well-to-do (worth £2000 to £5000) or wealthy (worth more than £5000). By the end of the war a great change had taken place among the legislators. The proportion of the wealthy had dropped from 46 to 22 per cent, members of old elite families had declined by more than one-half and even the proportion of the well-to-do or better off fell from four-fifths to about one-half. The electorate was increasingly selecting as its representatives men of more modest means such as farmers and artisans. Before the war they had comprised less than one-fifth of the legislature; afterwards they were more than two-fifths, rising to a majority in some northern legislatures. In the South the post-war legislators owned only about one-half the property of their colonial predecessors. As Main argues: 'Clearly the voters had ceased to confine themselves to an elite, but were selecting instead men like themselves'.[35]

One device for sustaining elite control proved to be very disappointing. Drafters of eleven constitutions incorporated an upper house or senate in the belief that it would permit the wisdom of the elite to mitigate what they feared would be the excesses of the more democratic lower house of legislature. Before the war colonial councils had been populated from the oldest and richest families, and their prime function had been the defence of royal authority, though within this constraint they had proved useful and efficient. Revolutionary state leaders hoped to retain their social supremacy by adapting upper houses to new circumstances, but made them more democratic than perhaps they intended. All except Maryland's upper houses were to be elected by voters rather than appointed or filtered, though the property qualification was generally set higher than for the lower houses. The new upper houses were also larger and geographically more representative, and like the lower houses the social status of their members drifted socially downwards. The number of farmers increased from 30 per cent to over one-half, and the number of merchants and lawyers was correspondingly reduced. Similarly the number of men possessing moderate property increased threefold to equal the number of the rich. The ranks of self-made men increased at the expense of the older

influential families who in some cases had been diminished
by loyalism. But the extent of the change should not be
exaggerated: the senates remained more elitist than democratic.[36]

There were also more obviously political reasons for the
dilution of elite control. Changes were notably clear among
officeholders. In Philadelphia the proprietary gentry had
generally opposed independence and in consequence lost their
power. The departure of many Loyalist officeholders created
vacancies for new men – a trend accentuated by the temporary absence of many Patriot leaders in Congress, the army,
and the diplomatic service. Among those who held the highest
offices (governors, lieutenant-governors, secretaries, treasurers,
chief and associate justices of the highest courts and councillors) the turnover ran to 77.5 per cent during the war, with
29 per cent of those who had held office during the closing
years of the colonial regime becoming neutral, and the
majority Loyalists. The turnover was especially high in the
proprietary and royal colonies, but less so in New England.
The older inter-related networks of wealth, status and family,
which had sustained elite control before the Revolution, were
severely damaged, all the more so since the exiles were men
with strong imperial associations who had become accustomed
to using their royal connections as counterweights to what
they had feared as democratic excesses. Even though there
was little change in local leadership in New England, the
effects were widely felt. In New Jersey and elsewhere the
tendency towards oligarchy was reversed, and new men like
John Hancock in Massachusetts, George Clinton in New York
and Patrick Henry in Virginia replaced the previous royal
governors. None were poor, but their success demonstrated
that the older deferential structure of authority was crumb-
ling. After the Revolution the wealthy remained disproportionately represented in high office, but their dominance had
diminished substantially, the proportion of the well-to-do had
increased, and in many states even those of average wealth
were represented. In Charleston, mechanics sat in the legislature and on the Board of Wardens. In Philadelphia they
provided seven out of ten elected officials in 1776–7 and by
1777 occupied half the seats in the municipal judiciary. In

New Hampshire the authority of the Revolutionary leaders depended on their capacity to satisfy local rather than imperial interests.[37]

The establishment of new governments brought significant changes in the balance between elites and their fellow white male citizens as well as between governments and the people. They flowed in part from conflicting uses of language. Elites often used the term 'the people', especially during the struggle against Britain, but did so as a synonym for 'community'; they did not intend it to imply equality of social status, political rights or participation in public affairs. During the Revolution it became clear that their choice of vocabulary was a bad mistake, for the word had several meanings and it opened the way for social inferiors to define it as including all citizens, thus implying equality of rights, if only for white males. They could also challenge elite supremacy.

Each state tackled the question of political equality differently, but in virtually all the old elite were challenged by their social inferiors and most deemed it prudent to take their interests and aspirations into account. Equality still did not mean complete equality of political influence or power, let alone equality of property, but it did mean that in theory every white man was entitled to equality of respect, equality of consideration for his interests, and equality of freedom from domination by others, though practice often fell short of principle. The extent of popular success varied from state to state. Conservatives were moderately successful in sustaining their position. But the consequences of the doctrines of equal rights and the sovereignty of the people were already evident. Voting was still almost entirely confined to those whose possession of a modicum of property gave them both the capacity to exercise independent judgement and a stake in society, but the boundaries of the political nation had been substantially extended. More men could vote and hold public office, and did so. Representatives were also responsible to the electorate, and though the logic of the new system had yet to lead to majoritarianism it had already brought about important changes. The old concept of prescriptive authority modified by the grant of special privileges and the consent of the governed that had characterised the British colonial system had been killed by the Revolution, and what replaced it was different. As members of independent states, the provincial elite could not claim authority as an automatic right of social status. Instead, both principles and circumstances obliged them to share their power with a wider range of their fellow citizens and permitted them to govern only as stewards responsible to the people for the administration of affairs in the interest of the communities as a whole. If they claimed that the general welfare was conterminous with their own interests, they would be called upon to prove the point. And the new constitutions permitted incremental reform and possessed machinery for modification should it be desired.

Attempts by the old social elites to retain power met with mixed success. Prevailing conditions in Revolutionary America left them no option but to concede the right of their social inferiors to participate in government, but they believed that the owners of large property should be entitled to special institutional protection against the jealousy of the masses, and rationalised their position by arguing that society was best served if its affairs were directed by the 'best' people. Jefferson attempted to distinguish between an aristocracy of talent, which was desirable, and an aristocracy of wealth; most members of the elite assumed they were identical. They had hoped to build their continued supremacy into the new constitutions by such devices as requiring differential property qualifications at each level of public office and establishing upper houses or senates which would be populated largely by rich property owners.

What happened was that political behaviour took an unexpected turn. Senates had been constructed on the assumption that the primary division in American politics would run along horizontal social divisions. In the event the division between the rich and the many proved to be only one among several. Jackson Turner Main has argued that the primary division was different. It was a separation between agrarian-localist interests on one side and commercial-cosmopolitan interests on the other. He persuasively demonstrates that identifiable voting blocs existed in every state: the cosmopolitans and localists of Massachusetts, Maryland and the Carolinas were almost identical to the Anti-Clintonians in New York,

the Republicans and Constitutionalists in Pennsylvania, and
divisions between Northern Neck and Southside interests in
Virginia, with comparable differences in remaining states.[38]

Divisions ran along cultural and locational lines as well as
economic and social ones. In the North the cosmopolitans
came from commercial areas and in the South they comprised
large property-owners. In both areas they included men who
were not farmers, but all lived along navigable rivers, had
connections in towns and with large-scale commerce, were
well-to-do or wealthy and above all had wide interests and
experience and a broader outlook than their fellow citizens.
They welcomed activist government (provided they could
direct it), applauded conservative monetary policies and
feared the agrarian democracy of their opponents. In their
view men of little property were unfit to govern. In contrast
the agrarian localists generally owned small properties in the
North, inhabited farming areas outside the main plantation
regions in the South, or had other especially local interests.
They generally lived in remoter interior areas that were
predominantly rural, and cultivated small farms which produced only limited marketable surpluses; on the whole they
were only moderately prosperous and had narrower intellectual, economic and social horizons. Their legislative delegates
sought primarily to help their fellow farmers, especially small
farmers. They were suspicious of government and much
preferred self-administration at local level. In particular they
argued for low-interest money and debtor relief when this
became a major problem; they opposed banking, business and
urban interests.

What was happening in response to the clash of different
interests in increasingly complex societies was the emergence
of proto-parties. The groupings were seldom organised –
though they were in Pennsylvania over the Constitution and
the Bank of North America, in Rhode Island over paper
money and in Massachusetts over monetary policy – and were
not as sophisticated in structure as the parties of the 1790s,
let alone the party systems of the nineteenth and twentieth
centuries. In this sense the term 'faction' is preferable to
'party' as a description. One of the most illuminating indica-
tors of the development was the changing relationship

between the two houses in the legislatures. Interest-group politics and the growth of proto-parties or factions encouraged the development of vertical factional lines across the two houses in place of the horizontal lines between them which it had been assumed would distinguish between the interests of property and numbers. The senates quickly ceased to possess any distinctive social characteristics and became only revisory bodies whose function was to evaluate and amend legislation passed by the lower house. Thus popular as well as conservative propertied groups were present in the upper houses, though conservatives were more elitist than the popular groups and were usually in a majority. Only in Maryland and South Carolina were the senates truly elitist in the manner originally assumed, and only in the former was the difference between the houses so great as to lead to continual disputes.[39]

Within a decade of the Declaration of Independence significant social and political developments had taken place in the states. All had constructed systems of government based on the principle of the sovereignty of the people. They had faced severe difficulties, many of which flowed from the demands of the war, and on the whole dealt with them successfully. Several states had introduced substantial reforms, though the curse of slavery still shackled the overwhelming majority of blacks. Above all the Revolution had encouraged the white lower orders (and some blacks and women) to demand substantial advances in their status within society. The American Revolution in the states did not achieve total democracy in the twentieth-century sense, but it had a profoundly democratising effect. The mass of white males had become active participants in politics, and the elites were obliged to share their power.

# 7

# PROBLEMS OF INDEPENDENCE

Far above all others, the central issue facing the United States during the remainder of the century and beyond was the growth of national union. The Revolutionary war had a powerfully nationalising effect, but independence was no guarantee of survival as a single society, and the 1780s has been aptly if misleadingly labelled the 'Critical Period'. Some conservative contemporaries and nineteenth-century historians (notably John Fiske, who popularised the term) argued that the United States was close to disintegrating, and placed much of the blame on what they considered as the inadequacy of the Articles of Confederation as a system of national government. In their view the union was saved only by nationalists who got a Convention called at Philadelphia in 1787 and drafted a new and more effective Constitution. More recently, progressive historians (notably Merrill Jensen) have challenged this thesis and pointed to the considerable number of successes achieved during the Confederation's brief life. There was indeed paradox, for by the end of 1781 many building blocks necessary for national development were in place and others were to be added, yet only a few years later many people shared George Washington's view that a crisis was imminent and things could not be allowed to continue as they were.[1]

Numerous problems faced the new regime and tested it from every direction. Some probed the sectional rivalries among states possessing different or opposed interests, others posed questions concerning the distribution of authority between Congress and the states, and others raised the issue of the balance between conservative and more democratic government. Foreign relations posed more problems, especially since their resolution often impinged on domestic affairs. Some difficulties (especially economic problems) were beyond the capacity of any government to overcome.

## I

Hardly surprisingly, the economy took a considerable time to recover from the destruction of war and separation from Britain. After a brief surge marking the end of fighting, the mid and late 1780s were years of post-war depression, though prospects were more promising at the close of the decade. Damage to many seaboard towns and large swathes of the interior had been severe; production, income and wealth had consequently suffered. Since the domestic economy was relatively small and dispersed, recovery depended largely on trade, and as late as 1790 commerce with Britain (a bellwether of prosperity) was less than it had been before the war. The United States no longer received from Britain the favoured treatment previously enjoyed by the colonies; to their great disadvantage American traders were excluded from the West Indies and their ships were regarded as foreign for the purpose of the Navigation Acts. All the South's major export crops – tobacco, rice, naval stores and indigo – suffered, and the northern iron, shipbuilding and whaling industries were even more severely damaged. Direct access to continental European markets was inadequate compensation for these losses. Economic difficulties were compounded by imports of large quantities of British goods, often at high prices and expensive credit charges. Between 1784 and 1786 the United States imported from Britain goods worth £7,591,935 but sold less than one-third of that in return. The consequences were shortages of money, commercial failures in major cities, depressed prices and wages, and reduced output. New England was hit hardest since it was very dependent on the carrying trade, but South Carolina, whose rice exports dropped by 46 per cent compared with the early 1770s, also suffered severely. Conditions were not as bad in other parts of the South and the Middle states, but when farm prices fell in 1785 considerable agrarian distress followed.[2] In the opinion of John J. McCusker and Russell Menard, economic performance during the severe contraction that lasted from 1782 to 1790 deteriorated by almost one-half compared with 1772 – a decline comparable to that of the Great Depression between 1929 and 1933.[3] The economic as well as other costs of independence were high.

Yet beneath the surface some benign secular processes were operating. Decennial demographic growth, which had dipped during the 1770s, accelerated to 41 per cent between 1780 and 1790 (the fastest in United States history), and the population increased from 2,781,000 to 3,929,214. Included within these numbers was substantial immigration to supplement natural increase. Another notable feature was rapid settlement west of the Appalachians and south of the Ohio; by 1790 the population of modern Kentucky rose to 73,677 and Tennessee reached 35,691.[4] Moreover, the economy slowly began to recover and seek new directions. British restrictions could be evaded – especially in the West Indies – and trade was expanding with continental Europe and even the Orient. Also, there is evidence suggesting that the disruption of overseas trade diverted attention to the domestic market and encouraged investment in internal improvements and manufacturing.[5] Furthermore, the groundworks of a sophisticated financial system were being laid in the form of several banks – the Bank of North America in Philadelphia, the Bank of New York and the Bank of Massachusetts in Boston. Unfortunately the full benefits could not be enjoyed for some years to come.

## II

The Articles of Confederation undoubtedly promised a more effective central government than the old Congress once they came into effect in 1781. First it was necessary to apply the principles of the Articles by constructing a system of government. This was the easiest task and was quickly done. Three executive departments were set up: finance, foreign affairs and war, with Robert Morris, Robert R. Livingston and Henry Knox as their respective heads. They functioned with varying success until replaced by the new government in 1789. At the same time, however, Congress ignored committee proposals that the Articles should be amended to permit it to use force to compel the states to fulfil their federal obligations. Similarly it rejected suggestions that it should be authorised to impose embargoes and impress property in wartime, appoint tax collectors and seize the property of delinquent states, the last of which in particular would have drastically altered the balance of power.[6] Attempts to coerce the states were totally impractical.

Finance posed the most demanding problems. On being appointed Superintendent of Finance in 1781, Morris tackled several related difficulties by developing a systematic financial policy. His programme contained three major elements. One was to develop sound paper money redeemable in specie. To do this he used the Congressionally chartered but privately financed Bank of North America by investing $254,000 of government specie to supplement inadequate private investment and encouraging it to issue notes and make loans to the government; he also issued additional notes backed by his private credit and reorganised army provisions contracts. Together these measures assisted materially in stabilising the currency. More importantly, Morris planned to restructure the national accounts and apportion war costs among the states, while retaining certain important obligations for Congress to provide a basis for a public debt; this, he argued in a report on public credit dated July 1782, would form the 'strongest cement' to keep the union intact. A regular revenue was an essential corollary, and he proposed an impost on trade, a poll tax, and taxes on land and distilled liquors. Morris's object was to give Congress political independence from the states by restoring credit, creating financial stability and encouraging economic growth; he did not particularly intend to diminish state power, nor did he propose extending Congressional authority to interstate and foreign trade, though both would have been a likely consequence of his programme.[7]

Unhappily, most of his high hopes were disappointed. The foreign loans which partly underpinned it dried up, and shortage of revenue caused constant difficulties. Morris's proposals for land, poll and excise taxes were rejected, though

Congress had already proposed an impost or import duty of 5 per cent in 1781. Since the impost was effectively an amendment to the Articles, it had to be approved by all 13 states. Rhode Island refused its assent in November 1782, and by that time Virginia had rescinded its earlier ratification. Congress consequently remained dependent on the states for revenue to meet its expenditures. The procedure by which it requisitioned funds was unsatisfactory since the states often failed to meet their obligations and could not be compelled to do so.

During the closing years of the war, difficulties with the army compounded Congress's other problems. Officers pressed hard for back pay and half-pay pensions, and the Connecticut line demanded in 1782 that unfulfilled promises of pay should be honoured. The most menacing challenge came from a group of officers (including several senior officers) at Newburgh, New York, during the winter of 1782–3. It hinted at a coup d'état backed by force, and was defused only by General Washington's use of his considerable personal authority. Later the same year, a group of dissatisfied soldiers surrounded the Pennsylvania State House while Congress was meeting and threatened its members. Congress was humiliated and obliged to abandon Philadelphia for a time, but otherwise the mutiny had little effect. News of the definitive peace treaty arrived in April, and the army was allowed to disperse. A proposal to retain an army of 896 men was fiercely criticised as inimical to American liberty, and numbers were halved, but in June 1784 all but 83 privates and a few officers were discharged.[8] For a time the only other armed forces were the state militias.

Partly in response to the army's demands for pay, Congress approved a second major financial programme on 18 April 1782. Once again an impost of 5 per cent was recommended, but with additional specific purposes. It was to be restricted to 25 years, and the revenue was intended to service the national debt in the states in which the revenue was raised. Military pensions were to be commuted and added to the debt, and it was intended that taxation should be shifted from land, as required by Article 8 of the Articles of Confederation, to population (including all free citizens and counting slaves

as three-fifths of a person for this purpose). Since the programme was in effect an amendment to the Articles, it was
once more felt to require unanimous consent. At one point the
impost again came close to ratification, but New York's
approval in 1786 was so qualified that Congress could not
accept it.[9] Morris had hoped that creation of a national debt
would justify a separate revenue for Congress, but he was
disappointed and left office in 1784.

Treatment of the Revolutionary debt continued to lie at the
heart of relations between Congress and the states, and thus
at the heart of the union. Congress had been obliged to share
its financial obligations with them in 1780, and this trend
continued throughout the decade. It made good sense in some
respects to allow the states to service much, though not all, of
the debt under Congress's direction. Most of the remaining
debt consisted of expenditures incurred for the general welfare
by the states as well as Congress; it was treated as common
charges, then distributed among the states according to the
land valuation formula. The complex task of settling accounts
between Congress and the states began in 1782, lasted
throughout the 1780s and was concluded only in 1793 after
the state debts were assumed by the federal government.
Another element requiring attention was the separate public
debt which had originated in loan certificates, and expanded
when other financial obligations such as the claims of the
Continental army and private citizens were settled. This
included the foreign debt. It was expected to be kept intact
and paid by the federal government, and was intended to be
met by Congress itself out of its own revenue.[10]

When faced with insistence that requisitions for servicing
the national public debt should be made partly in specie, the
states came under pressure from creditors. They began to
assume responsibility for servicing directly that part of the
debt held by their own citizens instead of responding to
Congressional requisitions for the same purpose – each state
suspecting (probably correctly) that not all the other states
would meet their obligations even if it did itself. The requirement to pay part of the debt in specie imposed severe burdens
on state taxpayers, especially since the states were also faced

with difficulty in dealing with their own debts. The system continued until 1788 and worked quite well. Congress obtained almost sufficient revenue to meet its normal expenses, and the states met the interest on the public debt under federal auspices. The result was that the Confederation was solvent, or nearly so, in domestic affairs, but was obliged to default on all but the Dutch section of the foreign debt. Nevertheless, Congress had been compelled to yield management of the debt to separate state action.[11]

Far more seriously, by 1786 the states had poached much of Congress's central function by incorporating the national debt into their state debts. Led by Pennsylvania, Maryland and New York, which by that time had appropriated nearly $9 million (almost one-third of the principal of the public debt) and New Jersey the states effectively took over the debt, though New England and the southern states apart from Maryland had been able to take over little. This appropriation also diminished Congress's claim to an independent revenue. The potential damage of this process to the status of Congress was prodigious, especially since the states were taking over financial responsibility at the request of public creditors. Had it continued, the states would have retired the debt using cheap finance methods. But Congress would have been left with depleted functions and little justification for seeking enlarged powers. The long-term consequences would have been incalculable.[12] It was also losing the political support of one of the most powerful interest groups in the country, and the gain to the states was a further centrifugal force dividing the nation since the revenues flowing from the operations were being used for local purposes. Financial and commercial difficulties in the states compounded the crisis.

### III

Linked firmly to the distribution of powers between the states and Congress was the problem of trade. In keeping with the limited nature of central authority under the Articles of Confederation, control over commercial matters was retained by the states. Immediately the Revolutionary war was over it became apparent that this was unsatisfactory especially since the United States was a weak country trading among major powers. Beginning in 1784 there were increasing demands that the Articles should be amended to allow Congress to regulate trade among the states as well as with foreign countries. The proposal aroused considerable intersectional rivalry since each area had different interests.[13] The mercantile interests of New England and the Middle states preferred a navigation act that would protect American shipping and trade and enable a commercial treaty to be negotiated with Britain, whose government was refusing to negotiate with Congress since it could not bind the individual states. Expanding industrial interests in the same areas argued for protective tariffs which would protect domestic products from British competition. In contrast southern states, as exporters of agricultural products, preferred free trade since they feared exploitation if the carrying trade were allowed to fall exclusively into northern hands instead of being competitively shared with Britain.

There is considerable evidence to suggest that economic pressures were compelling the states to adopt compatible policies without general regulation. By 1787 American goods were free from duties, and in instances where one or more states pursued especially severe policies they were forced to back down. Thus Connecticut and New Jersey were dominated by the rivalry of their more powerful commercial neighbour, New York, and efforts to prevent British vessels from loading in New Hampshire, Massachusetts and Rhode Island failed because Connecticut received them without penalty. In general, therefore, state legislation was moving rapidly towards reciprocity, and barriers to interstate trade were being dismantled by 1787. Nevertheless the situation was unsatisfactory, in good measure because of the inescapable uncertainty.[14] The logic of the situation led Massachusetts to call in 1785 for a convention to reorganise and strengthen commercial regulation, though at that point it was realised that a convention might open the way to a more general revision of the Articles in which southern influence would predominate.

## IV

The sensitivity felt by northern merchants towards British dominance of Atlantic trade was only one indication of American insecurity in the post-Revolutionary world. No matter how remarkable its success in persuading the world's most powerful maritime nation to abandon all attempts at suppressing its bid for independence, the United States was only a third-rank power in every important respect other than territorial extent; its population, production, wealth and especially military and naval power were considerably inferior to those of its rivals. Yet the new nation was obliged to share the continent with Britain to the north and Spain to the south and west, and France (which was less sympathetic towards America than its role in the Revolutionary War implied) was entrenched in the West Indies. Also, indigenous Indians continued to populate much of the area ceded to the United States in a peace treaty concluded between white men; they posed a threat of a different kind.

Congress's frailty had evident diplomatic consequences. John Adams, first American minister to Britain, was treated frostily by officials in London. The British government claimed there was little point in negotiating with the federal government, since Congress could not compel the states to implement its treaties; the point was confirmed by its inability to prevent the states from impeding the Loyalists' efforts to recover their property and collect debts owing to them. As well as refusing to negotiate a commercial treaty, Britain retained a chain of seven northwest forts within American territory running from the northern tip of Lake Champlain, round the southern shores of the Great Lakes to Fort Michilimackinac at the junction between Lakes Huron and Michigan. Ostensibly the forts were retained as bargaining counters to persuade the states to fulfil their treaty obligations to Loyalists; in reality the British government used them as an instrument for advancing its western interests. Elsewhere, American diplomacy had few successes to compensate for its inability to persuade Britain to evacuate the forts. It concluded commercial treaties with the Netherlands, Sweden and Prussia, but they had limited economic value.

Of all the diplomatic issues, problems posed by relations with Spain were the most complex and dangerous to American unity. They provoked conflicts of interest among the various regions in particularly acute form, and raised the possibility of secession by southwestern settlers. At the heart of the matter lay control of the Mississippi river. Under the peace treaty the United States and Britain had agreed that navigation should be free to both countries from the source of the Mississippi to the Gulf, and that the American southern boundary west of the Appalachian mountains should be 31 degrees latitude. Spain's position on the ground was strong. The Spanish commanded the entire west bank of the river, and controlled the east bank at New Orleans after ceding Florida to Britain in 1763, although the treaty obliged them to allow Britain navigation rights through Spanish territory. On recovering Florida in 1783 Spain extended its control of the east bank north to 31 degrees (and claimed as far upstream as Natchez) and thus controlled both banks for around 200 miles. Control of the river encouraged Spain to assert what it regarded as its lawful rights, denying that the United States could inherit British navigation rights through its territory, and claiming sovereignty over a huge triangular area north from the Gulf to the Tennessee and Ohio rivers.[15] Each side began negotiating with Indian tribes as a means of strengthening its diplomatic position.

Such a situation was highly unsatisfactory. For their part, southerners were moving rapidly into areas claimed by Spain, and in some instances establishing settlements and proto-governments. Security for these communities in the most rapidly developing area of the United States, and protection for the American fur trade, depended on retaining navigation rights on the river; it was also apparent that control of the lower Mississippi was the strategic key to the entire interior basin south and west of the Great Lakes. In particular, if the river were to be closed to American shipping it was feared that settlers would transfer their allegiance to Spain. The problem became yet more acute when the landed states began ceding their western lands to the Confederation between 1784 and 1786, and northerners began calculating that an acceptable price for a commercial treaty with Spain (which might encourage Britain and other countries to follow suit) might be abandonment of navigation on the Mississippi. Such an agreement with Spain would also have the potential advantage for northerners of discouraging the westward migration which they feared would debilitate their own population base and economy. Spain closed the Mississippi river to American shipping in 1784, and in negotiations with the Spanish representative Diego de Gardoqui in 1786, John Jay, of New York, who had replaced Livingston as Secretary for Foreign Affairs, felt obliged to recommend conceding the point as the price for a commercial treaty. The northern states were able to vote through a necessary revision in his instructions to permit this, but since the South clearly had sufficient votes to prevent ratification of any consequent treaty, the matter was allowed to drop.[16] Nevertheless, the failure to achieve a commercial treaty with Britain, the difficulties in implementing the peace treaty, the presence of the British in the northwest and the disputes with Spain in the southwest all demonstrated the weakness of Congress in foreign affairs.

## V

The one clear success for Congress was its western policy. Acquisition of land between the Appalachians and the Mississippi river created a huge area available for white colonisation once Indian claims had been extinguished. It immediately raised questions about the format of settlement, the legal structure of property rights and relationships with the original thirteen states and Congress. Several groups of settlers, encouraged by land speculators, had already attempted to organise themselves as legally constituted communities. Unlike Vermont none of these communities survived as states, but their brief existence caused considerable problems. Only Westsylvania was north of the Ohio; the others were in modern Kentucky and Tennessee. Watauga was the earliest community, formed in 1772 with articles of association based on those of the North Carolina Regulators and essentially democratic; it was readmitted to North Carolina as Washington County in 1777. As settlers entered the area after the war, another attempt to establish a state in eastern Tennessee was made under the title Franklin, and at one point the settlers drew up a virtually democratic constitution. Their efforts were frustrated, first by North Carolina's cession of its trans-Appalachian lands to Congress in 1784, and then by the parent state's insistence on reasserting authority over the area in 1786; it was the last attempt to establish a state by squatter sovereignty in the eighteenth century. To the north of Franklin most settlements established under the auspices of the Transylvania Company were absorbed into Virginia as the county of Kentucky.[17]

Development of these communities was a pressing reminder of the need to develop a coherent western policy. Crucially its prime purpose would be to bind the new western communities to the seaboard states at a time when many easterners, including men as different as Rufus King of Massachusetts and Thomas Jefferson, believed that separation was possible. A successful policy was required to take into account several considerations. One was the fact that western land was the greatest source of national wealth as well as a highly attractive magnet for settlers. A second was the need to balance the private interests of squatters and speculators against the public interest of a developing national union. It would be necessary therefore to establish a national market in western land. Economic development was desirable to encourage stronger links between new settlements and the older states based on reciprocity of interests. A third consideration was the need to avoid the sort of mistakes Britain had made when dealing with the colonies before the Revolution. Resolution of these problems required machinery that would encourage loyalty rather than provoke the separation of settlers who were geographically distant from the old centres of population and whose political relationship to the United States was similar to that of the colonists in relation to Britain before the war. In particular, land disposals would have to be orderly and controlled so as to bind commercial interests to the union. If the policy failed, loss of the western territories was expected to be certain.[18] All this suggested the need for central direction as well as local autonomy – a need strengthened by the preliminary necessity of extinguishing Indian title to the recently acquired lands.

Western policy developed in a series of Ordinances drafted during the 1780s. They were so successful that they provided a general model (even if it was not always used) for organising and admitting to statehood successive new territories as they came under American control. Such a fortunate outcome was partly the consequence of carefully thought out principles and in part a result of trial and error. John Dickinson's attempt to give Congress control of the west in the Articles of Confederation had failed, but in March 1784 Jefferson and a committee submitted a draft land ordinance which coincided with Virginia's final cession of land. It was approved with some amendments the following month. The Ordinance of 1784 covered roughly the area between the Appalachians and the Mississippi and from Florida to the Lakes. Working south from a baseline of 45 degrees latitude it proposed a grid pattern (somewhat modified by major topography) of 14 communities. Every territory would be self-governing from the start, its franchise would include all adult males and it could petition for admission to the Union as a state once its population reached that of the least populous of the original states. The proposed western states would be small since they extended no more than 2 degrees in latitude. In essence the plan proposed to solve the American colonial problem by allowing the new communities to organise themselves on republican principles and then to join the existing states on equal terms. In the event it was overtaken by the North West Ordinance of 1787 and never became operational, but apart from the franchise provision its principles remained intact. In the meantime Congress enacted a second Land Ordinance the following year.

The Land Ordinance of 1785 set out a basic survey system for the sale of land and organisation of local government. Once title had been acquired from the Indians, land would be surveyed before being offered for sale to settlers. Thus the New England pattern of orderly development (though not its custom of community settlement) was preferred to the more individualistic but confusing southern system by which settlers were allowed to set out their own boundaries which could then be registered with the state – and which often led to acrimonious disputes between rival claimants. Initially the procedure applied only north of the Ohio river, where there were few settlers as yet. Beginning at the intersection of the Pennsylvania state line and the river, seven ranges were to be surveyed along a geographer's base line running due west, with the range lines running south. Each range was divided into townships 6 miles square, and each township was sub-divided into sections of 640 acres (equivalent to a square mile) which were available for sale at public auction at a minimum price of $1 an acre. Within each township sections 8, 11, 26 and 29 were reserved to the United States, and section 16 for the maintenance of public schools. Both the surveying and the sale of land were slower than expected; nevertheless the rectangular system was confirmed by the Land Act of 1796. The geometric survey pattern ignored the topography of the new lands and produced many anomalies, but had several advantages. It provided a relatively quick and certain means of setting out lines in often difficult circumstances, and its precision of definition substantially reduced the potential for disputes among purchasers. Above all, the Ordinance estab-lished the principle that land was to be held freehold and could be freely sold; no services were due from purchasers, nor were any restrictions or covenants imposed upon them.[19]

Organisation of the West was completed with the passage of the North West Ordinance in July 1787. Jefferson's pre-vious ordinance, which had allowed as few as 500 settlers to organise a territorial legislature, had been too democratic for some members of Congress, and was accordingly rescinded and replaced by a new ordinance that retained many of its features but had a more conservative cast. The Ordinance divided the region northwest of the Ohio into either three or five territories, and established a procedure which, with adjustments to meet particular circumstances, became the model by which new areas were later organised and admitted to statehood. It consisted of three stages. The first was establishment of a territory administered by a governor, secretary and three judges under authority of Congress. As soon as there were 5000 free men in the area they were permitted to elect a House of Representatives which, with a governor and legislative council, was authorised to legislate for the territory. Once its population reached a total of 60,000 free inhabitants it could draft a constitution, receive a guarantee of republican government and apply to Congress for admission as a state on equal terms with existing states, with a proviso that it could be admitted earlier if appropriate. A mark of the conservatism of its principal author Nathan Dane was inclusion of modest property qualifications for voting and officeholding.[20] On the other hand, the measure also disposed of land in fee simple, incorporated protections for personal liberties drawn from the Massachusetts Constitution and prohibited slavery in the Territory.

For all the criticism directed against Congress both before and after ratification of the Articles of Confederation, much was achieved under its auspices. Independence was gained during an arduous war against a powerful enemy, and afterwards the nation sustained its integrity in a world dominated by great powers. The states were learning how to resolve territorial and navigation disputes. Connecticut and Pennsylvania accepted Congress as an adjudicator in the very difficult Wyoming Valley dispute. New York and Massachusetts managed to settle their boundary dispute, and Pennsylvania and New Jersey, and Virginia and Maryland settled navigation disputes on the Delaware and Potomac rivers respectively.

Nor was this all. A system for incorporating new territories was constructed, and a rudimentary bureaucracy established; moreover the new government developed significantly during its brief life. In spite of financial difficulties, national authority grew incrementally while permitting that high degree of local self-government which, with memories of the British regime in mind, was equated with the preservation and enjoyment of personal liberty. This process could have continued. Merrill Jensen has argued that the campaign to strengthen the Articles failed on the verge of success.[21] It is possible that reform could have been achieved, though procedural difficulties in ratifying amendments were a major impediment and arguably the crucial obstacle to change. In another dimension, several economic problems erroneously attributed to defects in the Articles – the post-war import surge and consequent depression, and commercial barriers to interstate trade erected by the states, for example – were being resolved.

Nevertheless, the 1780s were indeed a critical decade. The

nature of the federal system remained undetermined, and some forces were carrying the country towards a weak and limited union which might disintegrate under pressure. The alternatives were not encouraging. In spite of Congress's considerable achievements in wartime, there had been suggestions that Washington should be given dictatorial powers, though any attempt to erect an authoritarian regime probably would have provoked the very disintegration it was intended to avert. Other alternatives were equally dangerous. Early in 1786 Benjamin Lincoln argued that the United States would be more easily governed if it extended from east to west instead of north to south. Even so ardent a nationalist as James Madison feared that the union might collapse into a collection of regional confederacies.[22] When the individual states had become states, they had remained the primary units of social and political activity; in so far as economic interests united them, they did so in groups or sections rather than as a continental nation. Several, notably Virginia, could have survived easily as entirely autonomous nations, and a practicable alternative for others, notably the New England states, was regional grouping. If the example of Canada is any guide, it is reasonable to suppose that such confederations could have flourished. Each of these possibilities made considerable geographical and economic sense, and a false step could have precipitated it. National union was only embryonic, but 8 years after the Articles had been ratified, they were replaced by a new constitution predicated on much stronger national principles.

# VI

Agitation for a more national constitution and a stronger central government began even before the Articles of Confederation came into effect. Five years after the outbreak of fighting, final success still seemed distant in spite of the triumph at Saratoga in 1777 and the entry of France into the war. Congress was having increasing difficulty in directing and supplying the war effort, and being compelled more and more to rely on the states. The initial success of Britain's southern strategy suggested that victory was far from certain. The coming of independence and peace only temporarily allayed criticism, and a sense of crisis recurred during the mid-1780s.

Criticism of the Articles of Confederation came quickly from many sources. Merchants and businessmen found the economic controls irksome and ineffective. Army officers demanded a more efficient government that could supply the army with the equipment to win the war, and public creditors argued the need for a stronger central government capable of paying its debts. There was also a broader constituency of men concerned for stronger government at a time of national emergency. During the early years of the Confederation the group was perhaps best exemplified by Robert Morris although James Madison, Alexander Hamilton and Gouverneur Morris were more committed to reducing state powers. The strategy of this group was for Congress to retain as much of the national debt as possible, especially during the early 1780s when the states were assuming substantial portions of it, in order to bind the self-interest of creditors to the need to strengthen the union. A second benefit would be a simultaneous increase in the amount of capital available for business expansion. The economic nationalists lost ground in mid-decade but in the latter part of the 1780s they were among those most committed to revising the Articles, and their policies re-emerged in the new federal government.

Discontent with the Articles spread throughout the country. In cities such as Philadelphia, artisans supported a nationalist movement in the interests of commerce and trade. From the early 1780s onwards some states, notably New York led by Hamilton and Philip Schuyler in 1782, and Massachusetts in 1785, demanded a general convention, and individuals such as Madison and Washington of Virginia insisted that the union be strengthened. By 1786 it seemed that every section of the country was dissatisfied. Northern states were disappointed over the failure to give Congress the power to regulate trade. Southern states were alarmed by Jay's willingness as Secretary for Foreign Affairs to abandon the Mississippi navigation in favour of a commercial treaty, and were unhappy that most of the debt was held in the North. The weakness of America's position in foreign affairs, manifested especially by Congress's inability to secure a commercial treaty with Britain and eject it from the northwest forts, was alarming, as was Congress's continuing lack of an independent revenue and its shrivelling ability to make itself felt in domestic affairs.

There was a growing belief that a national interest existed superior to the states, but great difficulty in agreeing as to exactly what that interest was. The problem of definition was all the greater since many people shared a conviction that local autonomy was preferable to central authority. For them it was necessary that the direction of political affairs should be located primarily in local hands, and higher authority kept to a minimum. This sense of localism was by no means confined to small farmers. It was shared by men whose operations may have been substantial but were linked to local activities, and those whose political, social and economic interests were particularly associated with the states as entities. George Mason, a leading Virginia planter, feared that a stronger central government would replicate the British government at its worst and thus lead to the destruction of liberty, whose defence had lain at the heart of the American ideological agenda in 1776; in his view republicanism was equated with local self-direction. Others included men such as George Clinton, whose career as governor of New York was based on tying as many interests as possible to the welfare of the state, the Constitutionalists of Pennsylvania, and in Virginia those who had benefited from emancipation from British authority and creditors.[23] Among others with vested interests in state primacy were men engaged in western land speculation and debt holding. There was also a social dimension to the argument. Some men were obsessed with elitism and the dangers of aristocracy, as well as being frightened by what they believed were the perils of strong central government. They believed that elitism and centralism went hand in hand.

In face of this, nationalists realised it was prudent to move cautiously.[24] They were, of course, greatly concerned over what they regarded as the intractable political deficiencies of the Articles, but their criticism also possessed a deeper social dimension. James Otis had declared in 1776 that 'when the pot boils, the scum will rise', and recent experience appeared to vindicate his opinion. Their leaders were men of substance who were appalled by the unexpected social turbulence generated by the Revolution. They conceded the necessity of social mobility, but deplored its excesses. They were horrified by the type of new men who now populated so many seats in the state legislatures and appalled by what they considered to be the low standards of the consequent legislation. For them social hierarchy was not incompatible with republicanism but they believed the upwardly mobile should acquire wealth, education, experience and social connections as preliminary qualifications for political leadership.[25]

James Madison was among those nationalists who came to believe it was impractical to hope for amendments to the Articles. They could be rejected seriatim by the states, and it was therefore essential to call a convention. Another reason for his conviction was his feeling that much of the problem lay in the deficiencies of the states themselves. He listed them in a memorandum written in April 1787 to which he gave the title 'Vices of the Political System of the United States'. They included encroachments on federal authority, failure to comply with Congressional requisitions, infringement of treaties and the law of nations, and infringements on the rights of other states, including in particular economic rights and a lack of concern for the common interest. Other weaknesses which required correction in Madison's opinion were the multiplication of state laws and their mutability. He accepted that republican theory required that decisions were made by a majority, but was alarmed by the consequences that followed the absence of safeguards to protect minority interests. In particular he feared the possibility that an organised minority could manipulate the machinery of government to its own advantage. State laws were all too frequently unjust, because enlightened leaders were numerically overwhelmed by the multitude possessing limited vision and directed by narrow self-interest. In particular this led to violations of the rights and interests of minorities and of individuals.[26] The experience of Pennsylvania under the direction of the Constitutionalists and with a profoundly democratic constitution, the acute turbulence of Rhode Island and its legislature's apparent attempt to appropriate property by compelling creditors to accept paper money, the mistreatment of Loyalists and British merchants during the war and afterwards by the refusal of several states, especially in the South, to apply the terms of the peace treaty which required them to permit recovery of pre-war debts and property, and above all Shays's Rebellion in Massachusetts, all seemed to indicate the dangers of excessive popular power.

Where localists and republican purists believed the Revolution was most at risk from excessive central government and the recrudescence of aristocracy, the nationalists feared the Revolution would fail through its weaknesses and its excesses. In the early years of the Revolutionary War it had been possible to rely on the disinterested patriotism and good character of the people. This was no longer prudent, since the people had recently revealed their self-interested limitations. Under such circumstances the United States faced a paradox. A strengthened national government would have to draw its authority direct from the people, though the people could not be trusted; in Gordon Wood's words, 'Only a new continental republic that cut through the structure of the states to the people themselves and yet was not dependent on the character of that people could save America's experiment in republicanism.'[27]

Nevertheless, the advocates of a constitutional convention were not reacting crudely against the principles of 1776. Collectively, if not always individually, they applauded much of the Revolution's central ideology: popular sovereignty and representative government coupled to limits on government power; the attack on slavery; the disestablishment of religion; and the principle that republican government depended on public education for its citizens. But they derived much of their intellectual ancestry from the more conservative wing of American ideology – a conservatism that was radical by European standards. They believed that social order and hierarchy was an essential requisite for the enjoyment of liberty, but they also accepted the principle of equality in the sense that all citizens possessed rights and were entitled to equal esteem and equal protection of their interests. Like many localists they feared the potential excesses of government (though less than they feared the excesses of majoritarianism), but insisted that a higher degree of central authority was necessary than their opponents were prepared to concede. Also, being men of continental connections and experience rather than localists, they saw the need for stronger central government for policy reasons, particularly in relation to economic affairs, foreign policy and western development.

Not until 1786 did nationalist demands for a convention gain substantial influence. A committee proposal drawn up by Charles Pinckney of South Carolina was intended to give Congress substantial additional power but failed, thus allowing the nationalists to mount a campaign from outside. In January 1786 John Tyler, perhaps at Madison's suggestion, seized on the success of a conference held the previous year at Washington's home, Mount Vernon, at which Maryland and Virginia had settled disputes over navigation in Chesapeake Bay and on the Potomac and Pocomoke rivers. He persuaded Virginia to invite the other states to send delegates to Annapolis, Maryland, to discuss a broad range of commercial questions.[28] The Convention met for only four days, from 11 to 14 September, and was attended by delegates from only 5 states – Virginia, New York, Pennsylvania, New Jersey and Delaware (not even Maryland) but delegates included such key nationalists as Madison, Hamilton and Dickinson. A meeting of men who were known to desire stronger central government aroused considerable suspicion, and perhaps fortunately for their cause the paucity of delegates inhibited them from proposing specific amendments to the Articles. Instead, the Convention pointed out that any grant to Congress of authority to regulate trade would require adjustments to other sections of the Articles, and went on to recommend that a second convention should meet at Philadelphia in May 1787 to 'render the constitution of the Federal Government adequate to the exigencies of the union'.[29]

The recommendation was not acted upon until the new year. At first it was either rejected or ignored by Congress and most of the states, and only Virginia, Pennsylvania and New Jersey elected delegates.

What finally convinced waverers of the prudence of a

convention was Shays's Rebellion. At worst it was little more than a very violent protest movement whose political significance was local to Massachusetts, but it served as a propaganda gift to the nationalists. The rebellion appeared to exemplify all that was deficient in the structure of American government, and provided fortuitous but perfectly timed reinforcement for nationalist arguments about the alleged excesses and instability of the states and the consequent need for stronger central government. By the time Congress agreed to summon a convention to meet as recommended, the southern states had appointed delegates. Also, there was much more sympathy towards the proposal for a stronger central government than there had been at the time of previous attempts to strengthen the Confederation by the Morris plan of 1782–3, the revenue plan of 1783, the commercial amendments of 1784 and the committee reports of 1785–6. Above all, the time for relatively minor changes was over, and recent experiences reinforced the arguments of those who urged the necessity for substantial changes.[30] What those changes should be was a matter for vigorous debate, but few doubted that the time for reform had arrived.

# 8
# THE PHILADELPHIA
# CONVENTION

The Philadelphia Convention deliberated throughout the summer of 1787. Though due to begin its business on 14 May, it only commenced work on 28 May when seven states were represented. It concluded its deliberations on 17 September by recommending to Congress a draft constitution that altered the structure of national government and drastically changed its relationship to the states and the people.

## I

Members of the Convention were both unrepresentative and representative. The state legislatures appointed 74 delegates, but only 55 attended. Rhode Island, so ridden by factionalism that its legislature was unable to appoint any delegates, remained totally unrepresented. New Hampshire's delegates only arrived late in July, and New York's delegation was sharply divided and thus largely neutered. The delegates were far from a representative cross-section of contemporary American society. Discounting entirely the largest minorities – blacks and white women – important sections of the white male population were not represented by members of their own social status. There were no shopkeepers or artisans, no westerners, no tenant farmers and only one small farmer at the Convention. Also, some of the leading figures of the Revolution were absent. Thomas Jefferson and John Adams were representing the United States in Paris and London, and Richard Henry Lee and Patrick Henry were so suspicious of what would happen that they refused to serve. Among the major figures in Maryland politics, Samuel Chase and

Charles Carroll of Carrollton distrusted each other so deeply that they preferred to remain at home in order to keep an eye on what the other might do.[1] Neither Samuel Adams nor John Hancock was elected in Massachusetts.

The delegates who did attend were personally distinguished and well prepared, and in certain respects representative of their communities. They were representative in the sense that almost all were planters, merchants or lawyers and possessed broad experience of commercial affairs, thus representing the country's major economic interests and dominant social groups, and they were members of the elite within their respective states whose interests they could therefore claim to represent. Delegates already had much experience of national affairs since 39 of the 55 had sat in the Continental Congress, 21 had served in the army, 8 had signed the Declaration of Independence, and a handful had participated in the pre-war congresses. All had been active in state politics. At one point, John Dickinson declared 'experience must be our only guide', but leading delegates were well read in history and theory. Sir William Blackstone and the Baron de Montesquieu on the English Constitution, John Locke, David Hume, Adam Smith and the English radical writers were among those whose works were familiar to them.

A dozen or so delegates shaped the structure of debate. James Madison was especially influential, though he did not always get his own way. James Wilson and Gouverneur Morris of Pennsylvania, John Dickinson of Delaware, John Rutledge and Charles Pinckney of South Carolina, Oliver Ellsworth and Roger Sherman of Conecticut, Elbridge Gerry and Rufus King of Massachusetts, William Paterson of New Jersey and George Mason of Virginia all played significant parts, as did the idiosyncratic Luther Martin of Maryland. The presence of two men who said very little was profoundly important. Benjamin Franklin, by this time an old man of 81, seldom spoke but extended his great personal presţige to the proceedings and acted as an emollient at critical stages. Of central importance was the role of George Washington. He spoke in debate only once, but his record as commander-in-chief during the war coupled with his willingness to retire to Mount Vernon afterwards had given him a pre-eminent national reputation; his presence gave legitimacy to the Convention, and he was immediately elected president.[2]

As a group they were neither demi-gods, as some have suggested, nor notably self-interested as others have argued. They were, however, aware of the relationship between economic processes and political action, and the conflict between the disinterested advancement of public welfare and the pursuit of private gain. Like other men they possessed private interests, belonged to particular economic and social groups, and assumed they would share the benefits of national prosperity. Almost all were rich. Many stood to benefit from agricultural profitability, especially from the export of staples; several, including Washington, speculated heavily in western lands, more owned slaves, and some were engaged in overseas trade. Thirty owned public securities and stood to benefit if a new government led to an appreciation in their value. But Charles Beard, whose analysis has carried disproportionate influence since it was first published in 1913, was mistaken in arguing that debate centred on rivalry between the holders of personal property (money, public securities, manufactures and trade and shipping) and real property (the landed interest) and wrong to imply that delegates were powerfully driven by the self-interest of their particular economic group. Thus 30 members owned certificates of public debt and stood to gain from a rise in their market value under a new government, but 5 of the largest holders (including Gerry and Edmund Randolph of Virginia) voted against the Constitution.[3] Important though economic interests undoubtedly were, there were other central interests. They were not necessarily coincident.

The rules of procedure shaped the course of discussion. They reflected the reality of state power and community by requiring voting to be by state rather than delegate, with the proviso that if a delegation were equally divided its vote would be ignored. Recognising that decisions on later issues could affect those taken previously, flexibility of discussion was ensured by the principle that no vote would be considered final and by permitting any subject to be reopened for further discussion. Lastly, the debates were to be held in secret, thus enabling candour of expression and insulating delegates from outside public pressure.[4]

The Convention's instructions were clear. Congress had authorised it for 'the sole and express purpose of revising the Articles of Confederation' in order to strengthen the government and union.[5] But delegates immediately abandoned their instructions in favour of drafting a totally new Constitution. In formulating a new system of government they were called upon to resolve three principal conflicts, all of which had been wrestled with since independence and some for generations. They were obliged to balance local against national interests. Within this framework there were subdivisions between the large and small states, and between groups of states functioning as sections over issues such as slavery and commerce. They had to weigh the influence and security of the elite against the egalitarianism that had been a notable feature of the earlier years of the Revolution, and thirdly they had to consider the needs of effective government against the legitimate interests of the citizen. In addition it was necessary to construct a stable framework that would encourage social stability but enable change, and temper philosophical principles against pragmatic considerations under the influence of past experience and the pressures of contemporary interests. To achieve one objective might jeopardise another; compromise and concessions were essential to success.

There were several propositions on which virtually all delegates agreed. They were convinced of the necessity of imposing curbs on what they saw as the excessive democracy which had recently manifested itself in the states. It was also essential to construct a stronger central government that would bypass the states to operate directly on the people, and which would not depend on their capacity to behave disinterestedly. A paradox lay at the root of this latter proposition. They believed a republic could be made to work only by restraining popular influence. In this respect the social issue was between elitism and democracy.[6] There was also general agreement on two more particular points. The system would have to be grounded in the theory of natural rights. This theoretical base would make it clear that although the delegates' principles derived from the more conservative element in American Revolutionary ideology, they were neither aristocratic in the European sense of that term, nor were they obdurately opposed to every element of democratic theory. The second area of agreement concerned the necessity of extending the power of the federal government by granting it permission to raise its own tax revenue, authority to regulate international and interstate commerce, and the right to establish its own courts whose judges would adjudicate its laws. There was, however, disagreement as to exactly how powerful the federal government should be. Alexander Hamilton of New York held views that were so centralist and conservative (albeit brilliantly expressed) that they had little influence. In any case he was virtually neutralised by the opposing views of the other members of his delegation. Madison was convinced that it should be supreme over the states and argued unsuccessfully that Congress should possess a veto over state legislation; unlike Hamilton, however, he also believed that a distribution of powers was essential. He, Wilson and Gouverneur Morris were the principal nationalist leaders. Others such as Mason, Ellsworth and Rutledge wished to retain an important role for the states, while Sherman, Paterson and Gerry argued for merely strengthening the current system. Dickinson argued for a mixed system which would be partly national and partly based on the states.[7]

Substantive proceedings began with a series of 14 resolutions drafted by Madison, presented by Randolph on 29 May, and known as the Virginia Plan.[8] The first proposed that the Articles of Confederation should be corrected and enlarged so as to achieve their stated objects: 'common defence, security of liberty, and general welfare'; its phrasing was artful, for what was being recommended was a powerful national government dominated by Congress. The structure of representation lay at the heart of the matter and remained a central issue throughout the convention. Unsurprisingly, considering its origin in the largest state, the plan proposed a system favouring the larger states. Representation in the legislature would be determined either by contribution to government expenses (effectively wealth) or the number of free inhabitants, thus favouring states such as Virginia, Pennsylvania and Massachusetts, whose combined populations included almost half the country's total population, at the expense of smaller states such as Delaware, Maryland, Connecticut and

New Jersey. The legislature would have two houses, with the upper house apportioned on the same principle but elected by the lower house from among candidates nominated by state legislatures. To reinforce the supremacy of the central government over the states, the new legislature was to be vested with all the legislative powers of the old Congress, and the right to legislate in all areas where the states were incompetent. It was also given authority to veto state laws which in its opinion contravened the national constitution, a principle to which Madison attached great importance as a means of regulating state excesses, and authorised to use force against any state that failed to fulfil its duty under the constitution. A national executive was to be chosen by the legislature; it would enjoy all the executive rights possessed by the Confederation Congress and the authority to execute national laws. The plan was completed by a national judiciary. It would be submitted to state ratifying conventions. As in most states, the legislature would dominate the proposed system, but the executive and judiciary would form a council of revision with qualified power to veto its acts. On the following day the Convention approved the general principle 'that a *national* Government ought to be established consisting of a *supreme* Legislative, Executive & Judiciary'.[9] It left almost unlimited scope for debate and was never rescinded.

Representation occupied delegates' minds for many weeks. Several opposing arguments were advanced, for some delegates were sceptical about popular elections. Sherman believed that the people should have as little as possible to do with government and proposed that representatives should be elected by state legislatures, while Gerry was convinced that the nation's current problems flowed from an 'excess of democracy'. Conversely, Mason insisted that democratic principles required popular election, and Wilson wanted to raise 'the federal pyramid to a considerable altitude' and considered that it should have as broad a base as possible. He therefore argued from a conservative stance that only popular election would give the people confidence in central government; such a system would also emancipate it from the states. Madison for his part thought popular influence was desirable in the lower house and could be filtered in the selection of the upper house, executive and judiciary.[10] He also argued that enlargement of the scale of national government would provide a defence against the disadvantages of democracy that was consistent with a democratic form of government; it would do this both by taming the conflict of interest groups and by preventing the emergence of a dominant majority.

For their part, critics of the Virginia Plan were not averse to a stronger central government but wished to maintain the political integrity of the states. None of the previous arguments addressed the point insisted on by many of them that parity among the states should be retained from the old Congress in at least one branch of the legislature. John Dickinson early proposed that the upper house should be elected by state legislatures, but when the Convention approved a report based on the Virginia Plan on 13 June this concession proved insufficient for those delegates who believed the plan's implicit centralisation was excessive. Led by William Paterson of New Jersey, a group of small states accordingly proposed the so-called New Jersey Plan on 15 June.[11] Almost all the proposals for strengthening the central government were included; thus Congress would be granted the right to impose taxes and regulate commerce. In one respect the New Jersey Plan even went beyond the earlier ones by proposing that Congressional legislation and treaties should be the supreme law binding on the states, and authorising the federal executive to compel obedience by force if necessary. Its crucial feature was implicit rather than spelled out: the states would retain their equal representation in a single-house Congress, for in this respect the Articles of Confederation would not be amended.

This small-state plan exposed the division over proportional representation and state equality but did not last long in debate since it seemed to offer little advance on the existing system. In particular, it infuriated Alexander Hamilton, who believed both plans were far too democratic. In their place he recommended that the states should be reduced to subordinate divisions whose executives would be appointed by the national government. A chief executive would be elected for life by electors who were chosen by other electors who were chosen by popular vote; he would possess an absolute veto. A senate would also be elected for life.[12] His views and proposals were so extreme in their conservatism that they had little influence.

The first phase of the Convention came to a head on 19 June, when it rejected the New Jersey, or small state, Plan by 7 votes to 3 in favour of the nationalist, or large state, programme adumbrated in the Virginia Plan.[13] In retrospect this rivalry among states on grounds of size was ephemeral and largely confined to the Convention. In any case, as Forrest McDonald has pointed out, the disparity in population between large and small states was not great. The average population of the so-called small states was about 278,000; the average population of the large states was only about 10 per cent greater at 307,000.[14] It was quickly overtaken by the far more substantial dissension among the great regional sections of American society, the North, the South, and the West. Nevertheless, it took some time longer to resolve the dispute over representation.

Though the localist small-state group had lost, the nationalists had not truly won. For their part, the nationalists agreed to respect the continued importance of the states by substituting the words 'United States' for the term 'national'. But the small-state group continued to insist that the upper house should be elected by state legislatures. A further complication was that the senate, like its state counterparts, was expected to protect the property interest (especially land) against the political envy and levelling spirit of the masses.[15] Achievement of this end required senators to be insulated to some extent by allowing them a longer term of office than was customary for representatives in state legislatures. The issue was resolved by allowing them a six-year term. Complete resolution of the difficulty took until mid-July. A committee dominated by small-state delegates recommended on 5 July that representation in the lower house (the House of Representatives) should be by population. In the upper house (Senate) each state should have an equal vote; ultimately every state was given 2 senators. The big-state delegates had fought hard against the principle of state equality and it was only on 16 July that what is known as the Great Compromise (and sometimes described as the Connecticut Compromise since delegates from that state had been particularly influential in formulating it) was accepted.[16]

Resolution of several other issues accompanied settlement of the main principle of representation. In the lower house representation would be by numbers only, not by wealth as some of the richer delegates and states had wished. In the first instance 65 representatives would be distributed among the states according to a rough formula, but thereafter representation and direct taxation would be distributed according to the results of regular censuses. A major disagreement between North and South over whether slaves should be counted for either purpose (and, if so, in what way) was settled by following a Congressional formula of 1783 by which slaves would be counted as three-fifths of a person for both representation and the allocation of direct taxes. The proposal that representation should be determined by census had an added advantage for southerners since current population increases were mostly south of the Ohio river and they believed the South would soon overtake the current northern majority of population. It also made it easier to incorporate new western states into the legislature, and frustrated an attempt by Gouverneur Morris, a representative of commercial interests, to institutionalise the predominance of the original Atlantic states in the expanding nation.[17] Lastly, it was agreed that money bills should originate in the lower house. Although some members attached significance to the provision, it proved to be of little practical importance, since the Senate was permitted to amend them.

Success in dealing with the problem of representation marked a crucial stage in the Convention's debates but left much to discuss. The nationalists lost the Congressional veto over state legislation, but it was ironically Luther Martin of Maryland, a vociferous advocate of state rights, who unwittingly created one of the most powerful instruments of future national power by drawing from the New Jersey Plan the principle that acts and treaties of Congress 'shall be the supreme law of the respective states . . . and that the judiciaries of the several states shall be bound thereby in their decisions, anything in the respective laws of the individual States to the contrary notwithstanding.'[18] The proposal guaranteeing republican government in the states became acceptable when it was explained by Wilson that its purpose was to permit suppression of domestic violence.

In one important respect the nationalists began changing direction during the Convention. Delegates agreed on the desirability of a tripartite system of legislature, executive and judiciary, but had not worked out the way in which the balance among them would operate. The Virginia Plan had proposed a dominant legislature, as well as the supremacy of the nation over the states. Gradually this evolved into a new system in which the three components of government would be obliged to collaborate yet at the same time check and balance each other. In this way the English balance of estates – king, lords and commons – was transformed into a balance of functions which would protect both liberty and interests in a system in which all legitimate authority derived from the sovereignty of the single estate of the people. At first the nationalists wished to establish a powerful executive as a check on the legislature, for the behaviour of the states persuaded them that liberty was, in Gouverneur Morris's words, in 'greater danger from legislative usurpations than from any other source'.[19] By mid-July a majority favoured election by the states (whether by individuals or legislatures) for a time. Another, linked, question was whether there should be a plural or single executive. At least a dozen delegates, including Franklin, Mason, Sherman and Randolph, wished to neutralise the potential dangers inherent in executive authority by dispersing it among several persons. Conversely, Madison, Wilson and Morris argued that the need for vigorous executive power required that it should be vested in a single person, who could also act as a check on Congress. On 26 July the Convention accepted the argument for a single executive but reaffirmed that Congress should elect the President.[20]

Faced with this agreement in principle, the Convention instructed a Committee of Detail to prepare a draft constitution. The committee consisted for the most part of moderate nationalists, and included Rutledge of South Carolina in the chair, Randolph of Virginia, Wilson of Pennsylvania, Ellsworth of Connecticut and Gorham of Massachusetts. Many of the provisions, especially those assigning powers to Congress, were taken from the Articles; others were taken from earlier plans and state constitutions. The document, containing a preamble and 23 articles, provided a more concrete basis for discussion. In particular it enumerated the powers of Congress and imposed some limits on it, and specified the responsibilities of the President. While reaffirming the supremacy of United States legislation and treaties, it further sharpened the relationships between the central and state governments by giving some protection to state authority but imposing on it limitations such as prohibitions on coining money and making treaties.[21]

Debate on the report of the Committee of Detail occupied five weeks from 6 August to 10 September. Many amendments were matters of detail, though most had long-term importance in some way or another. Several delegates had proposed a freehold property qualification for the federal franchise and national officeholders, but in the end it was left to the states, though they were required to make it at least as broad as the franchise for the most popular branch of their own legislatures. One addition to the powers discussed previously had a powerfully nationalising potential but its significance was not appreciated at the time. This was a clause granting Congress the right 'to make all laws that shall be necessary and proper' for fulfilling its responsibilities under the Constitution; in the 1790s it provided grounding for Hamilton's doctrine of implied powers. A second crucial addition was Rutledge's proposal, accepted without debate on 23 August, that the Constitution as well as federal laws and treaties should be the supreme law of the United States, and thus superior to state constitutions and laws and binding on judges in the states.[22] Earlier, Luther Martin had proposed that national laws and treaties should be the supreme law, but that they should be enforced by state courts; had this been accepted the effectiveness of federal law would have been very seriously weakened. This new clause, when ratified as part of the Constitution, enabled development of the doctrine of judicial review (whereby the US Supreme Court later assumed the authority to interpret the Constitution and determine the constitutionality of the actions of the states and their courts,

Congress and the President) and permitted a massive extension of national law, especially in the twentieth century,
though neither seems to have been intended.

By contrast, there was bitter debate over the extent of
Congressional authority over interstate and especially foreign
commerce. One element was settled fairly quickly. Southern
states were opposed to the imposition of export taxes, believing that such duties would have an unfairly deleterious
effect on the overseas trade in agricultural products that was
essential to their prosperity. Their demand was conceded;
Congress was prohibited from imposing any such duties.[23]
The other issue was more bitter, and debate on it may have
masked the importance of the supremacy clause. It revolved
around slavery. George Mason spoke passionately against the
institution and warned of its consequences for the entire
nation. It was essential, he argued, that the general government should possess the power to limit it. Northern delegates
agreed, but since delegates from the lower South were horrified, there could be no question of using national authority to
eradicate the institution. Roger Sherman of Connecticut in
effect recommended that the issue should be left alone.
Blandly he pointed out that abolition was proceeding among
the states, though he failed to note that the process was taking
place only in the North.[24] In the end northern delegates and
some southerners such as Mason reluctantly recognised that
decisions on the status of slavery would have to be left with
the states as a price of continued national union, but their
concession left open the question of the continued importation
of slaves at a time when many states were moving towards
emancipation.

In face of the insistence of delegates from the Carolinas and
Georgia that they would never accept the new Constitution if
their right to import slaves was impaired, a major compromise
was necessary. Its other component was fashioned out of the
northern (and especially New England) states' desire for
navigation acts which would require American products to be
carried in American ships, and thus encourage their domestic
shipbuilding industry. A special committee was appointed to
consider the matter, and after debate the essence of its
recommendations was approved with amendments. Congress

would not be permitted to prohibit the importation of slaves (use of the word 'slave' was carefully avoided) until 1808 and in the meantime would not be allowed to levy an import duty of more than $10 per head on them. The southern states' reciprocal concession was to permit Congress to enact navigation laws by simple majority instead of the two-thirds majority they would have preferred. Once this was agreed the Convention also authorised Congress to enact fugitive slave laws.[25]

Since nationalist delegates had been especially concerned with what they regarded as the vices of the states, an important component of the new Constitution was to be restrictions on state power. Madison's original proposal to create a national veto on state legislation, for which he argued almost to the end, expired in face of the supreme law clause. However, a series of fiscal and economic restrictions were imposed; in particular the states were prohibited from issuing paper money, impairing the obligations of contracts and imposing revenue-raising import duties. They were also prohibited from enacting retrospective legislation (as was Congress) and from making agreements with other states or foreign countries without the consent of Congress. Furthermore, the requirement that states should give 'full faith and credit' to the official acts of other states, and the guarantee to citizens of other states of the privileges and immunities enjoyed by their own citizens, prevented them from developing discriminatory legislation in favour of their own citizens.[26] The Convention also agreed to allow admission of new states. Though it implicitly condoned the end of any privileged position for the original thirteen states it nevertheless permitted Congress to impose conditions before new states could be admitted to the union and required the consent of the parent state to the organisation and admission of any new state formed within its jurisdiction.[27] Another provision, which did not achieve its final form until the last minute, overcame what was perhaps the crucial deficiency of the Articles – the requirement for unanimous approval of the states before any change could be made. Under the new Constitution, amendments could be proposed by two-thirds of each house of Congress and ratified by a majority of three-fourths of the states.[28] The twofold intention was to prevent ill-considered amendments by making the process difficult but not impossible, and to incorporate an influential role for the states.

The presidency also required continued debate. Ultimately the President was made commander-in-chief and given the duty of making recommendations to Congress, but other components of executive power were divided. Congress was assigned authority to regulate commerce, establish law courts, appoint a treasurer and raise and regulate the armed forces. The President was given power to make treaties with the approval of two-thirds of senators, and the right to nominate judges and all other federal officials but only with the advice and consent of the senate. Some delegates proposed a council of state which would advise him, but this was rejected. On the other hand he was granted a veto over legislation, though this could be overturned by two-thirds of each house. Some of the more conservative and nationalist members urged a long term of office, but this was rejected in favour of a renewable four-year term. The manner of his election was only decided in the final stages. The original proposal that the President should be elected by the legislature was replaced by an electoral college whose members would be elected by the states. Under this system each state was required to elect the same number of electors as it had senators and representatives. The electors, who it was assumed would be men of broader experience and wisdom than the people, would then elect a candidate to office. If no candidate obtained a majority of electoral votes the House of Representatives, voting by states, would make a choice, thus bringing into the process a democratic element to balance the elitist electoral college.[29] It was expected, at least by Madison, that the final decision would normally go to the House. The cumbersome process was a compromise among the advocates of state interests, those who feared a strong executive, and those who believed the president should be elected by the legislature.

Of the three branches of federal government, the judiciary received least attention. It was agreed from the start that an independent national judiciary should be established, and that its judges should be appointed during good behaviour. Beyond that there was considerable disagreement, especially over two prime issues: the extent of its authority, and the

number of its tiers. For a time, the possibility was considered
of including the judiciary in a council of revision with the right
to veto legislation, but this was dropped. It can be argued that
many leading delegates, including Madison, Wilson, Gouverneur Morris and Mason believed that the courts would have
power to invalidate legislation that violated the Constitution.
The supremacy clause also suggested that delegates believed
the judiciary possessed similar authority over state actions.
But at one point Madison urged that the courts should be
limited to matters of a judicial character; this suggests that
the Convention did not intend them to have general authority
to expound the Constitution.[30] The subject is not listed in the
description of judicial power set out in Article Three; whether
it was intended or implied remains unproven. Similarly the
Convention could not agree whether the federal system should
include inferior courts or whether matters should be adjudicated initially in state courts and then passed to a single US
supreme court for determination on appeal. Rutledge and
Sherman persuaded delegates for a time that state courts
coupled to a single national supreme court would be adequate, but Madison and Wilson immediately and successfully
argued that Congress should be permitted to establish subordinate federal courts if it wished.[31]

By Saturday 8 September the draft was sufficiently close to
completion to justify tidying it into final form. A Committee
of Style was appointed to revise and arrange it, and most of
the work was done by Gouverneur Morris. One particularly
significant change was made to the preamble. The logic of
amending the Articles had suggested that the Constitution be
ratified unanimously, but instead Article Seven declared that
it would come into effect among only nine states as soon as
they had ratified it. This made the original formula of naming
the thirteen states inappropriate, so an essentially literary
device of opening the preamble with the phrase 'We the
People of the United States' was adopted, thus giving a
further unintentional boost to the Constitution's nationalising
tendency and encouraging a democratic interpretation of its
authority. On 17 September the Convention approved the
Constitution, with only Mason, Randolph and Gerry refusing
to sign.[32] In accordance with Article Seven it proposed to

side-step the probable obstructiveness of the state legislatures by recommending to Congress that it should be submitted for ratification to popularly elected conventions in each state.

Congress quickly accepted the recommendation but transmitted the Constitution to the states without any advice in either direction; supporters agreed not to demand an explicit recommendation in exchange for their opponents' abandonment of demands that it should be accompanied by amendments. The state legislatures approved the proposal, thus constructively meeting the requirement in the Articles of Confederation that amendments needed unanimous consent.[33]

## II

James Madison conceded that the Philadelphia Convention might not have drafted the best possible constitution, but insisted that the document was the best that could have been devised under the particular circumstances. It dramatically changed the balance of power between the national government and the states through the medium of the philosophically absurd but pragmatically convenient and flexible device of divided sovereignty. Article Six declared that the Constitution itself and the laws and treaties made under it were to be the supreme law of the land. Although the proposal that the national government should have a veto over state legislation had been dropped, judges in every state were to be bound by the Constitution and all federal and state officials and legislators were required to support it; in effect the state constitutions, actions of state legislatures and executives and decisions of state courts were required to be consistent with it. Yet the new federal government was not intended to be legally superior to the states, for the states could not be demoted to a status comparable to that of English counties with powers and even boundaries determined by national government. Rather, the federal government and individual state governments were intended to be parallel authorities; each was to be supreme within its own sphere, but both were subordinate to the United States Constitution and the ultimate sovereignty of the people – which was the sole fount of legitimate political authority.

In the new system the federal government was given powers lacked by the Confederation Congress. They included the right to raise its own taxes (including import duties, which were currently the most lucrative source of revenue for the states) instead of requisitioning funds from the states, authority to regulate foreign trade and interstate commerce within the country, and the right to establish its own courts through which federal laws could be enforced. Also, its authority was to operate directly on the people, thus avoiding many of the difficulties that had shackled the old Congress. But although the Constitution imposed restrictions on the states it also allowed them continued supremacy in important areas of jurisdiction and responsibility. On the one hand they were prohibited from concluding treaties with foreign countries, imposing import duties, coining money, emitting bills of credit or making anything except gold and silver legal tender in payment of debts, and they were enjoined from impairing the obligation of contracts. On the other hand, the states retained the right to regulate their own intrastate or internal commerce, and continued to exercise jurisdiction in many important areas of civil, criminal and family law; for many decades to come the daily life of citizens was impinged upon far more by state than by federal law. The Constitution also obliged each state to give full faith and credit to the proceedings of other states, and to grant to the citizens of other states the same privileges and immunities it granted to its own citizens.

On certain matters the Convention was obliged to concede that no matter how desirable it might be to define national policy, prudential considerations compelled them to allow local variations. All national elections were to be administered by the states, which were permitted to determine the extent of the franchise in elections to the House of Representatives. They also had an important role in the electoral college, especially during the period before the war of 1812 in which its members were selected by the legislatures, who continued to nominate senators until 1913.[34] At a time when religious belief and affiliation were central to community life, Congress was shortly prohibited by the first Amendment from establishing any church, but states were permitted to continue discriminatory policies if they wished. Thus the dominance of

the Congregational churches in Massachusetts and Connecticut enabled them to continue enjoying the privileges of
establishment well into the nineteenth century, and other
states continued to enforce more limited discriminatory laws
long after the Statute for Religious Freedom had eliminated
all forms of discrimination in Virginia. For many years religious tests formed a residual element of electoral qualifications.

But by far the most important issue that had to be left to
the states was the question of slavery. Although Congress was
permitted to prohibit the importation of more slaves after
1808, and northern delegates and some southerners such as
Madison, Washington and Mason were prepared to use the
opportunity to begin the process of general emancipation, the
delegates from the lower South indicated that their states
would secede rather than permit it. Since it was clear that
neither the new national government nor the remaining states
possessed sufficient coercive power to prevent such a move,
they were obliged to concede the point.

Members of the Convention had been concerned to protect
the liberty of the citizen as well as to create a government
sufficiently powerful to perform its necessary duties. Article
One of the Constitution already contained restrictions on
Congress such as prohibition of bills of attainder and *ex post
facto* laws, and the suspension of the right to the writ of habeas
corpus except in the exceptional circumstances of invasion or
rebellion. Members agreed that a Bill of Rights argued for by
some delegates was redundant, but since several states made
ratification conditional on the addition of such protection, one
was approved in 1791 as the first ten amendments. Further
rights protected by the Bill of Rights included freedom of
speech and the press, the rights of peaceable assembly and
petitioning, and a series of procedural protections associated
with the investigation and trial of criminal offences.

But the primary protection of the liberty of the citizen lay
in the structure of the federal government itself. Following the
precedents of the state constitutions (especially Massachusetts
and New York) but applying the principles more systematic-
ally and rigorously, the three elements of legislature (Congress), executive (the President and federal government), and

judiciary were established in a framework of checks and balances. The separation of powers was intended to permit the other two branches of government to check the third (normally assumed to be the President) should it exceed its authority. Each was to be independent of the other, so that unlike the British parliamentary system members of the executive branch were denied membership of the legislature. But the Constitution also provided for considerable overlapping of powers, and Congress and the President were obliged to cooperate if the conduct of public business was to proceed. Thus most powers were lodged in Congress though the President was expected to propose policy. In some instances this cooperation was formalised – thus the President was given the power to nominate federal judges and officials but his recommendations required confirmation by the Senate. Similarly negotiation of treaties was made a presidential responsibility but treaties required ratification by the senate, and only Congress was given authority to declare war. It was assumed that the need for effective government would lead to cooperation through negotiation.

If the Constitution offered promising solutions to the problems of creating a stronger central government yet protecting the interests of the states and individual citizens, the Philadelphia Convention's success in imposing limits on what most of its members regarded as the excessive democracy evident in the states was more questionable. The senate was half-heartedly intended to protect the interests of property as well as represent the states, and it was assumed that the device of an electoral college for electing the President would allow voters to participate by electing more sophisticated electors, who could apply their superior wisdom to selecting a suitable candidate for office. At no time, however, did the electors function in this way. Instead, with only very rare exceptions, they have always felt themselves bound by the evident wishes of those who elected them. In practice the elitism that continued to operate in American politics was a function of the structure of society itself. The Constitution was ideologically neutral though ironically its opening phrase 'We the People' became a prop for future democratic interpretation.

Yet for all the Convention's efforts and its members'

concern to construct detailed systems in certain areas, much of the Constitution was couched in general terms and many major issues were left open. In particular, Article Three left large gaps in the structure and functions of the federal judiciary by creating a supreme court but leaving Congress to decide whether there should be any inferior courts. Within the federal government the division of authority between Congress and President was imprecise, and more importantly, the boundaries between federal and state power within the system of divided sovereignty were far from sharply defined. In each case the inevitable wrestling for primacy posed the problem of defining the Constitution. In some respects the states had the most powerful claim to exercising the right to arbitrate on the meaning of the Constitution since they could argue that they had created the union and that their sover- eignty had been expressly recognised in the Articles of Con- federation. Both the President and Congress often claimed to be able to interpret the Constitution, but although the docu- ment made no mention of the possibility, the United States Supreme Court during the Chief Justiceship of John Marshall from 1801 to 1835 successfully claimed the right to be the final arbiter, and the doctrine of judicial review became a central component of American constitutionalism.

The problem of applying the Constitution also raised other matters of interpretation on which the document failed to provide unambiguous guidance. It was unclear whether the Constitution should be strictly constructed or more loosely interpreted. Thus section 8 of Article One could be inter- preted in two distinct ways. If it was strictly constructed it meant that Congress possessed the power to do only those things that were specifically mentioned: to establish Post Offices and post roads but not construct canals, for example. Conversely, the 'general welfare' and 'necessary and proper' clauses suggested that the federal government possessed im- plied powers that would enable it to select whatever means it found convenient (providing they were not clearly illegal) in achieving its constitutional objectives. These and other mat- ters quickly became the subject of intense debate and have given rise to an extensive superstructure of constitutional interpretation which has largely displaced the formal process of amendment as a method of applying the Constitution to particular circumstances and adjusting it to the needs of successive generations.

The new Constitution created a general framework of government and an incomplete set of rules within which future political activity and national growth could take place. But of itself the document was inert and inanimate: it enabled solutions to be found to a multitude of problems, but was not itself a solution to any. Being a product of intense debate and many compromises and concessions, it lacked total consistency of systematic theory and institutional logic, except in the most general sense. It required animation and a set of processes which would operationalise it. Put differently, the Convention had constructed the skeleton of a federal system; it became the duty of those who would bring it to life to provide a muscular network and central nervous system. These essential elements were created during the 1790s, and only then was the Revolution complete. But first it was necessary for the Constitution to be ratified. There was no certainty that it would be.

# 9
# THE REVOLUTION COMPLETED

Completion of the Revolution required ratification and then implementation of the federal Constitution. The process of ratification was slow and uncertain and provoked bitter public debate. Not until June 1788 did the ninth state necessary for it to come into effect ratify; the major states of Virginia and New York were not among them. Neither North Carolina nor Rhode Island ratified before the new regime came into operation in April 1789. Disagreements centred on three elements: ideology, socio-economics and political tactics. All were interactive, and all were especially concerned with the issues involved in strengthening the union. But ratification was only a necessary stage, not a conclusion. It remained to give the union life, for the principles, procedures and allocation of powers so carefully devised at Philadelphia were little more than statements of hope and intent; they were anything but self-enforcing. A new government had to be constructed which could operationalise the new regime. This was the literally vital contribution of the first President and Congress. National politics under the Constitution also needed structures and organs through which a multitude of competing interests could be articulated. This was the function of the party system which developed during the 1790s.

## I

Disagreement over the Constitution quickly resolved into two rival camps. At the most fundamental level its advocates and opponents could agree, for they shared a common view of human nature and the purposes of political society; they agreed that protection of individual rights was best achieved through a form of limited representative government.[1] Beyond that, however, they had major disagreements, especially over the machinery by which theoretical principles could be articulated into an effective system of government in a society as extensive as the United States. The arguments were intense and the political manoeuvring often bruising; neither side could be confident of victory.

The heart of the Federalists' argument lay in the nationalist programme at the Convention. They argued that it was essential to curb state sovereignty if the manifest weaknesses of American government were to be cured. Their deepest fear was that rejection of the proposed new system would lead to collapse of the union, anarchy and interstate warfare and ultimately the loss of American independence.[2]

To the Anti-Federalists the proposed cure was worse than the disease. Like their opponents they feared that American politics would be destabilised, though for opposite reasons. The core of their argument was the belief that the Constitution created a consolidated national government which blended the powers of the executive and legislature and gave vast and excessive power to the federal government; it would emasculate the sovereignty of the states and put American republicanism at risk. For them the primary purpose of government was the protection of liberty. Thus they deplored the absence of a Bill of Rights which would give procedural protection to citizens in the legal process and ensure them the enjoyment of liberty of conscience and freedom of the press.

But arguably the Anti-Federalists were more concerned for state rights than individual rights. They were convinced that only in a small republic could government be made sufficiently responsible to the people, and only a small republic could form citizens who would maintain republican government. The Anti-Federalists argued that union was necessary only for limited purposes: defence against enemies, the promotion and protection of American commerce, and the maintenance of order among the states. They were aware of the problems of the 1780s but believed they were exaggerated and argued that the Constitution would not solve them. Government power should be restricted, and although a central government was necessary for limited purposes, the states had their own responsibilities and were the best defenders of individual liberties.[3] Whether their judgement was correct or not, the contrast with their opponents was stark. James Madison, who emerged as the Constitution's principal publicist just as he had been the Convention's most influential member, argued that republican principles could be better preserved and encouraged in an extended nation, and insisted that in spite of the restrictions that had been placed on the states in order to eradicate their vices the new system still allowed a division of authority.[4]

Because of their adherence to the traditional argument that republicanism could only survive in small communities, Anti-Federalists concluded that local uncentralised government was essential. They also insisted that the diversity of interests among states as different from each other as those in New England, Pennsylvania and South Carolina was so great that it was impossible to construct a legal code applicable to them all. The Anti-Federalists attached even greater importance to local self-direction than to order or to personal rights. They were horrified by the implications of the supremacy and the necessary and proper clauses (in Articles Six and One respectively); in their eyes the Constitution established a centralised and national, not federal and limited, form of government. Their alarm was reinforced by the grant of taxation power to Congress coupled with the failure to reserve powers to the states, and they deplored the implication that the federal Supreme Court would interpret the Constitution to the detriment of the states. Moreover, Anti-Federalist writers such as Richard Henry Lee of Virginia, James Winthrop of Massachusetts and Melancthon Smith of New York argued that a central government would necessarily lead to aristocratic government at the expense of the people. In their view the Constitution was calculated to increase the power and wealth of those who already had it, and they contended that under a consequent aristocracy the liberty of the common people would disappear. What they regarded as the excessive authority granted to the President reinforced their fears. The distinction between localism and personal rights was, ironically, seen most clearly in criticism of the two houses of Congress. The

Senate, which following traditional patterns would be expected to function as a bastion of aristocracy, was tolerable since it also represented the states, but the role of the House of Representatives was at risk since its smallness threatened to make it a dependency of aristocracy even though it was popularly elected. The state legislatures, they argued, were more representative of the people.[5] Their arguments were almost persuasive.

Having taken the initiative at the opening of the Convention, the nationalists retained it until ratification was achieved. In spite of considerable opposition they were able to shape the terms of debate in many states. The first brilliant move was to appropriate the title 'Federalist' for themselves. Since it implied an articulation of authority between states and national government, it would have been a more apt title for their opponents, who were immediately placed on the defensive by having to identify themselves as 'Anti-Federalists'. The nationalists' second strategic decision was to move as quickly as possible, and where necessary to coordinate action in the various states. In this strategy they had several advantages. The nationalist group had been in informal existence for several years and included major leaders, among them George Washington; they also offered an explicit programme in the shape of the Constitution which several of them had recently helped to draft at Philadelphia. By their nature the group had a broad nationalist vision to promote and extensive continental connections through which it could be articulated. Also, their supporters controlled a majority of the newspapers (whereas only a dozen supported the Anti-Federalists) or were able to apply sufficient pressure to restrict the publication of their opponents' arguments, as they did in Boston, New York and Philadelphia.[6]

For their part the Anti-Federalists were dispersed and their efforts to coordinate action were less effective. Among the most active opponents of the Constitution was Richard Henry Lee of Virginia. He met the New York delegation to Congress and Elbridge Gerry from Massachusetts, who had refused to sign the Constitution at Philadelphia, and wrote to potential supporters in every region. They developed a strategy consisting of three elements. The state legislatures would be persuaded to delay action until spring 1788 and then summon the conventions to meet simultaneously. When the conventions met the Anti-Federalists would coordinate tactics, agree on a specific set of amendments and demand a second convention. This would be accompanied by a propaganda campaign, including *Letters of a Federal Farmer*, which was possibly written by Lee himself. With some justice they believed the Constitution could be defeated at the conventions, for although the Federalists possessed majorities in 7 states and needed only 2 more for victory, the Anti-Federalists controlled New York, Rhode Island and Virginia, and also needed only 2 more states to achieve their objective of preventing ratification in the required 9 states. This they achieved for a time. They mounted extensive and coordinated campaigns in Massachusetts, New Hampshire and Pennsylvania, and won the first two. Their problem was that they were unable to sustain their victories.[7]

Success in the campaign to achieve ratification required careful calculation by the Federalists. Four states were crucial both for their importance and their location. Pennsylvania, Massachusetts and Virginia were the largest and most influential, with New York not far behind. Each occupied a vital point in the geographical chain of states; without any one of them the union could scarcely have survived even if the Constitution had been approved by the nine states necessary for it to become operational. A second consideration was the need for protagonists of the Constitution to avert the build-up of opposition by moving as quickly as possible. On 7 December 1788 Delaware unanimously became the first state to ratify, though its reasons are unclear. The nature of the Federalists' tactical problem in Pennsylvania was evident from the moment Congress transmitted the Constitution to the states with the instruction to elect a ratifying convention. Political factions were finely balanced, and a state legislature which was currently Federalist in its sympathies was about to expire. Opponents planned to delay the convention until after the annual elections in the hope that a fresh legislature would reject the Constitution. Their tactics failed, but only by kidnapping two Anti-Federalist delegates and holding them in their places to make a quorum were the Federalists able to

ensure that the Assembly would summon a convention.[8]
When this body met the Federalists enjoyed a comfortable
46:23 victory; had it failed to ratify, the Constitution would
probably have died. New Jersey ratified on 18 December, and
by early January 1788 Georgia had ratified unanimously and
Connecticut by 128:40, but three of the four key states had
still to decide.

Massachusetts was the second crucial state, and the first in
which the issue was in doubt. Commercial interests in Boston
and along the coast, which normally dominated the state,
were convinced of the value of the Constitution but the
interior was still racked by the bitterness associated with
Shays's Rebellion. Many voters were horrified by the manner
in which it had been suppressed, and although they were
poorly organised, Anti-Federalists turned out in large numbers at the elections.[9] Important leaders such as Elbridge
Gerry, Samuel Adams and James Warren publicly opposed
it, while John Hancock carefully reserved his position by
remaining silent. Attempts to bounce the state into quick
ratification failed and the convention did not meet until
January 1788. This gave opponents more time to organise.
The consequence was evident, for when the convention met
the Federalists were faced with a hostile majority of twenty
or more. Vigorous arguments and efforts to detach delegates
from the Anti-Federalist majority having been insufficient, the
Federalists succeeded only by making important concessions
and offering future political support to John Hancock. The
decisive move was to concede the possibility of amendments
including addition of a Bill of Rights as a condition of
ratification. It was sufficient to swing perhaps twenty votes,
but even so the decision was narrow, at 187 to 168.[10] Probably
a majority of the population remained opposed.

Somewhat surprisingly, ratification was easier in Maryland
and South Carolina, the first two southern states other than
Georgia to come to a decision. Maryland possessed some of
the most prominent critics of the Constitution, including John
Francis Mercer and Luther Martin who had left the Convention in disgust, Samuel Chase and William Paca, but they
wrote little and organised less. In spite of the state's potential
for a strong Anti-Federalist vote (suggested by its sectional

divisions), opponents carried only three counties in the elections to the ratifying convention and quickly lost the argument by 63 votes to 11. This outcome had its repercussions elsewhere. Although the South Carolina legislature had voted by the narrowest margin to hold a convention and its traditional adherence to state rights and local dignity should have favoured the Anti-Federalists, it voted by a margin of two to one (149:73) in favour of ratification. Perhaps the key lay in the choice of venue, for the convention took place in Charleston, the heart of the state's commercial region which was staunchly Federalist, whereas the interior backcountry was similarly Anti-Federalist.[11] A similar sectional division is also evident in New Hampshire. Here, it was in general the commercial townships along the coastline (including the major town of Portsmouth) and the Connecticut river towns which voted Federalist, and the interior which voted Anti-Federalist. Once New Hampshire ratified on 21 June 1788, the requirement of approval by nine states had been met.[12] The Constitution formally became operational among those states and the process of holding elections for office and establishing the new system could begin.

Yet important gaps in the new system remained. Four states still had to ratify, and although the inability of North Carolina and Rhode Island to ratify before the new establishment began to function was immaterial to its success, the assent of the other two states was vital. Had either Virginia or New York failed to ratify, the combination of their respective political importance and geographical locations would almost certainly have prevented continuance of the union. In Virginia the outcome was so uncertain that when the Convention opened on 2 June neither side dared call for a ballot; in New York fifteen days later the Anti-Federalists held a 2:1 majority.[13] Partly in consequence of these factors, partly because each state included the most articulate advocates of the Constitution as well as, in Virginia, its most intellectually able opponents, the standard of public discussion reached its highest point. Madison led for the Federalists and Richard Henry Lee articulated the Anti-Federalist case in Virginia, and Madison, Alexander Hamilton and John Jay published the *Federalist* papers, the most profound commentaries on the Constitution produced during the entire debate, in New York.

As Virginia was both physically extensive and contained many diverse interests, the divisions were especially complex. Apart from the Federalists' ownership of more slaves, there was not a great deal to choose between the wealth of the two groups; each recruited its delegates from the same strata of society. In geographical terms the Anti-Federalists had a majority east of the Blue Ridge (though the Federalists dominated the Northern Neck). The Shenandoah Valley and some western counties were Federalist, partly because of links with the Northern Neck and partly because they hoped for national protection against the British, who still occupied the north-west forts, and their Indian allies. In essence the division was between the commercial Tidewater counties plus particular western counties on one side, and the less well-developed regions on the other. The debates were sufficiently influential, especially given the Federalists' willingness to add a Bill of Rights, to persuade a number of waverers to support the Constitution. It was finally ratified by 89 votes to 79 on 25 June – just in time to influence the New York Convention at Poughkeepsie.[14]

In that state the division between commercial and local economies was at its sharpest. New York City and its surrounding counties were Federalist, but the rest of the state, including Hudson Valley counties that might have been expected to have voted with the Federalists, was Anti-Federalist. Similarly most merchants and rich landowners and those who had received a college education supported the Constitution while their opponents were generally less well off and less well educated. But Governor George Clinton, the state's most effective politician, and his organisation opposed the Constitution, and initially the Anti-Federalists had a majority of 46:19 in the Convention. As in Virginia, the debate was crucial, although in spite of their later reputation the *Federalist* papers had little direct influence. Both sides organised strongly, but ultimately the terms of debate dis-advantaged the Anti-Federalists. Their localist interests placed them in a difficult position, and some were sympathetic provided amendments were made. Once Virginia had ratified, the real choices facing them were union or separation and the further prospect that if the Constitution were rejected the city and lower counties might secede from the state. Persuaded by these considerations sufficient delegates from Dutchess County switched sides – a move made easier once again by the prospect of the addition of a Bill of Rights and the possibility of amendments. New York ratified by the narrow margin of 30 to 27 on 26 July.[15]

Ratification was, in spite of North Carolina's and Rhode Island's dilatoriness, effectively complete once New York had approved the Constitution, yet it had been a slow and uncertain process. The best rough estimate, by Jackson Turner Main, suggests that the Anti-Federalists may have been in a slight majority among all voters. More certainly they outnumbered the Federalists by as much as four to one in Rhode Island and South Carolina, and by perhaps three to one in New York and North Carolina, and they were slightly more than a majority in Massachusetts and Virginia.[16] Nevertheless, the Federalists were able to persuade between 60 and 75 delegates of the prudence of ratification.

In part their success was a product of better organisation and tactics, their dominance of the newspapers, and the greater prestige of their leaders. Those Anti-Federalists who were closer in character to the Federalists than the majority of the Constitution's opponents were susceptible to persuasion, and the support of more obscure delegates was sufficient to turn the decision in its favour. In comparison with the positive programme offered by the Federalists, the Anti-Federalist position was politically weak, though ironically their insistence on individual autonomy and limited central government was compatible with the reigning political orthodoxy during much of the nineteenth century. They supported the union and were prepared to strengthen it, yet they deplored the potential centralisation implicit in the new Constitution. Both their alternative proposals – continuation under the Articles of Confederation or a second convention – put the future of the union at risk. They were much concerned for the protection of individual liberties and severely criticised the Constitution for its lack of a Bill of Rights, but their arguments were not decisive. Many Federalists had resisted the proposition for a Bill of Rights at Philadelphia, but found it easy to turn the Anti-Federalists' flank by agreeing to add one as the price of ratification in the crucial states of Massachusetts, Virginia and New York. As a political manoeuvre it was brilliant for it was a persuasive concession yet left the Federalists' major objective – strengthening of the central government – intact.

Social divisions over the Constitution were complex. Virtually everyone acknowledged the connection between economic interests and political action, and appreciated that economic consequences would flow from ratification of the Constitution. They assumed that a new government would address the problems of the Revolutionary debt and that those who held it would benefit from a consequent rise in its value. Yet some of the largest holders of public debt opposed the Constitution. Probably more important was the prohibition on the states' issuing of paper money and impairing private contracts; it was these policies that had horrified conservatives in the 1780s. Since the document gave the federal government control over interstate and foreign trade, it had economic implications which made it highly attractive to the mercantile community from Baltimore northwards. The debate was thus not simple in economic terms; still less was it merely a conflict between two types of property – personal and real – as Beard argued.

However, social status did have some importance in influencing decisions, especially in rural areas. In the North it was common for men of greater wealth to be Federalists. Almost all the richer men supported ratification in the small states of New Jersey, Delaware and Georgia, and in Pennsylvania the Federalist delegates to the Convention owned substantially more land and other taxable property than their opponents, while creditors also were assumed to be Federalists. But in Maryland and Virginia some of the most prominent Anti-Federalist leaders – men like Samuel Chase and Luther Martin in Maryland and George Mason, Richard Henry Lee and Patrick Henry in Virginia – were also members of the elite. To a considerable extent, therefore, the substantive debate took place within the upper echelons of society rather than between the elite and their social inferiors. Also, and significantly, the class division broke down in the towns, where virtually the entire body of voters supported the Federalists.[17] In that respect it was a contest between men of local focus and those of national vision.

Setting aside personal idiosyncrasies, the most persuasive general model of social and economic divisions over the Constitution centres on this split between localism and cosmopolitanism. In economic terms it overlapped the political boundaries of the states in favour of a division between those areas with commercial economies linked to an expanding national economy and foreign markets, and those whose economies were local in their focus. Thus the towns (all commercial) and the commercial farming regions of the Chesapeake, eastern North Carolina and the lower South supported the Constitution, while the interior counties of Massachusetts, North Carolina and the Virginia southside and west generally voted against, as did the rural sections of Rhode Island. However, the correlation is imperfect. Even though much of upstate New York had excellent commercial links with the city down the Hudson river, it supported the Anti-Federalist cause, as did Anne Arundel and Baltimore Counties at the head of the Chesapeake in Maryland – though the towns of Annapolis and Baltimore voted Federalist. Conversely, interior sections of Connecticut surprisingly voted Federalist. So, more explicably, did the interior sections of Georgia, those sections of Virginia (including the Shenandoah and modern West Virginia), and the northern tier of Pennsylvania counties; all needed strong central support against local threats from Indians and the British. A further geographical distinction was the support given by those smaller states which were most sensitive about their integrity in relation to more powerful neighbours – Connecticut, New Jersey, Delaware and Georgia – and those which had been occupied for long periods by the British.[18]

Beyond this, the division over the Constitution was more personal. Even in states such as Virginia and Maryland, where there was little to choose between Federalist and Anti-Federalist leaders on social grounds, there were significant cultural differences between the groups. Federalists often had commercial as well as agricultural interests and social and economic connections out-of-state, and many of their leaders had served in Congress or the Continental army and were in many instances well educated. Their opponents were more modest and provincial and had less formal education or other broadening experience. Also, on political grounds there were divisions between men such as New York Governor George Clinton and his supporters whose political activities focused on state politics, and his opponents the Philip Schuyler–Alexander Hamilton faction whose interests were also national. Perhaps the prime examples of this were in Massachusetts, where Hancock's continental ambitions and hopes of high office ultimately persuaded him to endorse ratification, and Virginia, where George Washington's known support for the Constitution gave powerful impetus to the campaign run by James Madison. There was, however, irony in this, since if it was the Federalists who possessed the broader and more confident vision of a national future, it was the more timid Anti-Federalists who were closer to the members of their local communities. Neither group were democrats according to later definitions of that term, but it can be argued, as Cecelia M. Kenyon has done, that the Anti-Federalists lacked their opponents' faith and vision to extend their principles nationwide.[19]

The old Congress took its time in extinguishing itself. For much of 1788 it conducted business on a limited scale. Its principal concern was with the request by settlers in the Kentucky area of Virginia to be admitted as the fourteenth state, but members felt it was an issue that should be left to their successors. During the summer all thirteen states were represented simultaneously for the first time in several years. Once ratification was completed, attention focused on arrangements for the new system. After much manoeuvring New York was selected as the location of the government. Elections were held in the states during the fall, and from October onwards Congress was never quorate, though the executive departments maintained an exiguous existence.[20]

## II

The new regime was inaugurated, a month late, in April 1789. Facing it was the task of implementing the Constitution as well as responsibility for developing policy and conducting day-to-day affairs. Implementation of the Constitution included three prime elements: the deliberate processes of establishing the institutions of federal government (including a demonstration of its capacity to enforce its lawful authority), the formulation of a financial programme with political as well as fiscal purposes, and the unexpected and initially unwelcome emergence of a coherent and organised political party system.

Without doubt the new government entered office with several advantages not enjoyed by its predecessor. Some were barely evident. The worst of the post-war depression was over, and the economy was expanding, if somewhat slowly. Although they had yet to approach pre-Revolutionary levels, exports to Britain had increased by more than half since 1784, and the proportion carried in foreign ships had diminished somewhat. In spite of continued discrimination, even trade with the British West Indies was developing. The 1790s were about to prove to be a boom decade, especially once the outbreak of European wars increased demands for American goods. The Constitution had important domestic economic consequences in that it created a unified national market within which persons, goods and capital could move freely and equally.[21] There was also general willingness to allow things to work themselves out and a common recognition that there was no practical alternative to the new Constitution. Substantive amendments which had been the price of ratification in several states were quickly and quietly dropped. Other advantages were obvious.

The first elections were a great Federalist success. Only 3 or perhaps 4 senators and 11 out of 59 members of the House of Representatives were Anti-Federalists, and Anti-Federalism as a faction was destroyed. First the electorate, then their representatives, accepted the new Constitution and were prepared to make it successful. Also, 44 out of 91 members of the first Congress had assisted in writing and ratifying the Constitution, and more than half the Convention's members served as legislators, administrators or judges.[22] Among these was Madison, who was serving in the House of Representatives since he had been outmanoeuvred in elections for Virginia's senators. Above all there was George Washington who, as expected, had been elected first President. His public commitment to the new regime and contribution to government policy gave them legitimacy, just as his membership had given authority to the Philadelphia Convention.

On the other side of the account, however, some serious handicaps remained. It was far from clear that a republican government could control an area as vast as the United States, with its scattered population, poor communications and often divergent economic and social interests. During the campaign to ratify the Constitution in New York, Madison had argued brilliantly in *Federalist* number 10 that size and diversity would take the sting out of the inescapable conflict of interests and that a republican government could harness their latent energies to national benefit: diversity could be an advantage. In so doing he formulated a profoundly perceptive analysis of the dynamics of American politics. But the received wisdom of the period remained against him, and much evidence supported the sceptics. Two gaps rendered the union incomplete. Rhode Island was sufficiently small to pose no great difficulty, and arrangements were put in train to treat it as a separate state. North Carolina was large enough to pose a potential difficulty, but did not do so; by the end of 1789 it had ratified the Constitution, though Rhode Island did not do so for another year. Overseas the country was still held in low esteem by European powers, two of which (Spain and Great Britain) each occupied far more of the continent than the United States did; North America remained for some time a field of action for the rivalries of outside empires. Within the country, the Confederation government had come to a virtual halt by 1789, public credit was in acute disarray, and the available currency was so various that a normal means of exchange was bills of credit drawn on a London bank.

## III

The first stage in completing the nationalisation of the Revolution was establishment of machinery of government capable of meeting the challenge of fresh problems, adapting to respond to new ones and above all giving substance to the aspirations contained within the terms of the Constitution. Washington realised his actions would be interpreted as precedents. He attached great importance to the need to create a vigorous and effective executive under his direction, and his policies did much to determine the direction in which development would move. At a psychological level he used his popularity to give credibility to the new regime. On two occasions, in 1789 and 1791, he made grand tours to the North and South in order to publicise the existence of the new government and display his commitment to it. He held regular levees in Philadelphia for the same purpose, though after inconclusive discussion in Congress he settled for the plain title of Mr President rather than one of the grandiose titles proposed by some members.[23]

Recognising that for most people judgement on the federal government would be judgement on its local officials, Washington took considerable care to ensure that they would be men capable of bringing credit to it. More obviously he selected major figures who could represent different areas as his principal officers. In particular he appointed Thomas Jefferson of Virginia as Secretary of State and Alexander Hamilton of New York as Secretary of Treasury, though neither was his first choice. A third more overtly political criterion, which was applied in the selection of local officials, was the need to choose men who would promote the interests of the new government. Senior officers in the Customs service wielded considerable political influence in their respective states, and to a lesser extent this was true of post office officials and federal judges. Washington appointed his supporter Benjamin Lincoln to the Collectorship of Customs in Boston, but reluctantly nominated William Paca as US District Judge for Maryland since he had initially opposed the Constitution and openly hesitated before voting for it at the state ratifying convention. Similarly Federalists in Rhode Island used federal office and Washington's visit in 1790 to bolster their position in a state in which Anti-Federalism was strong. During the 1790s 63 per cent of federal officials whose political affiliations are known were Federalists. Many also had strong Revolutionary associations; only 17 were identifiable Loyalists.[24]

The machinery of government needed urgent development.

The residual machinery of the old Confederation was exiguous in anticipation of its replacement and in consequence of its lack of public funds. Congress established three initial departments, Foreign Affairs (soon renamed the Department of State), War, and Finance (entitled the Treasury Department), in each case with a single head; but it permitted the President authority to remove their officials at will. By 1792 the civil service was in full working order but was small in numbers. It employed about 780 persons, of whom about 660 were employed by the Treasury in its offices throughout the country.[25] At this point there were effectively three possible lines of executive development. The Senate could function as an executive council as had been common in the colonies before 1776 and as councils were expected to act in a number of states. Alternatively a collectivity of ministers subordinate to a semi-ceremonial President could take responsibility for initiating as well as administering legislation, a system clearly preferred by Alexander Hamilton. Each of these systems would have initially subordinated the executive to the legislature, thus continuing the practice customary in the states but breaking the balance of powers carefully constructed at Philadelphia and possibly leading to a system approximating to the British ministerial system. Washington rejected these alternatives in favour of a single executive to whom, he believed, Article Two had given a grant of power as well as responsibility for implementing Congressional legislation. He insisted that members of his cabinet were his subordinates, and his right to dismiss them was reluctantly conceded by Congress. While he permitted them administrative autonomy he retained active responsibility for policy decisions.[26]

Relations with Congress posed delicate problems. It quickly became prudent and necessary (and thus established practice) for the President to consult Senators about federal appointments. After an embarrassingly unsuccessful attempt to seek personally the Senate's advice and consent to negotiations with southern Indian tribes, Washington insisted on the executive's sole right to conduct foreign policy, though he recognised the Senate's constitutional right to approve or reject a treaty. He argued in 1793 that although Congress possessed the exclusive right to declare war, the avoidance of war through a Proclamation of Neutrality was an integral component of the executive's foreign policy power. He also refused to give the House of Representatives papers concerned with the negotiation of Jay's treaty with Britain in 1794.[27] As yet, Washington was uneasy in his relations with Congress, though members of his administration, notably Hamilton, were active in advocating and advancing public policy and his friend Madison functioned virtually as a government leader in the House of Representatives. Thus balance was achieved.

One area in which Congress was required to implement the Constitution was in establishing a national system of courts. Prepared in private session by the Senate, the Judiciary Act of 1789 gave substance to the very general terms of Article Three of the Constitution which states that there should be a federal supreme court but left it to Congress either to establish inferior courts or to permit state courts to function as inferior federal courts. The Act established a Supreme Court with District Courts in each state and Circuit Courts with appellate jurisdiction in between. The structure was an important victory for the nationalists. They defeated the state rights localists who had wished to confine the Supreme Court almost entirely to appellate jurisdiction and had argued that state courts would be competent to try federal issues under the jurisdiction of the United States Constitution as well as their local law. By creating an entire apparatus, the Act ensured that federal laws and rights would be adjudicated uniformly throughout the nation and exclusively in national courts. This system reinforced the principle that the new government would act directly on individuals, by-passing the states. Section 25 of the Act further reinforced national authority by permitting appeals from state courts to the Supreme Court on matters where the supremacy of the Constitution and laws and treaties made under it were at issue, though efforts to construct a single nationwide system failed. Instead, federal lower courts were allowed limited original jurisdiction and a considerable amount of concurrent jurisdiction; state courts retained considerable authority.[28]

A major item of business outstanding from the ratification debate was the addition of a Bill of Rights to the Constitution. Most members of the Philadelphia Convention had believed a Bill of Rights redundant on the grounds that the Constitution itself provided adequate protection for citizens' rights and because they feared that any statement of rights would be interpreted as an exclusive and limited list, thus implying that citizens possessed no others. Voters and many delegates to the ratifying conventions disagreed; and Virginia and Massachusetts in particular made such amendments a virtual condition of ratification. Madison, perhaps more fearful that demands for a second convention would unravel the work of the previous two years than convinced of the necessity of a bill, reduced the many proposals to nineteen. By the time they had passed the two houses of Congress and been ratified by the states in December 1791 they had been reduced to ten. Eight out of the ten remaining were largely concerned with procedural protection for individual rights, mainly drawn from the state declarations, though the first amendment included a prohibition on the establishment of any religion by Congress. Madison's wish that the protections be extended to the states was rejected. Had it been accepted the consequences for national supremacy would have been profound, and its rejection demonstrated the continuing wish to protect state interests. However, the tenth amendment, reserving powers neither granted to the United States nor prohibited by it to the states, to the people or the states respectively, was approved without the crippling addition of the word 'expressly' before the verb 'delegated'.[29] The insertion of this adverb would have drastically curtailed interpretation of the Constitution by preventing growth of the doctrine of implied powers, and restricted the development of federal power. It was a major defeat for state-rights interests.

## IV

Once the structure of federal government had been erected it was possible to move to the second stage of completing the union by developing appropriate public policies. Their centrepiece was Alexander Hamilton's financial programme. Presumptuously conceiving of himself as prime minister to Washington's ceremonial presidency, Hamilton had the broadest possible vision of public policy. His programme had five principal elements: the linked funding of the national debt and the assumption and funding of the states' Revolutionary war debts (both achieved in 1790); the establishment of the Bank of the United States (chartered in 1791); an excise tax designed to finance the funding programme by supplementing the original tariff of 1789 (enacted in 1791); and a protective as opposed to a revenue-raising tariff intended to encourage domestic manufactures (the only proposal not implemented). His object was only partly to place government finances on a sound basis; it was also intended to promote commercial development and sustain a conservative social ideology. Pre-eminently it had the grand purpose of strengthening the union, particularly by tying creditor and commercial interests to the new regime: the programme was a work of political economy as well as financial policy.

There was general agreement that the chaotic financial obligations entered into by Congress during the war would have to be funded. After Hamilton reorganised it, it became evident that the foreign debt had held its value well. The Confederation Congress had recognised the importance of maintaining the nation's credit with overseas creditors and had accordingly made the Dutch debt a prime charge on public revenue; it remained worth its $12 million face value. In contrast, domestic debts incurred by Congress had depreciated significantly – from their face value of $40 million to a market value of no more than $13 million – all with nominal interest of 6 per cent. New stock was issued on different terms once the debt had been organised and funded. A central principle was that creditors would be entitled to receive payment in western lands or some other means, but would be paid in specie if they wished. A second was Hamilton's argument that holders would prefer the more certain prospect of payment even if the interest rate was reduced. Accordingly, when he exchanged new stock for old, he issued two-thirds at 6 per cent and the remaining one-third at 6 per cent deferred for ten years, with interest certificates payable at 3 per cent, making an average interest rate of 4 per cent.

Disagreement was not directed at the central principle but at its application. There were two principal issues: whether it should be funded at face value, instead of at the substantial current market discount, and whether the policy should discriminate in favour of the original holders (many of whom were soldiers and similar deserving people) by paying them in full, and against their successors in title, who were frequently speculators. Hamilton insisted that the debts should be funded at par, regardless of who the current holders were, in order to establish the government's financial credit and thus the political credibility of the new regime. The policy was immediately successful in that the value of the new bonds rose sharply. By June 1791 the market value went above par, and by February 1792 the 6 per cent stock traded at $1.20 on the dollar.[30]

Discussion of the second element of Hamilton's proposals for public credit was far more bitter. Hamilton believed that Revolutionary war debts incurred by the states were logically part and parcel of the general war debt, and that since the most lucrative sources of revenue (import duties) were now exclusively in the hands of Congress the states would encounter difficulty in servicing them. Also, in the context of political economy, he feared the political consequences for national unity of the existence of a disaffected creditor class attached to the states, whereas his grand constitutional objective was to bind commercial interests to the federal government. Only Massachusetts and South Carolina, each of which had substantial outstanding war debts, supported assumption of these Revolutionary debts by the federal government. Other states, notably Maryland, Virginia, North Carolina and Georgia, were afraid that they would be obliged to shoulder excessive burdens since they had already paid off most of their debts. The remaining states were indifferent. The amount of the debt assumed came to $21,500,000. Assumption was approved only after very difficult negotiation and bargaining in Congress, since its opponents understood very clearly its political consequences for their states. Ultimately the accounting problem was solved at the general settlement of Revolutionary debts in 1793 by allowing generous settlements to every state.[31]

In the end assumption revolved around the satisfaction of state rather than economic interests, but gained important political consequences by establishing the federal government as worthy of support by commercial interests. The pre-eminence of the federal government was further strengthened ironically by the creditor states' acceptance of payment in federal stock; by becoming creditors they drew large revenues from the federal government. Thus the political authority of the states was denied once more, to the great advantage of the union. Similarly, much of the debt became the property of a relatively small number of people. As intended, creditors, especially the rich, were bound to the union.[32]

Once it came into effect, the success of Hamilton's funding and assumption programme, and thus the financial reputation of the new government, depended on one critical factor: the capacity of the federal government to meet its financial obligations. The commitment to payment at par and in specie a debt worth about $80 million, much of which could have been retired in 1786 for far less, imposed a substantial burden and required commitment of such large sums that over two-fifths of national revenue was committed to payment of interest alone during the 1790s.[33] If the government proved unable to impose its authority by raising the necessary taxes, its own credibility as well as the scheme itself would collapse.

The matter was shortly put to the test. Since the original tariff of 1789 was insufficient to meet the government's revenue needs, Congress raised an excise duty on whiskey in 1791. The duty aroused considerable opposition in western Pennsylvania. Living in an area in which specie was in short supply and whose major crop, grain, was bulky and thus difficult to transport eastwards across the mountains, its farmers had customarily converted their product into whiskey, which could be more easily transported and became in effect a monetary medium. The excise imposed a considerable burden on men with few resources, and their resentment ultimately led to open rebellion in 1794. As in so many instances, other matters complicated the issue, but Hamilton interpreted it as an open challenge to the new government's authority and determined to exploit it to his advantage. Suppression of the so-called Whiskey Rebellion was easy, but the political benefit of victory was substantial. He succeeded in demonstrating that, unlike its predecessor during the

Confederation era, the federal government was capable of imposing its will on its citizens if challenged.[34]

The final element of Hamilton's programme to be implemented was the establishment of a national bank under the title of the Bank of the United States. Again the objectives were political as well as financial and commercial. In 1790 there were only three banks in the United States – the original Bank of North America in Pennsylvania, the Bank of New York with which Hamilton himself was associated, and the Bank of Massachusetts. Taking the Bank of England as his prime model, Hamilton hoped to create capital and encourage commercial and industrial growth. At the same time he intended to reinforce once again the ties of the financial classes to the new regime, perform the government's financial business, and exercise control over banks chartered by the states. As established by Congress in 1791, one-fifth of the bank's capital of $10 million was subscribed by the government, which was permitted to appoint five directors; the remainder of the capital was to be subscribed by private investors, including $2 million in coin and $6 million in United States securities.

In all respects the Bank was successful. It was highly profitable and contributed to economic development. By attracting the support of men such as Thomas Willing, one of the richest merchants in Philadelphia, and establishing branches in the commercial centres of Boston, New York, Baltimore and Charleston as well as Philadelphia, it strengthened the national economy and thus the national union. Necessarily also, the financial programme, based as it was on specie, required the establishment of a national mint and currency. This was done by the Coinage Act of 1792. Although provision was made for gold coinage, in practice the currency became one based on silver. However, it was still insufficient for business requirements, a problem which Hamilton had anticipated by allowing the Bank of the United States to issue paper currency in the form of bank notes which maintained their value because he allowed them to be converted into specie and accepted them at par in payment of taxes.[35]

A by-product of the establishment of the bank was central to the development of a strongly national as opposed to localist government. Before the Bank could be chartered it was necessary to determine whether the United States possessed legal authority to do so. It was far from self-evident that the Constitution had granted Congress the right to charter a bank, although it certainly had not prohibited one. Section 8 of Article One enumerated many powers such as the right to coin money and establish a Post Office, but made no mention of a bank. Moreover the Philadelphia Convention had rejected a proposal that construction of canals should be authorised, thus implying that the enumerated list was an exclusive list. When invited to sign the Bank bill, Washington requested the advice of his Secretary of State Thomas Jefferson and his Attorney General Edmund Randolph. Both argued that the Constitution should be strictly construed as a grant of particular enumerated powers. In their opinion the authority to establish a bank could not be inferred from any expressly specified power, and could be regarded as no more than convenient rather than necessary and proper within the terms of the Constitution. They accordingly concluded that the federal government lacked the power to charter a bank. In contrast, Washington found Hamilton's argument that the Constitution should be broadly construed as more persuasive. This interpretation, which became the reigning view that permitted massive development of federal authority in the centuries to follow, argued that the federal government possessed implied powers to achieve its objectives as well as those particular powers enumerated in the Constitution. In Hamilton's view the term 'necessary' included useful as well as essential; thus the federal government possessed the right to use any 'necessary and proper' (that is, convenient) means to achieve its legitimate Constitutional objectives, providing they were not forbidden by the Constitution or contrary to the essential ends of government. While remaining doubtful about aspects of Hamilton's advice, Washington signed the bill, thus completing another stage in the implementation of the Constitution.[36]

## V

One further element was needed to make the new national regime viable. It was necessary to create a medium through which the two-way relationship between electorates and government could operate, the national executive and legislature collaborate, and political, social and economic interests at all levels connect with the formulation of public policy. At a mundane level, institutions were needed through which candidates could compete for support and, from the opposite perspective, electorates could select candidates and get them elected in a society which lacked a dominant tradition of prescriptive authority and deference but had wide and complex electorates.[37] That medium was the system of competing political parties which emerged during the 1790s. Unexpected, since they were not discussed at Philadelphia and not mentioned in the Constitution, they were initially unwelcome. Yet within three years of Washington's inauguration a party system was clearly visible, and in the 1800 elections both presidential and congressional contests brought a transfer of power from one party to its successful rival. Parties quickly came to possess a powerful nationalising potential and became an important informal component of American constitutionalism; they turned out to be essential vehicles that enabled a physically large and diverse aggregation of communities to be woven into a single if diversified nation.

Their ancestry went back many decades. Several colonies – though by no means all – had long possessed political organisations. Thus politics revolved around family connections in New York, contests between supporters and opponents of the Proprietor and between Quakers and their critics in Pennsylvania, and in Rhode Island especially round the bitter rivalry between the Ward faction based in Newport and the Hopkins faction in Providence. But these factional activities were with some justice considered as self-interested and potentially dangerous to the public welfare. During the prewar crisis, political organisation developed rapidly at all levels and began to change character. Samuel Adams's Boston Caucus played a central role in mobilising resistance in Massachusetts, and committees of correspondence made possible a broader coordination of activity throughout the colonies, as did the Congresses from the Stamp Act Congress of 1765 to the First and Second Continental Congresses of 1774 and 1775 – though even the need to collaborate against

Britain was insufficient to make factional politics fully respect-able.

Factional rivalries continued everywhere after independ-ence. They were clearest perhaps in New York, where the Clintonians established a powerful control over state politics, and Pennsylvania, where politics were dominated by the conflict between Constitutionalists and Republicans over the 1776 Constitution, but existed in all states. Such divisions were less explicit in Congress during the Revolution, but here too voting patterns were cohesive, even if they were not formally and publicly acknowledged.[38] The evidence thus suggests that many individuals and interest-groups often voted together consistently during the Revolution and that collaboration was essential if policy success was to be achieved. Also, application of the principle that ultimate authority in the new regime lay with the people, and the constant fear of excessive power in the executive branch suggested the need for organised opposition. Reciprocally, the existence of formed opposition implied need for government organisation.

Yet these voting blocs were limited in character compared with the parties that developed after 1789. Many were specific in purpose and some were only short-lived; even the national-ist movement which achieved fulfilment with the Philadelphia Convention should not be called a party in the later sense, though the contest between Federalists and Anti-Federalists over ratification had many characteristics of party operations. In any case, divisions over the Constitution did not continue along the same lines once the issue had been resolved. Moreover, the electorate was still profoundly and continually suspicious of party activity; any organised and sustained grouping was equated with faction, assumed to oppose the current regime, and regarded as inherently dangerous. The most potent memory of the dangers of rivalry came from the Revolutionary war itself, when the bitter dispute between Patriots and Loyalists went to the heart of the republic's existence, and the opposition was dedicated to its destruction. In such a context the protection of citizens against the excesses of government and rival interests was expected to be provided by such institutional devices as checks and balances.

American society in 1789 was at first sight ill-fitted for party development. Its diversity was obvious: from ethnic and religious distinctions to differences between men owning much property and those with little or none, creditors and debtors, and merchants and great planters. The vast territorial extent of the United States posed additional problems, and all were overlaid by the growing sectional rivalry between North and South and the increasing importance of the West. Madison described America in *Federalist* 10 as a congeries of competing interests, and argued that a well-constructed union was essential, in his words, to 'break and control' the violence inherent in faction and harness its latent forces; the Philadelphia Convention had not intended to construct a government of parties, but a constitutional government that would curb them.[39]

The complexity of American society suggested that a multi-party system would emerge. For a time after the first nation-wide national elections, voting blocs took shape in the first Congress along the earlier three-way regional lines. At the same time, elections were conducted for the most part on a personal basis, a traditional practice not conducive to party formation. The key to success was a reputation for integrity, political independence and commitment to the public welfare – as demonstrated by the unanimous election of Washington to be first President.

The potent sense of national unity generated by Washington's inauguration soon evaporated, even though those who had opposed ratification of the Constitution now accepted its legitimacy. By the end of 1791 a two-party structure began replacing the older sectional divisions. Its origins were located partly in local and partly in national politics.

Most of the impetus came from national affairs. From the beginning, organisation increasingly affected behaviour in the House of Representatives, though cohesive voting on the previous pattern preceded party discipline. Divisions had strong ideological components and frequently turned explicitly on policy issues (to a far greater extent than later party systems) and on interpretation of the Constitution. All politicians were committed to making the new Constitution work but disagreed vehemently as to its character.[40] To men like Hamilton it was an expansive grant of power for national purposes and could be implemented only by constructing a central government committed to activist politics. To Madison, Jefferson and others it offered a limited grant of powers to the federal government, and was intended to protect and preserve the liberty of individual citizens and the autonomy of the states; they wished for a strong union but not a powerful activist federal government. Both sides in the contest became convinced that the integrity of republican society was at stake and believed their opponents were determined to destroy it.

Not surprisingly under these circumstances parties grew principally (but not entirely) from growing opposition to Hamilton's financial policies. Though he had begun as *ad hoc* government leader in the lower house of the first Congress, Madison opposed the Treasury Secretary's decision to treat all current holders equally when the federal debt was funded, and moved into open opposition in the interest of Virginia over assumption of state debts. The split widened over establishment of the Bank of the United States and its essential prerequisites, the broad construction of the Constitution and the doctrine of implied powers. By the end of 1791 the cabinet was irrevocably divided. On one side were the opposition, led by Secretary of State Jefferson with Madison supporting him in the House, and known as Republicans (or sometimes Democrats), and on the other the party of government directed by Hamilton and taking the title Federalists; Washington continued to protest that he was a national leader who deplored party factionalism. Each party had its own caucus in Congress, and its own press; John Fenno's *Gazette of the United States* represented the Federalist interest and Philip Freneau's *National Gazette* spoke for the Republicans.[41] Outside Congress the Federalists' greatest strength lay in the commercial regions of New England, coastal Virginia and South Carolina, and the Republicans were strongest in New York and other parts of Virginia.

The 1792 elections marked a halfway stage. There were few manifestations of party organisation in most states, largely because the complexity of multiple elections made it difficult, but significant developments in a few. In New York John Jay's unsuccessful challenge to George Clinton for the governorship

stimulated the development of party organisation. Committees of correspondence were set up, and mobilisation of
support for Jay was coordinated by the Albany Committee;
although the contest was largely personal in character, it
was recognised that Clinton represented the Republican
interest.[42]

Pennsylvania also saw the emergence of nominating committees for statewide elections, the distribution of circular letters
intended to whip up support for particular candidates, and
the composition of election tickets which listed slates of nomi-
nees for use by electors. Signs of the new developments were
clearer in national politics. In addition to the contests in Congressional seats, Republicans hoped to replace John Adams as
Vice-President by someone more congenial. Their leaders in
New York, Pennsylvania and Virginia agreed on a common
candidate and began to organise a campaign on his behalf.[43]

Differences over foreign relations aggravated the quarrel.
They began with disagreement over the significance of the
French Revolution after it moved into its most radical phase
between those who continued to see it as functioning within
the reform tradition of their own Revolution and those who
increasingly believed it posed a threat to liberty and stability
everywhere, even in the United States. France's declaration
of war on Britain in 1793 heightened the tension. Residual
bitterness deriving from memories of the struggle for independence, resentment at continuing discrimination against
American trade, and annoyance at their persistent refusal to
evacuate the northwest forts in defiance of the 1783 peace
treaty incited continuing hostility towards the British. But
while its opponents preferred France, the government was
more sympathetic towards Britain, partly from its inherent
conservatism, partly because its members appreciated the
importance of British trade to American prosperity, and
partly because they understood the strategic implications for
the United States (which was still militarily very weak) of
Britain's dominant naval power in the Atlantic Ocean. The
dispute came to a head in 1794 when Jay negotiated a
settlement with Britain in the treaty which bears his name; it
was ratified only after a bitter struggle. By the Third Congress
of 1793–5, sectional voting blocs had changed into a two-bloc
division which cohered over a broad range of issues.[44]

As divisions on domestic and foreign policy deepened, so did differences of opinion over the relationship between government and people. Critics argued that in a republic administered by limited government it was unavoidable, and indeed essential and desirable, that those in power should be constantly responsive to the will of the community, and that public policy should be open to debate and subject to criticism even of the most virulent kind. By contrast, the government which had entered office under Washington's presidency as a government of national interest argued along traditional conservative lines that liberty required stability and order, and that the government had been elected to office in order to administer public affairs according to its own interpretation of the national good – especially since it was composed by definition of the 'better' sort of men. Continual criticism, especially if virulent, was considered potentially dangerous and destabilising; it was the people's duty to accept direction by their officials, subject only to their right of judgement at elections.

Party politics continued to develop throughout the decade. Washington condemned parties in his Farewell Address of 1795, but his advice was ignored. The Federalists, having occupied the high ground of government at the beginning of the new regime, were slower to organise than their opponents but established limited organisations in a number of states, notably New York, New Jersey, Pennsylvania, Delaware and Virginia. Their machinery became highly sophisticated at the beginning of the next century, with a network of caucuses and state, county and local committees in their strongest areas.[45] The 1796 presidential contest was the first to be openly fought on party grounds. In the end the Federalist candidate John Adams secured a narrow victory over the Republican nominee Thomas Jefferson but his success exacerbated rather than dampened the quarrel. Battles over major issues in domestic and foreign affairs continued raging with unabated intensity, and success swung from one party to the other. Four years later, the logic of party politics reached its zenith when the Republicans reversed the previous verdict by securing Jefferson's election as President. The election of 1800 was the first occasion on which political power was peacefully transferred from an incumbent party to an opposition party after a contest; it was not so much a revolution in itself as fulfilment of a revolution which had already taken place.

Important though ideological differences were in setting an agenda for national politics, they were less important than structural developments. The emergent machinery of party activity was essential in the long run. The frequency and intensity of competition for elective offices and the need to marshal support for the enactment of legislation paradoxically encouraged political collaboration; different interest groups found it prudent to make concessions to each other in hopes of partial success rather than working for total victory but risking total failure. The numerous levels at which political activity operated added complexity to the system and made it necessary to articulate action from the most local levels through the states to the highest levels of national government. In spite of the frequently venomous rhetoric and hostility which characterised political battles during the 1790s, the parties helped to channel the processes of government and tame dissension; in so doing they secured the union. Factionalism was naturally divisive and centrifugal but parties defused and harnessed it to the national interest. They provided routes by which interest groups could influence public policy and, in particular, means by which different areas in a physically extended society could cooperate; they dampened potentially dangerous forces and made it possible to link local conflicts over local concerns to national debates over national issues and thus encouraged compromise. In another political dimension, deferential acceptance of official leadership encouraged elitism but parties provided acceptable channels for criticism and routes by which new men could challenge for power. Within this context it is difficult to see how a Hamiltonian government could have imposed its will successfully on such a diverse and dispersed society. By 1800 the party system had demonstrated its viability as a vehicle for action and change. It gave life to the Constitution and permitted the politics of union and national growth. The Revolution was complete.

# TABLES

## 1 Estimated population ('000s)

|               |                         | 1770 | 1790 |
|---------------|-------------------------|------|------|
| New England   | Maine[1]                | 31   | 97   |
|               | New Hampshire           | 62   | 142  |
|               | Vermont[2]              | 10   | 85   |
|               | Massachusetts           | 235  | 379  |
|               | Rhode Island            | 58   | 69   |
|               | Connecticut             | 184  | 238  |
|               | Total                   | 580  | 1009 |
| Middle States | New York                | 163  | 340  |
|               | New Jersey              | 117  | 184  |
|               | Pennsylvania            | 240  | 434  |
|               | Delaware                | 35   | 59   |
|               | Total                   | 555  | 1017 |
| South (upper) | Maryland                | 203  | 320  |
|               | Virginia[3]             | 447  | 748  |
|               | North Carolina          | 197  | 394  |
| (lower)       | South Carolina          | 124  | 249  |
|               | Georgia                 | 23   | 83   |
|               | Total                   | 994  | 1795 |
| Southwest     | Kentucky                | 16   | 74   |
|               | Tennessee               | 1    | 36   |
|               | Total                   | 17   | 110  |
| Total in area of 1790 |                 | 2148 | 3929 |

[1] Part of Massachusetts until 1820.
[2] Area contested by New York and New Hampshire; admitted to statehood 1791.
[3] Includes modern West Virginia.

Source:   US Bureau of the Census, *Historical Statistics of the United States* (Washington DC, 1975).

## 2 Private physical wealth, 1774
(aggregates in £'000s sterling)

|  | Total (1) | Non-human (2) | Slaves and servants (3) |
|---|---|---|---|
| (1) Thirteen colonies combined | 109,570 | 88,106 | 21,463 |
| (2) New England | 22,238 | 22,136 | 101 |
| (3) Middle colonies | 26,814 | 25,782 | 1,032 |
| (4) South | 60,518 | 40,188 | 20,330 |

Source: Alice Hanson Jones, *Wealth of a Nation to Be*, Table 3.1.

## 3 Distribution of total physical wealth by decile. Free and non-free potential wealthholders, thirteen colonies, 1774

|  | Value at lower bound (£ sterling) | Share held (percentages) |
|---|---|---|
| 100th percentile (richest 1%) | 1946.2 | 14.5 |
| 99th percentile (next richest 1%) | 1459.8 | 8.5 |
| 10th decile (richest 10%) | 482.1 | 56.4 |
| 9th decile | 279.6 | 18.0 |
| 8th decile | 190.7 | 11.5 |
| 7th decile | 107.6 | 7.6 |
| 6th decile | 48.9 | 3.6 |
| 5th decile | 23.8 | 1.7 |
| 4th decile | 11.3 | 0.8 |
| 3rd decile | 0.0 | 0.3 |
| 2nd decile | 0.0 | 0.0 |
| 1st decile (poorest 10%) | 0.0 | 0.0 |

Note:   Value of slaves and servants is included as part of wealth of their free owners and masters in the fourth and higher deciles. Potential wealthholders include adult male slaves and servants, but exclude children and married women.

Source:   Alice Hanson Jones, *Wealth of a Nation to Be*, Table 6.15.

**4 Racial, ethnic and regional distribution of population, 1790**

| | All whites (%) | English (%) | Welsh (%) | Scotch Irish [Ulster] (%) | Scottish (%) | Irish [South] (%) | Germans (%) | Dutch (%) | French (%) | Swedish (%) | All blacks (%) | Regional distribution (%) | Total numbers ('000s) |
|---|---|---|---|---|---|---|---|---|---|---|---|---|---|
| New England | 98.4 | 82.0 | 3.0 | 6.0 | 3.0 | 2.9 | 0.4 | 0.1 | 1.0 | – | 1.7 | 25.7 | 1010 |
| Middle States | 93.8 | 37.6 | 3.4 | 10.5 | 5.3 | 5.3 | 19.9 | 8.9 | 2.4 | 0.6 | 6.2 | 25.9 | 1017 |
| South | 63.1 | 35.2 | 3.8 | 8.5 | 4.2 | 5.2 | 3.9 | 0.3 | 1.7 | 0.2 | 36.9 | 45.6 | 1794 |
| Ky & Tenn | 84.5 | 45.1 | 3.4 | 14.3 | 7.2 | 7.5 | 4.6 | 1.0 | 1.1 | 0.2 | 15.5 | 2.8 | 110 |
| US | 80.7 | 47.9 | 3.5 | 8.5 | 4.3 | 4.7 | 7.2 | 2.1 | 1.7 | 0.2 | 19.3 | 100.0 | 3929 |

Figures have been rounded and do not sum to 100 per cent.

Sources: US Bureau of the Census, *Historical Statistics of the United States* (Washington DC, 1975), Table A195. Thomas Purvis, 'The European Ancestry of the United States Population, 1790', *William and Mary Quarterly*, 3rd ser., 41, 980.

# DOCUMENTS

## THE DECLARATION OF INDEPENDENCE

The Unanimous Declaration of the Thirteen United States of America

When in the Course of Human Events it becomes necessary for one people to dissolve the political bands which have connected them with another, and to assume among the Powers of the earth, the separate and equal station to which the Laws of Nature and of Nature's God entitle them, a decent respect to the opinions of mankind requires that they should declare the causes which impel them to the separation.

We hold these truths to be self-evident, that all men are created equal, that they are endowed by their Creator with certain unalienable Rights, that among these are Life, Liberty and the pursuit of Happiness. That to secure these rights, Governments are instituted among Men, deriving their just Powers from the consent of the governed, That whenever any Form of Government becomes destructive of these ends, it is the Right of the People to alter or to abolish it, and to institute new Government, laying its foundation on such principles and organizing its Powers in such form, as to them shall seem most likely to effect their Safety and Happiness. Prudence, indeed, will dictate that Governments long established should not be changed for light and transient causes; and accordingly all experience hath shewn, that mankind are more disposed to suffer, while evils are sufferable, than to right themselves by abolishing the forms to which they are accustomed. But when a long train of abuses and usurpations, pursuing invariably the same Object evinces a design to reduce them under absolute Despotism, it is their right, it is their duty, to throw off such Government, and to provide new Guards for their future security. Such has been the patient sufferance of these Colonies; and such is now the necessity which constrains them to alter their former Systems of Government. The history of the present King of Great Britain is a history of repeated injuries and usurpations, all having in direct object the establishment of an absolute Tyranny over these States. To prove this, let Facts be submitted to a candid world.

He has refused his Assent to Laws, the most wholesome and necessary for the public good.

He has forbidden his Governors to pass Laws of immediate and pressing importance, unless suspended in their operation till his Assent should be obtained; and when so suspended, he has utterly neglected to attend to them.

He has refused to pass other Laws for the accommodation of large districts of people, unless those people would relinquish the right of Representation in the Legislature, a right inestimable to them and formidable to tyrants only.

He has called together legislative bodies at places unusual, uncomfortable, and distant from the depository of their Public Records, for the sole Purpose of fatiguing them into compliance with his measures.

He has dissolved Representative Houses repeatedly, for opposing with manly firmness his invasions on the rights of the People.

He has refused for a long time, after such dissolutions, to cause others to be elected; whereby the Legislative Powers, incapable of Annihilation, have returned to the People at large for their exercise; the State remaining in the mean time exposed to all the dangers of invasion from without, and convulsions within.

He has endeavoured to prevent the Population of these States; for that purpose obstructing the Laws of Naturalization of Foreigners; refusing to pass others to encourage their migrations hither, and raising the conditions of new Appropriations of Lands.

He has obstructed the Administration of Justice, by refusing his Assent to Laws for establishing Judiciary Powers.

He has made Judges dependent on his Will alone, for the tenure of their offices, and the amount and payment of their salaries.

He has erected a multitude of New Offices, and sent hither swarms of Officers to harass our people, and eat out their substance.

He has kept among us, in times of peace, Standing Armies without the Consent of our legislatures.

He has affected to render the Military independent of and superior to the Civil Power.

He has combined with others to subject us to a jurisdiction foreign to our constitution, and unacknowledged by our laws; giving his Assent to their Acts of pretended Legislation:

For Quartering large bodies of armed troops among us:

For protecting them, by a mock Trial, from Punishment for any Murders which they should commit on the Inhabitants of these States:

For cutting off our Trade with all parts of the world:

For depriving us in many cases, of the benefits of Trial by Jury:

For transporting us beyond Seas to be tried for pretended offences:

For abolishing the free System of English Laws in a neighbouring Province, establishing therein an Arbitrary government and enlarging its Boundaries so as to render it at once an example and fit instrument for introducing the same absolute rule into these Colonies:

For taking away our Charters, abolishing our most valuable Laws, and altering fundamentally the Forms of our Governments:

For suspending our own Legislatures, and declaring themselves invested with Power to legislate for us in all cases whatsoever.

He has abdicated Government here, by declaring us out of his Protection, and waging War against us.

He has plundered our seas, ravaged our Coasts, burnt our towns, and destroyed the lives of our people.

He is at this time transporting large Armies of foreign Mercenaries to compleat the works of death, desolation and tyranny, already begun with circumstances of Cruelty and perfidy scarcely paralleled in the most barbarous ages, and totally unworthy the Head of a civilized nation.

He has constrained our fellow Citizens taken Captive on the high Seas to bear Arms against their Country, to become the executioners of their friends and Brethren, or to fall themselves by their Hands.

He has excited domestic insurrections amongst us, and has endeavoured to bring on the inhabitants of our frontiers, the merciless Indian Savages, whose known rule of warfare, is an undistinguished destruction of all ages, sexes and conditions.

In every stage of these Oppressions We have Petitioned for Redress in the most humble terms: Our repeated Petitions have been answered only by repeated injury. A Prince, whose character is thus marked by every act which may define a Tyrant, is unfit to be the ruler of a free People.

Nor have We been wanting in attentions to our British brethren. We have warned them from time to time of attempts by their legislature to extend an unwarrantable jurisdiction over us. We have reminded them of the circumstances of our emigration and settlement here. We have appealed to their native justice and magnanimity, and we have conjured them by the ties of our common kindred to disavow these usurpations, which, would inevitably interrupt our connections and correspondence. They too have been deaf to the voice of justice and of consanguinity. We must, therefore, acquiesce in the necessity which denounces our Separation, and hold them, as we hold the rest of mankind, Enemies in War, in Peace Friends.

WE, THEREFORE, the Representatives of the UNITED STATES OF AMERICA, in General Congress, Assembled, appealing to the Supreme Judge of the world for the rectitude of our intentions, do, in the Name, and by Authority of the good People of these Colonies, solemnly publish and declare, That these United Colonies are, and of Right ought to be FREE AND INDEPENDENT STATES; that they are Absolved from all Allegiance to the British Crown, and that all political connection between them and the State of Great Britain, is and ought to be totally dissolved; and that, as Free and Independent States, they have full Power to levy War, conclude Peace, contract Alliances, establish Commerce, and to do all other Acts and Things which Independent States may of right do. And for the support of this Declaration, with a firm reliance on the protection of divine Providence, we mutually pledge to each other our Lives, our Fortunes and our sacred Honor.

## THE VIRGINIA DECLARATION OF RIGHTS
### 12 JUNE 1776

AT A GENERAL CONVENTION of Delegates and Representatives, from the several counties and corporations of Virginia, held at the Capitol in the City of Williamsburg on Monday the 6th May 1776.

*A Declaration of Rights made by the representatives of the good people of Virginia, assembled in full and free Convention; which rights do pertain to them and their posterity, as the basis and foundation of government.*

1. That all men are by nature equally free and independent, and have certain inherent rights, of which, when they enter into a state of society, they cannot by any compact deprive or divest their posterity; namely, the enjoyment of life and liberty, with the means of acquiring and possessing property, and pursuing and obtaining happiness and safety.

2. That all power is vested in, and consequently derived from, the people; that magistrates are their trustees and servants, and at all times amenable to them.

3. That government is, or ought to be instituted for the common benefit, protection, and security of the people, nation, or community; of all the various modes and forms of government, that is best which is capable of producing the greatest degree of happiness and safety, and is most effectually secured against the danger of maladministration; and that when any government shall be found inadequate or contrary to these purposes, a majority of the community hath an indubitable, unalienable and indefeasible right to

reform, alter or abolish it, in such manner as shall be judged most conducive to the public weal.

4. That no man, or set of men, are entitled to exclusive or separate emoluments or privileges from the community, but in consideration of publick services; which, not being descendible, neither ought the offices of magistrate, legislator or judge to be hereditary.

5. That the legislative and executive powers of the state should be separate and distinct from the judiciary; and that the members of the two first may be restrained from oppression, by feeling and participating the burthens of the people, they should, at fixed periods, be reduced to a private station, return into that body from which they were originally taken, and the vacancies be supplied by frequent, certain, and regular elections, in which all, or any part of the former members to be again eligible or ineligible, as the laws shall direct.

6. That elections of members to serve as representatives of the people in assembly, ought to be free; and that all men having sufficient evidence of permanent common interest with, and attachment to the community, have the right of suffrage, and cannot be taxed or deprived of their property for publick uses, without their own consent, or that of their representatives so elected, nor bound by any law to which they have not, in like manner, assented for the public good.

7. That all power of suspending laws, or the execution of laws, by any authority without consent of the representatives of the people, is injurious to their rights, and ought not to be exercised.

8. That in all capital or criminal prosecutions a man hath a right to demand the cause and nature of his accusation, to be confronted with the accusers and witnesses, to call for evidence in his favour, and to a speedy trial by an impartial jury of his vicinage, without whose unanimous consent he cannot be found guilty; nor can he be compelled to give evidence against himself; that no man be deprived of his liberty, except by the law of the land or the judgement of his peers.

9. That excessive bail ought not be required, nor excessive fines imposed, nor cruel and unusual punishments inflicted.

10. That general warrants, whereby an officer or messenger may be commanded to search suspected places without evidence of a fact committed, or to seize any person or persons not named, or whose office is not particularly described and supported by evidence, are grievous and oppressive, and ought not to be granted.

11. That in controversies respecting property, and in suits between man and man, the ancient trial by jury is preferable to any other, and ought to be held sacred.

12. That the freedom of the press is one of the great bulwarks of liberty, and can never be restrained but by despotick governments.

13. That a well-regulated militia, composed of the body of the people trained to arms, is the proper, natural and safe defence of a free state; that standing armies in time of peace should be avoided as dangerous to liberty; and that in all cases the military should be under strict subordination to, and governed by, the civil power.

14. That the people have a right to uniform government; and, therefore, that no government separate from, or independent of the government of Virginia, ought to be erected or established within the limits thereof.

15. That no free government, or the blessings of liberty, can be preserved to any people, but by a firm adherence to justice, moderation, temperance, frugality and virtue, and by frequent recurrence to fundamental principles.

16. That religion, or the duty which we owe to our Creator, and the manner of discharging it, can be directed only by reason and conviction, not by force or violence; and therefore all men are equally entitled to the free exercise of religion, according to the dictates of conscience; and that it is the mutual duty of all to practise Christian forbearance, love, and charity towards each other.

## THE CONSTITUTION OF THE UNITED STATES OF AMERICA

We the People of the United States in Order to form a more perfect Union, establish Justice, insure domestic Tranquility, provide for the common defence, promote the general Welfare, and secure the Blessings of Liberty to ourselves and our Posterity, do ordain and establish this Constitution for the United States of America.

### ARTICLE I

**Section 1.** All legislative Powers herein granted shall be vested in a Congress of the United States, which shall consist of a Senate and House of Representatives.

**Section 2.** The House of Representatives shall be composed of Members chosen every second Year by a People of the several States, and the Electors in each State shall have the Qualifications requisite for Electors of the most numerous Branch of the State Legislature.

No person shall be a Representative who shall not have attained to the Age of twenty five Years, and been seven Years a Citizen of the United States, and who shall not, when elected, be an Inhabitant of that State in which he shall be chosen.

Representatives and direct Taxes shall be apportioned among the several States which may be included within this Union, according to their respective Numbers, which shall be determined by adding to the whole Number of free Persons, including those bound to Service for a Term of Years, and excluding Indians not taxed, three fifths of all other Persons. The actual Enumeration shall be made within three Years after the first Meeting of the Congress of the United States, and within every subsequent Term of ten Years, in such Manner as they shall by Law direct. The Number of Representatives shall not exceed one for every thirty Thousand, but each State shall have at least one Representative, and until such enumeration shall be made, the State of New Hampshire shall be entitled to chuse three; Massachusetts eight; Rhode-Island and Providence Plantations one, Connecticut five, New-York six, New Jersey four, Pennsylvania eight, Delaware one, Maryland six, Virginia ten, North Carolina five, South Carolina five, and Georgia three.

When vacancies happen in the Representation from any State, the Executive Authority thereof shall issue Writs of Election to fill such Vacancies.

The House of Representatives shall chuse their Speaker and other Officers; and shall have the sole Power of Impeachment.

**Section 3.** The Senate of the United States shall be composed of two Senators from each State, chosen by the Legislature thereof, for six Years; and each Senator shall have one Vote.

Immediately after they shall be assembled in Consequence of the first Election, they shall be divided as equally as may be into three Classes. The Seats of the Senators of the first Class shall be vacated at the Expiration of the second Year, of the second Class at the Expiration of the fourth Year, and of the third Class at the Expiration of the sixth Year, so that one third may be chosen every second Year; and if Vacancies happen by Resignation, or otherwise, during the Recess of the Legislature of any State, the Executive thereof may make temporary Appointments until the next Meeting of the Legislature, which shall then fill such Vacancies.

No Person shall be a Senator who shall not have attained to the Age of thirty Years, and been nine Years a Citizen of the United States, and who shall not, when elected, be an Inhabitant of that State for which he shall be chosen.

The Vice-President of the United States shall be President of the Senate, but shall have no Vote, unless they be equally divided.

The Senate shall chuse their other Officers, and also a President pro tempore, in the Absence of the Vice President or when he shall exercise the Office of President of the United States.

The Senate shall have the sole Power to try all Impeachments. When sitting for that Purpose, they shall be on Oath or Affirmation. When the President of the United States is tried, the Chief Justice shall preside: And no Person shall be convicted without the Concurrence of two thirds of the Members present.

Judgment in Cases of Impeachment shall not extend further than to removal from Office, and disqualification to hold and enjoy any Office of honor, Trust or Profit under the United States: but the Party convicted shall nevertheless be liable and subject to Indictment, Trial, Judgment and Punishment, according to Law.

**Section 4.** The Times, Places and Manner of holding Elections for Senators and Representatives, shall be prescribed by each State by the Legislature thereof, but the Congress may at any time by Law make or alter such Regulation, except as to the Places of Chusing Senators.

The Congress shall assemble at least once in every Year, and such Meeting shall be on the first Monday in December, unless they shall by Law appoint a different Day.

**Section 5.** Each House shall be the judge of the Elections, Returns and Qualifications of its own Members, and a Majority of each shall constitute a Quorum to do Business; but a smaller Number may adjourn from day to day, and may be authorized to compel the Attendance of absent Members, in such Manner, and under such Penalties as each House may provide.

Each House may determine the Rules of its Proceedings, punish its Members for disorderly Behaviour, and, with the Concurrence of two thirds, expel a Member.

Each House shall keep a Journal of its Proceedings, and from time to time publish the same, excepting such Parts as may in their Judgment require Secrecy; and the Yeas and Nays of the Members of either House on any question shall, at the Desire of one fifth of those Present, be entered on the Journal.

Neither House, during the Session of Congress, shall, without the Consent of the other, adjourn for more than three days, nor to any other Place than that in which the two Houses shall be sitting.

**Section 6.** The Senators and Representatives shall receive a Compensation for their Services, to be ascertained by Law, and paid out of the Treasury of the United States. They shall in all Cases, except Treason, Felony and Breach of the Peace, be privileged from Arrest during their Attendance at the Session of their respective Houses, and in going to and returning from the same; and for any Speech or Debate in either House, they shall not be questioned in any other Place.

No Senator or Representative shall, during the Time for which he was elected, be appointed to any civil Office under the Authority of the United States, which shall have been created, or the Emoluments whereof shall have been encreased during such time; and no Person holding any Office under the United States, shall be a Member of either House during his Continuance in Office.

**Section 7.** All Bills for raising Revenue shall originate in the House of Representatives; but the Senate may propose or concur with Amendments as on other Bills.

Every Bill which shall have passed the House of Representatives and the Senate shall, before it become a Law, be presented to the President of the United States; If he approve he shall sign it, but if not he shall return it, with his Objections to that House in which it shall have originated, who shall enter the Objections at large on their Journal, and proceed to reconsider it. If after such Reconsideration two thirds of that House shall agree to pass the Bill, it shall be sent, together with the Objections, to the other House, by which it shall likewise be reconsidered, and if approved by two thirds of that House, it shall become a Law. But in all such Cases the Votes of both Houses shall be determined by yeas and Nays, and the Names of the Persons voting for and against the Bill shall be entered on the Journal of each House respectively. If any Bill shall not be returned by the President within ten Days (Sundays excepted) after it shall have been presented to him, the Same shall be a Law, in like Manner as if he had signed it, unless the Congress by their Adjournment prevent its Return, in which Case it shall not be Law.

Every Order, Resolution, or Vote to which the Concurrence of the Senate and House of Representatives may be necessary (except on a question of Adjournment) shall be presented to the President of the United States; and before the Same shall take Effect, shall be approved by him, or being disapproved by him shall be repassed by two thirds of the Senate and House of Representatives, according to the Rules and Limitations prescribed in the Case of a Bill.

**Section 8.** The Congress shall have Power To lay and collect Taxes, Duties, Imposts and Excises, to pay the Debts and provide for the common Defence and general Welfare of the United States; but all Duties, Imposts and Excises shall be uniform throughout the United States.

To borrow Money on the credit of the United States;

To regulate Commerce with foreign Nations, and among the several States, and with the Indian Tribes;

To establish an uniform Rule of Naturalization, and uniform Laws on the subject of Bankruptcies throughout the United States;

To coin Money, regulate the Value thereof, and of foreign Coin, and fix the Standard of Weights and Measures;

To provide for the Punishment of counterfeiting the Securities and current Coin of the United States;

To establish Post Offices and post Roads;

To promote the Progress of Science and useful Arts, by securing for limited Times to Authors and Inventors the exclusive Right to their respective Writings and Discoveries;

To constitute Tribunals inferior to the supreme Court;

To define and punish Piracies and Felonies committed on the high Seas, and Offences against the Law of Nations;

To declare War, grant Letters of Marque and Reprisal, and make Rules concerning Captures on Land and Water;

To raise and support Armies, but no Appropriation of Money to that Use shall be for a longer Term than two Years;

To provide and maintain a Navy;

To make Rules for the Government and Regulation of the land and naval Forces;

To provide for calling forth the Militia to execute the Laws of the Union, suppress Insurrections and repel Invasions;

To provide for organizing, arming, and disciplining the Militia, and for governing such Part of them as may be employed in the Service of the United States, reserving to the States respectively, the Appointment of the Officers, and the Authority of training the Militia according to the discipline prescribed by Congress;

To exercise exclusive Legislation in all Cases whatsoever, over such District (not exceeding ten Miles square) as may, by Cession of particular States, and the Acceptance of Congress, become the Seat of the Government of the United States, and to exercise like Authority over all Places purchased by the Consent of the Legislature of the State in which the Same shall be, for the Erection of Forts, Magazines, Arsenals, dock-Yards, and other needful Buildings;–And

To make all Laws which shall be necessary and proper for carrying into Execution the foregoing Powers, and all other Powers vested by this Constitution in the Government of the United States, or in any Department or Officer thereof.

**Section 9.** The Migration or Importation of such Persons as any of the States now existing shall think proper to admit, shall not be prohibited by the Congress prior to the Year one thousand eight hundred and eight, but a Tax or duty may be imposed on such Importation, not exceeding ten dollars for each Person.

The Privilege of the Writ of Habeas Corpus shall not be suspended, unless when in Cases of Rebellion or Invasion the public Safety may require it.

No Bill of Attainder or ex post facto Law shall be passed.

No Capitation, or other direct, Tax shall be laid, unless in Proportion to the Census or Enumeration herein before directed to be taken.

No Tax or Duty shall be laid on Articles exported from any State.

No Preference shall be given by any Regulation of Commerce or Revenue to the Ports of one State over those of another; nor shall Vessels bound to, or from, one State be obliged to enter, clear, or pay Duties in another.

No Money shall be drawn from the Treasury, but in Consequence of Appropriations made by Law; and a regular Statement and Account of the Receipts and Expenditures of all public Money shall be published from time to time.

No Title of Nobility shall be granted by the United States: And no Person holding any Office of Profit or Trust under them, shall, without the Consent of the Congress, accept of any present, Emolument, Office, or Title, of any kind whatever, from any King, Prince or foreign State.

**Section 10.** No State shall enter into any Treaty, Alliance or Confederation; grant Letters of Marque and Reprisal; coin Money; emit Bills of Credit; make any Thing but gold and silver Coin a Tender in Payment of Debts; pass any Bill of Attainder, ex post facto Law, or Law impairing the Obligation of Contracts, or grant any Title of Nobility.

No State shall, without the Consent of the Congress, lay any Imposts or Duties on Imports or Exports, except what may be absolutely necessary for executing its inspection Laws: and the net Produce of all Duties and Imposts, laid by any State on Imports or Exports, shall be for the Use of the Treasury of the United States; and all such Laws shall be subject to the Revision and Controul of the Congress.

No State shall, without the Consent of Congress, lay any Duty of Tonnage, keep Troops, or Ships of War in time of Peace, enter into any Agreement or Compact with another State, or with a foreign Power, or engage in War, unless actually invaded, or in such imminent Danger as will not admit of delay.

**ARTICLE II**

**Section 1.** The executive Power shall be vested in a President of the United States of America. He shall hold his Office during the Term of four Years, and, together with the Vice President, chosen for the same Term, be elected, as follows:

Each State shall appoint, in such Manner as the Legislature thereof may direct, a Number of Electors, equal to the whole Number of Senators and Representatives to which the State may be entitled in the Congress; but no Senator or Representative, or Person holding an Office of Trust or Profit under the United States, shall be appointed an Elector.

The Electors shall meet in their respective States, and vote by Ballot for two Persons, of whom one at least shall not be an inhabitant of the same State with themselves. And they shall make a List of all the Persons voted for, and of the Number of Votes for each; which List they shall sign and certify, and transmit sealed to the Seat of the Government of the United States, directed to the President of the Senate. The President of the Senate shall, in the Presence of the Senate and House of Representatives, open all the Certificates and the Votes shall then be counted. The Person having the greatest Number of Votes shall be the President, if such Number be a Majority of the whole Number of Electors appointed; and if there be more than one who have such Majority, and have an equal Number of Votes, then the House of Representatives shall immediately chuse by Ballot one of them for President; and if no Person have a Majority, then from the five highest on the List the said House shall in like Manner chuse the President. But in chusing the President, the Votes shall be taken by States, the Representation from each State having one Vote; A quorum for this Purpose shall consist of a Member or Members from two thirds of the States, and a Majority of all the States shall be necessary to a Choice. In every Case, after the Choice of the President, the Person having the greatest Number of Votes of the Electors shall be the Vice President. But if there should remain two or more who have equal Votes, the Senate shall chuse from them by Ballot the Vice President.

The Congress may determine the Time of chusing the Electors, and the Day on which they shall give their Votes; which Day shall be the same throughout the United States.

No Person except a natural born Citizen, or a Citizen of the United States, at the time of the Adoption of this Constitution, shall be eligible to the Office of President, neither shall any Person be eligible to that Office who shall not have attained to the Age of thirty five Years, and been fourteen Years a Resident within the United States.

In Case of the Removal of the President from Office, or of his Death, Resignation, or Inability to discharge the Powers and Duties of the said Office, the Same shall devolve on the Vice President, and the Congress may by Law provide for the Case of Removal, Death, Resignation or Inability, both of the President and Vice President, declaring what Officer shall then act as President, and such Officer shall act accordingly, until the Disability be removed, or a President shall be elected.

The President shall, at stated Times, receive for his Services, a Compensation, which shall neither be increased nor diminished during the Period for which he shall have been elected, and he shall not receive within that Period any other Emolument from the United States, or any of them.

Before he enter on the Execution of his Office, he shall take the following Oath or Affirmation: – "I do solemnly swear (or affirm) that I will faithfully execute the Office of President of the United States, and will to the best of my Ability, preserve, protect and defend the Constitution of the United States."

**Section 2.** The President shall be Commander in Chief of the Army and Navy of the United States, and of the Militia of the several States, when called into the actual Service of the United States; he may require the Opinion, in writing of the principal Officer in each of the executive Departments, upon any Subject relating to the Duties of their respective Offices, and he shall have Power to grant Reprieves and Pardons for Offences against the United States, except in Cases of Impeachment.

He shall have Power, by and with the Advice and Consent of the Senate, to make Treaties, provided two thirds of the Senators present concur; and he shall nominate, and by and with the Advice and Consent of the Senate, he shall appoint Ambassadors, other public Ministers and Consuls, Judges of the supreme Court, and all other Officers of the United States, whose Appointments are not herein otherwise provided for, and which shall be established by Law: but the Congress may by Law vest the Appointment of such inferior Officers, as they think proper, in the President alone, in the Courts of Law, or in the Heads of Departments.

The President shall have Power to fill up all Vacancies that may happen during the Recess of the Senate, by granting Commissions which shall expire at the End of their next Session.

**Section 3.** He shall from time to time give to the Congress Information of the State of the Union, and recommend to their Consideration such Measures as he shall judge necessary and expedient; he may, on extraordinary Occasions, convene both Houses, or either of them, and in Case of Disagreement between them, with Respect to the Time of Adjournment, he may adjourn them to such Time as he shall think proper; he shall receive Ambassadors and other public Ministers; he shall take Care that the Laws be faithfully executed, and shall Commission all the Officers of the United States.

**Section 4.** The President, Vice President and all civil Officers of the United States, shall be removed from Office on Impeachment for, and Conviction of, Treason, Bribery, or other high Crimes and Misdemeanors.

### ARTICLE III

**Section 1.** The judicial Power of the United States, shall be vested in one supreme Court, and in such inferior Courts as the Congress may from time to time ordain and establish. The Judges, both of the supreme and inferior Courts, shall hold their Offices during good Behaviour, and shall, at stated Times, receive for their Services, a Compensation, which shall not be diminished during their Continuance in Office.

**Section 2.** The judicial Power shall extend to all Cases, in Law and Equity, arising under this Constitution, the Laws of the United States, and Treaties made, or which shall be made, under their Authority; – to all Cases affecting Ambassadors, other public Ministers and Consuls; – to all Cases of admiralty and maritime Jurisdiction; – to Controversies to which the United States shall be a Party; – to Controversies between two or more States; – between a State and Citizens of another State; – between Citizens of different States – between Citizens of the same State claiming Lands under Grants of different States, and between a State, or the Citizens thereof, and foreign States, Citizens or Subjects.

In all Cases affecting Ambassadors, other public Ministers and Consuls, and those in which a State shall be Party, the supreme Court shall have original Jurisdiction. In all the other Cases before mentioned, the supreme Court shall have appellate Jurisdiction, both as to Law and Fact, with such Exceptions and under such Regulations as the Congress shall make.

The Trial of all Crimes, except in Cases of Impeachment; shall be by Jury; and such Trial shall be held in the State where the said Crimes shall have been committed; but when not committed within any State, the Trial shall be at such Place or Places as the Congress may by Law have directed.

**Section 3.** Treason against the United States, shall consist only in levying War against them, or in adhering to their Enemies, giving them Aid and Comfort. No Person shall be Convicted of Treason unless on the Testimony of two Witnesses to the same overt Act, or on Confession in open Court.

The Congress shall have Power to declare the Punishment of Treason, but no Attainder of Treason shall work Corruption of Blood, or Forfeiture, except during the Life of the Person attainted.

**ARTICLE IV**

**Section 1.** Full Faith and Credit shall be given in each State to the public Acts, Records, and judicial Proceedings of every other State; And the Congress may by general Laws prescribe the Manner in which such Acts, Records and Proceedings shall be proved, and the Effect thereof.

**Section 2.** The Citizens of each State shall be entitled to all Privileges and Immunities of Citizens in the several States.

A Person charged in any State with Treason, Felony or other Crime, who shall flee from Justice, and be found in another State, shall on Demand of the executive Authority of the State from which he fled, be delivered up, to be removed to the State having Jurisdiction of the Crime.

No Person held to Service or Labour in one State, under the Laws thereof, escaping into another, shall, in Consequence of any Law or Regulation therein, be discharged from such Service or Labour, but shall be delivered up on Claim of the Party to whom such Service or Labour may be due.

**Section 3.** New States may be admitted by the Congress into this Union; but no new State shall be formed or erected within the Jurisdiction of any other State, or any State be formed by the Junction of two or more States or parts of States, without the Consent of the Legislatures of the States concerned as well as of the Congress.

The Congress shall have Power to dispose of and make all needful Rules and Regulations respecting the Territory of other Property belonging to the United States; and nothing in this Constitution shall be so construed as to Prejudice any Claims of the United States, or of any particular State.

**Section 4.** The United States shall guarantee to every State in this Union a Republican Form of Government and shall protect each of them against Invasion; and on Application of the Legislature, or of the Executive (when the Legislature cannot be convened) against domestic Violence.

## ARTICLE V

The Congress, whenever two thirds of both Houses shall deem it necessary, shall propose Amendments to this Constitution, or, on the Application of the Legislatures of two thirds of the several States, shall call a Convention for proposing Amendments, which, in either Case, shall be valid to all intents and Purposes, as Part of this Constitution, when ratified by the Legislatures of three fourths of the several States, or by Conventions in three fourths thereof, as the one or the other Mode of Ratification may be proposed by the Congress; Provided that no Amendment which may be made prior to the Year One thousand eight hundred and eight shall in any Manner affect the first and fourth Clauses in the Ninth Section of the first Article; and that no State, without its Consent, shall be deprived of its equal Suffrage in the Senate.

## ARTICLE VI

All Debts contracted and Engagements entered into, before the Adoption of this Constitution, shall be as valid against the United States under this Constitution, as under the Confederation.

This Constitution, and the Laws of the United States which shall be made in Pursuance thereof; and all treaties made, or which shall be made, under the Authority of the United States, shall be the supreme Law of the Land; and the Judges in every State shall be bound thereby, any Thing in the Constitution or Laws of any State to the Contrary notwithstanding.

The Senators and Representatives before mentioned, and the Members of the several State Legislatures, and all executive and judicial Officers, both of the United States and of the several States, shall be bound by Oath or Affirmation, to support this Constitution; but no religious Test shall ever be required as a Qualification to any Office or public Trust under the United States.

## ARTICLE VII

The Ratification of the Conventions of nine States, shall be sufficient for the Establishment of this Constitution between the States so ratifying the Same.

Done in Convention by the Unanimous Consent of the States present of the Seventeenth Day of September in the Year of our Lord one thousand seven hundred and Eighty seven and of the Independence of the United States of America the Twelfth. In witness whereof We have hereunto subscribed our Names.

G.º Washington – Presid.ᵗ
and deputy from Virginia

| | |
|---|---|
| **New Hampshire** | John Langdon |
| | Nicholas Gilman |
| **Massachusetts** | Nathaniel Gorham |
| | Rufus King |
| **Connecticut** | Wm. Saml. Johnson |
| | Roger Sherman |
| **New York** | Alexander Hamilton |
| **New Jersey** | Wil: Livingston |
| | David Brearley |
| | Wm. Paterson |
| | Jona: Dayton |
| **Pennsylvania** | B. Franklin |
| | Thomas Mifflin |
| | Robt Morris |
| | Geo. Clymer |
| | Thos. FitzSimons |
| | Jared Ingersoll |
| | James Wilson |
| | Gouv Morris |
| **Delaware** | Geo: Read |
| | Gunning Bedford jun |
| | John Dickinson |
| | Richard Bassett |
| | Jaco: Broom |
| **Maryland** | James McHenry |
| | Dan of St. Thos. Jenifer |
| | Danl Carroll |

**Virginia**     John Blair-
James Madison Jr.

**North Carolina**     Wm. Blunt
Richd. Dobbs Spaight
Hu Williamson

**South Carolina**     J. Rutledge
Charles Cotesworth Pinckney
Charles Pinckney
Pierce Butler

**Georgia**     William Few
Abr. Baldwin

Attest William Jackson Secretary

Articles in Addition to, and amendment of, the Constitution of the United States of America, Proposed by Congress, and Ratified by the Legislatures of the Several States, Pursuant to the Fifth Article of the Original Constitution.

*Amendment I*
Congress shall make no law respecting an establishment of religion, or prohibiting the free exercise thereof; or abridging the freedom of speech, or of the press; or the right of the people peaceably to assemble, and to petition the Government for a redress of grievances.

*Amendment II*
A well regulated Militia, being necessary to the security of a free State, the right of the people to keep and bear Arms shall not be infringed.

*Amendment III*
No Soldier shall, in time of peace, be quartered in any house, without the consent of the Owner, nor in time of war, but in a manner to be prescribed by law.

*Amendment IV*
The rights of the people to be secure in their persons, houses, papers, and effects, against unreasonable searches and seizures, shall not be violated, and no Warrants shall issue, but upon probable cause, supported by Oath or affirmation, and particularly describing the place to be searched, and the persons or things to be seized.

*Amendment V*

No person shall be held to answer for a capital or otherwise infamous crime, unless on a presentment or indictment of a Grand Jury, except in cases arising in the land or naval forces, or in the Militia, when in actual service in time of War or public danger; nor shall any person be subject for the same offence to be twice put in jeopardy of life or limb; nor shall be compelled in any criminal case to be a witness against himself, nor be deprived of life, liberty, or property, without due process of law; nor shall private property be taken for public use, without just compensation.

*Amendment VI*

In all criminal prosecutions, the accused shall enjoy the right to a speedy and public trial, by an impartial jury of the State and district wherein the crime shall have been committed, which district shall have been previously ascertained by law, and to be informed of the nature and cause of the accusation; to be confronted with the witnesses against him; to have compulsory process for obtaining witnesses in his favor, and to have the Assistance of Counsel for his defence.

*Amendment VII*

In suits at common law, where the value in controversy shall exceed twenty dollars, the right of trial by jury shall be preserved, and no fact tried by a jury, shall be otherwise reexamined in any Court of the United States, than according to the rules of the common law.

*Amendment VIII*

Excessive bail shall not be required, nor excessive fines imposed, nor cruel and unusual punishments inflicted.

*Amendment IX*

The enumeration in the Constitution, of certain rights, shall not be construed to deny or disparage others retained by the people.

*Amendment X*

The powers not delegated to the United States by the Constitution, nor prohibited by it to the States, are reserved to the States respectively, or to the people.

# NOTES

**Abbreviations**   The following abbreviations are used throughout the notes:

AHR   *American Historical Review*
JAH   *Journal of American History*
WMQ   *William and Mary Quarterly*


INTRODUCTION

1. D. J. Boorstin, *Genius of American Politics* (Chicago: University of Chicago Press, 1953), p. 75.
2. A. Koch (ed.), *The American Enlightenment* (New York: George Braziller, 1965), p. 228.
3. L. H. Butterfield (ed.), *Letters of Benjamin Rush*, 2 vols (Princeton, NJ: Princeton University Press, 1951), I, 388.
4. Koch (ed.), *American Enlightenment*, p. 229.


I   LAND, PEOPLES AND THE ECONOMY

1. US Geological Survey, *The National Atlas of the United States of America* (Washington, DC: Government Printing Office, 1970), pp. 97,100,102; J. H. Paterson, *North America*, 6th edn (New York: Oxford University Press, 1979), pp. 1–5, 20–9; R. H. Brown, *Historical Geography of the United States* (New York: Harcourt, Brace & World, 1948), pp. 93–8.
2. A. H. Jones, *Wealth Of A Nation To Be* (New York: Columbia University Press, 1980), p. 46.
3. See L. J. Cappon *et al.* (eds), *Atlas of Early American History* (Princeton, NJ: Princeton University Press, 1976), p. 23.
4. Quoted in *Perspectives in American History*, 10 (1976), 11.
5. W. R. Jacobs, 'The Tip of an Iceberg', *WMQ*, 3rd ser., 31 (1974), 123–32; G. B. Nash, *Red, White and Black* (Englewood Cliffs, NJ: Prentice-Hall, 1974), p. 17; E. J. Perkins, *Economy of Colonial America* (New York: Columbia University Press, 1980), p. 9.

274

6. W. E. Washburn, *Indians in America* (New York: Harper & Row, 1975), pp. 156–8.

7. R. C. Simmons, *The American Colonies* (London: Longman, 1976), pp. 20–74, 192–3.

8. J. Potter, 'The Growth of Population in America', in *Population in History*, ed. D. V. Glass and D. E. C. Eversley (London: Edward Arnold, 1965), pp. 631–5, 643–63.

9. *Ibid.*, pp. 639–40.

10. Potter, 'Growth of Population', p. 651; US Department of Commerce, *Historical Statistics of the United States* 1789–1945 (Washington, DC: Government Printing Office, 1949), Series B30.

11. J. Potter, 'Demographic Development and Family Structure' in *Colonial British America*, ed. J. P. Greene and J. R. Pole (Baltimore: Johns Hopkins University Press, 1984), pp. 139–45; and 'Growth of Population', p. 662; W. T. K. Nugent, *Structures of American Social History* (Bloomington: Indiana University Press, 1981), pp. 49, 54–6.

12. Potter, 'Growth of Population', pp. 643, 645; and 'Demographic Development', p. 136.

13. Nugent, *Structures*, pp. 47–8; A. R. Ekirch, 'Bound for America', *WMQ*, 3rd ser., 42 (1985), 188, 194.

14. Potter, 'Demographic Development', pp. 136–7, and 'Growth of Population', p. 641.

15. Figures derived from US Bureau of the Census, *Historical Statistics of the U.S.* (Washington, DC: Government Printing Office, 1975), Table A195, and T. L. Purvis, 'The European Ancestry of the United States Population, 1790', *WMQ*, 3rd ser., 41 (1984), 98. Purvis suggests that his figures may underestimate the English population.

16. See Cappon *et al.* (eds), *Atlas*, pp. 24, 102.

17. D. W. Galenson, *White Servitude in Colonial America* (Cambridge, UK: Cambridge University Press, 1981), p. 119.

18. Potter, 'Growth of Population', p. 640, and 'Demographic Development', p. 139.

19. *Historical Statistics of the United States* (1975), Series Z 1-190.

20. Perkins, *Economy*, p. 35; J. F. Shepherd and G. M. Walton, *Shipping, Maritime Trade, and the Economic Development of Colonial North America* (Cambridge, UK: Cambridge University Press, 1972), pp. 7–13.

21. M. Egnal, 'The Economic Development of the Thirteen Continental Colonies', *WMQ*, 3rd ser., 32 (1975), 201–3, 217–21.

22. A. H. Jones, *Wealth*, p. 48; J. J. McCusker and R. R. Menard, *The Economy of British America, 1607–1789* (Chapel Hill: University of North Carolina Press, 1985), pp. 81–3.

23. McCusker and Menard, *Economy of British America*, p. 53; A. H. Jones, *Wealth*, p. 73.

24. A. H. Jones, *Wealth*, pp. 54–8.

25. McCusker and Menard, *Economy of British America*, pp. 130, 174, 199, 208; Shepherd and Walton, *Shipping*, p. 47.

26. Perkins, *Economy*, pp. 26–7.

27. A. H. Jones, *Wealth*, p. 51.

28. Ibid., pp. 51–4.

29. D. C. Klingaman, 'The Significance of Grain in the Development of the Tobacco Colonies', *Journal of Economic History*, 29 (1969), 271–3; C. Earle and R. Hoffman, 'Staple Crops and Urban Development in the Eighteenth Century South', *Perspectives in American History*, 10 (1976), 48–68. J. M. Price, 'Economic Function and the Growth of American Port Towns in the Eighteenth Century', *Perspectives in American History*, 7 (1974), 163–72.

30. McCusker and Menard, *Economy of British America*, p. 174.

31. A. C. Land, 'Economic Base and Social Structure', *Journal of Economic History*, 25 (1965), 646–53; J. T. Main, 'The One Hundred', *WMQ*, 3rd ser., 11 (1954), 356.

32. A. H. Jones, *Wealth*, pp. 51–8.

33. Cappon *et al.*, *Atlas*, p. 97; D. L. Jones, *Village and Seaport* (Hanover, NH: University Press of New England, 1981), pp. 4–6.

2  SOCIAL, POLITICAL AND INTELLECTUAL PATTERNS

1. A. H. Jones, *Wealth of A Nation To Be* (New York: Columbia University Press, 1980), p. 191.

2. Ibid., p. 259.

3. G. B. Nash, *The Urban Crucible* (Cambridge, Mass.: Harvard University Press, 1979), p. 257; Jones, *Wealth*, p. 314.

4. Jones, *Wealth*, p. 316.

5. Ibid., p. 210.

6. J. T. Main, *The Social Structure of Revolutionary America* (Princeton, NJ: Princeton University Press, 1965), pp. 7–10, 45.

7. W. M. Wiecek, 'The Statutory Law of Slavery and Race in the Thirteen Mainland Colonies of British America', *WMQ*, 3rd ser., 34 (1977), 262–4; Jones, *Wealth*, p. 403.

8. R. Hofstadter, *America at 1750* (London: Jonathan Cape, 1972), pp. 127–30; A. Kulikoff, *Tobacco and Slaves* (Chapel Hill: University of North Carolina Press, 1986), pp. 341–51.

9. A. C. Land, 'The Tobacco Staple and the Planters' Problems', *Agricultural History*, 43 (1969), 78–9; Kulikoff, *Tobacco and Slaves*, pp. 136, 337; Jones, *Wealth*, pp. 104, 109.

10. A. Zilversmit, *The First Emancipation* (Chicago: University of

Chicago Press, 1967), pp. 4–5; Nash, 'Forging Freedom', in *Slavery and Freedom in the Age of the American Revolution*, ed. I. Berlin and R. Hoffman (Charlottesville: University Press of Virginia, 1983), Table 2.

11. Jones, *Wealth*, p. 39; D. W. Galenson, *White Servitude in Colonial America* (Cambridge, UK: Cambridge University Press, 1981), p. 178.

12. B. G. Smith, 'The Material Lives of Laboring Philadelphians, 1750–1800', *WMQ*, 3rd ser., 38 (1981), 201–20; G. B. Nash *et al.*, 'Labor in the Era of the American Revolution', *Labor History*, 24 (1983), 435.

13. P. D. Hall, *The Organization of American Culture, 1700–1900* (New York: New York University Press, 1982), p. 42.

14. Main, *Social Structure*, pp. 91, 102, 87–8; T. M. Doerflinger, *A Vigorous Spirit of Enterprise* (Chapel Hill: University of North Carolina Press, 1986), p. 158.

15. E. J. Perkins, *The Economy of Colonial America* (New York: Columbia University Press, 1980), p. 43; S. K. Kim, *Landlord and Tenant in Colonial New York* (Chapel Hill: University of North Carolina Press, 1978), pp. vii, 278; G. A. Stiverson, *Poverty in a Land of Plenty* (Baltimore: Johns Hopkins University Press, 1977), pp. 137–40; D. A. Williams, 'The Small Farmer in Eighteenth Century Virginian Politics', *Agricultural History*, 43 (1969), 92.

16. Stiverson, *Poverty*, p. 96; Land, 'Tobacco Staple', 79.

17. Kulikoff, *Tobacco and Slaves*, p. 141; Main, *Social Structure*, pp. 65, 62, and 'The One Hundred', *WMQ*, 3rd ser., 11 (1954), 355.

18. Perkins, *Economy*, p. 56; Main, *Social Structure*, pp. 58–9; Jones, *Wealth*, p. 190.

19. R. D. Brown, 'The Emergence of Urban Society in Rural Massachusetts', *JAH*, 41 (1974), 382; M. Zuckerman, 'The Social Context of Democracy in Massachusetts', *WMQ*, 3rd ser., 25 (1968), 526–38; S. G. Wolf, *Urban Village* (Princeton, NJ: Princeton University Press, 1976), pp. 329–37; E. S. Morgan, *American Slavery, American Freedom* (New York: W. W. Norton, 1975), pp. 369, 376, 380–7.

20. C. S. Sydnor, *American Revolutionaries in the Making* (New York: Collier Books, 1962), p. 74; R. M. Zemsky, 'Power Influence and Status', *WMQ*, 3rd ser., 26 (1969) 513.

21. Main, *Social Structure*, p. 8.

22. P. Oliver, *Origin and Progress of the American Rebellion*, ed. D. Adair and J. A. Schutz (Palo Alto, Cal.: Stanford University Press, 1961), p. 65.

23. C. C. Bonwick, 'The American Revolution as a Social Movement Revisited', *Journal of American Studies*, 20 (1986), 357–60.

24. T. H. Breen, 'Horses and Gentlemen', *WMQ*, 3rd ser., 34 (1977), 242–7, 256–7; R. Isaac, *The Transformation of Virginia, 1740–1790* (Chapel Hill: University of North Carolina Press, 1982), pp. 88–114.

25. J. Appleby, 'The Social Origins of American Revolutionary Ideology', *JAH*, 64 (1978), 956.

26. P. V. Bonomi and P. R. Eisenstadt, 'Church Adherence in the Eighteenth-Century British American Colonies', *WMQ*, 3rd ser., 39 (1982), 275.

27. L. J. Cappon *et al.* (eds), *Atlas of Early American History* (Princeton, NJ: Princeton University Press, 1976), pp. 36–8, 116–19.

28. L. W. Labaree, *Royal Government in America* (New York: Frederick Ungar, 1958), pp. 8, 30–1.

29. B. Bailyn, *The Origins of American Politics* (New York: Alfred A. Knopf, 1968), pp. 59–91.

30. J. P. Greene, *The Quest for Power* (Chapel Hill: University of North Carolina Press, 1963), Parts II–V.

31. C. Williamson, *American Suffrage from Property to Democracy, 1760–1860* (Princeton, NJ: Princeton University Press, 1960), p. 19; R. J. Dinkin, *Voting in Provincial America* (Westport, Conn.: Greenwood Press, 1977), pp. 28–34.

32. Williamson, *American Suffrage*, pp. 12–16.

33. Ibid., pp. 40–5; Dinkin, *Voting in Provincial America*, pp. 51–61.

34. W. E. Nelson, *Americanization of the Common Law* (Cambridge, Mass.: Harvard University Press, 1975), pp. 14–17, 19; Bailyn, *Origins of American Politics*, pp. 68–9.

35. J. M. Murrin, 'Political Development', in *Colonial British America*, ed. J. P. Greene and J. R. Pole (Baltimore: Johns Hopkins University Press, 1985), pp. 434–41.

36. R. C. Simmons, *The American Colonies* (London: Longman, 1976), pp. 229–30; Cappon *et al.*, *Atlas*, pp. 109–15.

37. C. A. Barker, *American Convictions* (Philadelphia: Lippincott, 1970), pp. 189–218; A. Koch, 'Pragmatic Wisdom and the American Enlightenment', *WMQ*, 3rd ser., 18 (1961), 323–9.

38. Barker, ibid., pp. 12, 45; C. B. Cowing, *The Great Awakening and the American Revolution* (Chicago: Rand McNally, 1971), pp. 192–8.

39. B. Bailyn, *The Ideological Origins of the American Revolution* (Cambridge, Mass.: Harvard University Press, 1967), pp. 22–54; H. T. Colbourn, *The Lamp of Experience* (Chapel Hill: University of North Carolina Press, 1965), pp. 21–39; R. E. Shalhope, 'Toward a Republican Synthesis', *WMQ*, 3rd ser., 29 (1972), 49–80; J. G. A.

Pocock, *Virtue, Commerce, and History* (Cambridge, UK: Cambridge University Press, 1985), pp. 73–88; C. Robbins, *The Eighteenth-Century Commonwealthman* (Cambridge, Mass.: Harvard University Press, 1961), pp. 385–6; Appleby, 'Social Origins', 953–8.

40. G. S. Wood, *The Creation of the American Republic, 1776–1789* (Chapel Hill: University of North Carolina Press, 1969), pp.48–70.

41. E. S. Morgan, 'The Puritan Ethic and the Coming of the American Revolution', *WMQ*, 3rd ser., 24 (1967), 3–8.

42. Robbins, *Commonwealthman*, pp. 336–7.

43. T. W. Tate, 'Social Contract in America, 1774–1787', *WMQ*, 3rd ser., 22 (1965), 379; Appleby, 'Social Origins', 937–44.

## 3  THE COMING OF THE REVOLUTION

1. J. J. McCusker and R. R. Menard, *The Economy of British America 1607–1789* (Chapel Hill: University of North Carolina Press, 1985), p. 63; M. Egnal, 'The Economic Development of the Thirteen Continental Colonies, 1720–1775', *WMQ*, 3rd ser., 32 (1975), 193, 217; G. B. Nash, *The Urban Crucible* (Cambridge, Mass.: Harvard University Press, 1979), pp. 246–8.

· 2. A. Kulikoff, *Tobacco and Slaves* (Chapel Hill: University of North Carolina Press, 1986), p. 129–30.

3. B. C. Daniels, 'Economic Development in Colonial and Revolutionary Connecticut', *WMQ*, 3rd ser., 37 (1980), 432; K. A. Lockridge, 'Land, Population, and the Evolution of New England Society, 1630–1790', *Past and Present*, 39 (1968), 68.

4. Kulikoff, *Tobacco and Slaves*, p. 136; D. C. Skaggs, *Roots of Maryland Democracy, 1753–1776* (Westport, Conn.: Greenwood Press, 1973), pp. 39–42; C. V. Earle, *The Evolution of Tidewater Settlement System* (Chicago: University of Chicago Department of Geography, 1975), pp. 216–18.

5. Kulikoff, *Tobacco and Slaves*, p. 123; T. H. Breen, 'The Culture of Agriculture', in *Saints and Revolutionaries*, ed. D. D. Hall *et al.* (New York: W. W. Norton, 1984), pp. 251–2; M. Egnal, 'The Origins of the Revolution in Virginia', *WMQ*, 3rd ser., 33 (1980), 403–5.

6. A. H. Jones, *Wealth of A Nation To Be* (New York: Columbia University Press, 1980), pp. 258–9; G. B. Nash *et al.*, 'Labor in the Era of the American Revolution', *Labor History*, 24 (1983), 420; Nash, 'Urban Wealth and Poverty in Pre-Revolutionary America', *Journal of Interdisciplinary History*, 6 (1976), 550, 560–3.

7. J. K. Martin, *Men in Rebellion* (New Brunswick, NJ: Rutgers University Press, 1973), p. 24–32.

8. J. P. Greene, 'Virtus et Libertas', in *The Southern Experience in the American Revolution*, ed. J. J. Crow and L. E. Tise (Chapel Hill: University of North Carolina Press, 1978), p. 71; Greene, 'Society, Ideology, and Politics', in *Society, Freedom and Conscience*, ed. R. M. Jellison (New York: W. W. Norton, 1976), pp. 54–65; T. H. Breen, *Tobacco Culture* (Princeton, NJ: Princeton University Press, 1985), p. 173.

9. P. U. Bonomi, *A Factious People* (New York: Columbia University Press, 1971), pp. 279–82; M. Klein, in *Perspectives on Early American History*, ed. A. T. Vaughan and G. A. Billias (New York: Harper & Row), 1973, p. 144.

10. R. M. Brown, 'Violence and the American Revolution', in *Essays on the American Revolution*, ed. S. G. Kurtz and J. H. Hutson (Chapel Hill: University of North Carolina Press, 1973), P. Maier, 'Popular Uprisings and Civil Authority in Eighteenth Century America', *WMQ*, 3rd ser., 27 (1970), 4–13.

11. S. B. Kim, *Landlord and Tenant in Colonial New York* (Chapel Hill: University of North Carolina Press, 1978), pp. 413–15; M. Kammen, *Colonial New York* (New York: Scribner, 1975), p. 280.

12. J. P. Whittenberg, 'Planters, Merchants and Lawyers', *WMQ*, 3rd ser., 34 (1977), 238; A. R. Ekirch, *'Poor Carolina'': Politics and Society in Colonial North Carolina, 1729–1776* (Chapel Hill: University of North Carolina Press, 1981), pp. 161–78.

13. W. G. McLoughlin, 'Role of Religion in the Revolution', in *Essays*, ed. Kurtz and Hutson, pp. 199–201; C. B. Cowing, *The Great Awakening and the American Revolution* (Chicago: Rand McNally, 1971), p. 202; H. S. Stout, 'Religion, Communications and the Ideological Origins of the American Revolution', *WMQ*, 3rd ser., 34 (1977), 540.

14. R. L. Bushman, *From Puritan to Yankee* (New York: W. W. Norton, 1970 [orig. 1967]), p. 231; R. Isaac, *The Transformation of Virginia, 1740–1790* (Chapel Hill: University of North Carolina Press, 1982), pp. 147–8, 161–77, 263, 354–5, 358; Isaac, 'Evangelical Revolt: The Nature of the Baptists' Challenge to the Traditional Order in Virginia, 1765 to 1775', *WMQ*, 3rd ser., 31 (1974), 354–5, 358.

15. D. Boorstin, *The Americans: The Colonial Experience* (Harmondsworth, Middx: Penguin Books, 1965), p. 349.

16. D. Hoerder, *Crowd Action in Revolutionary Massachusetts, 1765–1780* (New York: Academic Press, 1977), p. 115.

17. J. P. Greene, 'Search for Identity', *Journal of Social History*, 3 (1970), 205–18.

18. J. P. Greene, 'Independence, Improvement, and Authority',

in *An Uncivil War*, ed. R. Hoffman *et al.* (Charlottesville: University Press of Virginia, 1985), pp. 10–18.

19. R. J. Taylor, 'Trial at Trenton', *WMQ*, 3rd ser., 26 (1969), 521–3.

20. A. Burnaby, *Travels through the Middle Settlements in North America* (1775, reprinted Ithaca, NY: Cornell University Press, 1960), p. 114.

21. J. P. Greene, *Pursuits of Happiness* (Chapel Hill: University of North Carolina Press, 1988), pp. 170–1; R. L. Merritt, *Symbols of American Community: 1735–1775* (New Haven, Conn.: Yale University Press, 1966), pp. 54, 125, 146–7, 180, 182.

22. I. R. Christie, *Crisis of Empire* (London: Edward Arnold, 1966), pp. 39–45.

23. J. L. Bullion, ' "The Ten Thousand in America" ', *WMQ*, 3rd ser., 43 (1986), 646–57; J. Shy, *Toward Lexington* (Princeton, NJ: Princeton University Press, 1965), pp. 67–8.

24. M. Jensen (ed.), *Tracts of the American Revolution* (Indianapolis: Bobbs-Merrill, 1967), pp. 28–34.

25. P. Maier, *From Resistance to Revolution* (London: Routledge & Kegan Paul, 1973), pp. 85–9.

26. Christie, *Crisis of Empire*, pp. 63–4.

27. B. Bailyn, *The Ideological Origins of the American Revolution* (Cambridge, Mass.: Harvard University Press, 1967), pp. 213–15.

28. M. Jensen (ed.), *English Historical Documents*, vol. 9 (London: Eyre & Spottiswoode, 1955), pp. 701–2.

29. Jensen (ed.), *Tracts*, pp. 150–60.

30. P. G. D. Thomas, *The Townshend Duties Crisis* (Oxford: Oxford University Press, 1987), p. 137.

31. R. C. Simmons, *The American Colonies* (London: Longman, 1976), p. 318.

32. C. Bridenbaugh, *Mitre and Sceptre* (New York: Oxford University Press, 1962), pp. 335–8.

33. I. R. Christie and B. W. Labaree, *Empire or Independence, 1760–1776* (Oxford: Phaidon Press, 1976), p. 190.

34. M. Jensen, *The Founding of A Nation* (New York: Oxford University Press, 1968), p. 463.

35. R. D. Brown, *Revolutionary Politics in Massachusetts* (New York: W. W. Norton, 1976 [orig. 1970]), p. 200.

36. J. N. Rakove, *The Beginnings of National Politics* (Baltimore: Johns Hopkins Press, 1979), p. 27.

37. Ibid., pp. 22–7; Simmons, *American Colonies*, p. 346.

38. W. P. Adams, *The First American Constitutions* (Chapel Hill: University of North Carolina Press, 1980), p. 39.

39. Rakove, *Beginnings*, pp. 47–8.

40. Ibid., p. 61.
41. Ibid., p. 60.

4  ACHIEVING INDEPENDENCE

1. D. Higginbotham, *The War of American Independence* (Bloomington: Indiana University Press, 1977), p. 66.
2. E. C. Burnett, *The Continental Congress* (New York: W. W. Norton, 1964 [orig. 1941]), pp. 70–1.
3. I. R. Christie, *Wars and Revolutions* (London: Edward Arnold, 1982), pp. 112–13.
4. E. McInnes, *Canada*, 4th edn (Toronto: Holt, Rinehart & Winston of Canada, 1982), pp. 166, 169–71; G. Lanctot, *Canada and the American Revolution* (Toronto: Clarke Irwin, 1967), pp. 217–21.
5. McInnis, *Canada*, pp. 167–8.
6. Paine, *Common Sense*, Penguin Books edn (Harmondsworth, Middx, 1976), p. 87.
7. Burnett, *Continental Congress*, pp. 154–68.
8. M. Jensen (ed.), *English Historical Documents*, vol. 9 (London: Eyre & Spottiswoode, 1955), p. 854.
9. Ibid., pp. 867–8.
10. Burnett, *Continental Congress*, p. 188.
11. C. L. Becker, *The Declaration of Independence* (New York: Vintage Books, 1958 [orig. 1922]), pp. 25–6.
12. R. M. Calhoon, *The Loyalists in Revolutionary America: 1760–1781* (New York: Harcourt Brace Jovanovich, 1973), p. 342.
13. P. H. Smith, 'The American Loyalists: Notes on Their Organization and Numerical Strength', *WMQ*, 3rd ser., 25 (1968), 267–9.
14. Calhoon, *Loyalists*, pp. 502–3.
15. J. S. Tiedemann, 'Patriots by Default', *WMQ*, 3rd ser., 43 (1986), 36–7; T. L. Purvis, 'High-born, Long-Recorded Families', *WMQ*, 3rd ser., 37 (1980), 614; Calhoon, *Loyalists*, p. 360–1.
16. W. H. Nelson, *The American Tory* (Boston: Beacon Press, 1964 [orig. 1961]), p. 86.
17. J. K. Martin, *Men in Rebellion* (New Brunswick, NJ: Rutgers University Press, 1973), p. 44.
18. Nelson, *American Tory*, p. 91.
19. A. G. Condon, 'Marching to a Different Drummer', in *Red, White and True Blue*, ed. E. Wright (New York: AMS Press, 1976), p. 18.
20. J. N. Rakove, *The Beginnings of National Politics* (Baltimore: Johns Hopkins University Press, 1979), pp. 17, 19.

21. Ibid., 196–7.

22. Ibid., p. 201.

23. E. J. Ferguson, *The Power of the Purse* (Chapel Hill: University of North Carolina Press, 1961), p. 333.

24. J. J. McCusker and R. R. Menard, *The Economy of British America, 1607–1789* (Chapel Hill: University of North Carolina Press, 1985), pp. 338–9.

25. Ferguson, *Power of the Purse*, pp. 26–30.

26. Ibid., p. 32; Rakove, *Beginnings*, p. 165.

27. E. Foner, *Tom Paine and Revolutionary America* (New York: Oxford University Press, 1976), pp. 172–8.

28. Ferguson, *Power of the Purse*, pp. 51, 44.

29. J. R. Dull, *A Diplomatic History of The American Revolution* (New Haven, Conn.: Yale University Press, 1985), pp. 53–6.

30. Ibid., pp. 90–1.

31. P. D. G. Thomas, *Lord North* (London: Allen Lane, 1976), pp. 128–32.

32. This and the previous paragraph are based on J. Shy, 'Military Conflict', in *Essays on the American Revolution*, ed. S. J. Kurtz and J. H. Hutson (Chapel Hill: University of North Carolina Press, 1973), pp. 126–51.

33. A. Kulikoff, *Tobacco and Slaves* (Chapel Hill: University of North Carolina Press, 1986), pp. 311–12; C. M. Jedrey, *The World of John Cleaveland* (New York: W. W. Norton, 1979), p. 138.

34. J. Shy in *Legacies of the American Revolution*, ed. L. R. Gerlach *et al.* (Logan: [Utah State University], 1978), pp. 45–6.

35. J. Lemisch, 'Listening to the Inarticulate', *Journal of Social History*, 3 (1969), 1–29.

36. F. Anderson, 'A People's Army', *WMQ*, 3rd ser., 40 (1983), 506–7; C. Royster, *A Revolutionary People at War* (Chapel Hill: University of North Carolina Press, 1979), pp. 215–16; Shy in *Legacies*, p. 58.

37. C. P. Nettels, *The Emergence of a National Economy, 1775–1815* (New York: Holt, Rinehart & Winston, 1962), p. 45.

38. J. M. Price, 'Reflections on the Economy of Revolutionary America' in *The Economy of Early America*, ed. R. Hoffman *et al.* (Charlottesville: University Press of Virginia, 1988), p. 318; McCusker and Menard, *Economy*, pp. 361–2; Nettels, *Emergence*, p. 14; A. H. Jones, *Wealth of A Nation To Be* (New York: Columbia University Press, 1980), pp. 82–3.

39. Nettels, *Emergence*, p. 12.

5   FRAMING NEW GOVERNMENTS

1. J. Adams, 'Thoughts on Government', in *The American Enlightenment*, ed. A. Koch (New York: George Braziller, 1965), p. 250.
2. R. L. Bushman, *King and People in Provincial Massachusetts* (Chapel Hill: University of North Carolina Press, 1985), pp. 212–14; J. G. Marston, *King and Congress* (Princeton, NJ: Princeton University Press, 1987), pp. 129–30.
3. W. P. Adams, *The First American Constitutions* (Chapel Hill: University of North Carolina Press, 1980), pp. 53–6.
4. Ibid., pp. 58–9.
5. J. R. Daniell, *Experiment in Republicanism* (Cambridge, Mass.: Harvard University Press, 1970), pp. 109–11; J. J. Nadelhaft, *The Disorders of War* (Orono: University of Maine Press, 1981), pp. 27–9; I. H. Polishook, *Rhode Island and the Union, 1774–1795* (Evanston, Ill.: Northwestern University Press, 1969), p. 22.
6. G. Jones (ed.), *The Sovereignty of the Law* (London: Macmillan, 1973), pp. 71–2.
7. C. M. Kenyon, 'Republicanism and Radicalism in the American Revolution', *WMQ*, 3rd ser., 19 (1962), 165–6.
8. Nadelhaft, *Disorders*, p. 184–5.
9. S. E. Patterson, *Political Parties in Revolutionary Massachusetts* (Madison: University of Wisconsin Press, 1973), p. 118.
10. R. J. Taylor (ed.), *Massachusetts* (Chapel Hill: University of North Carolina Press, 1961), pp. 27–8, 45; W. P. Adams, *First American Constitutions*, p. 88.
11. Taylor (ed.), *Massachusetts*, p. 116.
12. W. P. Adams, *First American Constitutions*, p. 93.
13. J. R. Pole, *Pursuit of Equality* (Berkeley: University of California Press, 1978), p. 15; G. S. Wood, *The Creation of the American Republic, 1776–1787* (Chapel Hill: University of North Carolina Press, 1969), p. 47.
14. R. Hofstadter, *The American Political Tradition and the Men Who Made It* (New York: Vintage Books, 1958), pp. 6–7.
15. B. J. Bernstein (ed.), *Towards a New Past* (New York: Pantheon Books, 1968), p. 13.
16. D. Ammerman, *In the Common Cause* (Charlottesville: University Press of Virginia, 1974), pp. 103–9.
17. E. Foner, 'Tom Paine's Republic', in *The American Revolution*, ed. A. F. Young (DeKalb, Ill.: Northern Illinois University Press, 1976), pp. 210–16; S. Rosswurm, 'The Philadelphia Militia, 1775–1783', in *Arms and Independence*, ed. R. Hoffman and P. J. Albert (Charlottesville: University Press of Virginia, 1984), pp. 76–

86; R. A. Ryerson, *The Revolution is Now Begun* (Philadelphia: University of Pennsylvania Press, 1978), pp. 66, 87–8, and 'Political Mobilization and the American Revolution: The Resistance Movement in Philadelphia, 1765–1776', *WMQ*, 3rd ser., 31 (1974), 584.

18. W. P. Adams, *First American Constitutions*, pp. 76–8.

19. Foner, 'Tom Paine's Republic', p. 209.

20. F. N. Thorpe (ed.), *The Federal and State Constitutions*, 7 vols (Washington DC: Government Printing Office, 1909), pp. 3082–5.

21. W. L. Bockleman and O. S. Ireland, 'The Internal Revolution in Pennsylvania', *Pennsylvania History*, 41 (1974), 126–49; T. M. Doerflinger, *A Vigorous Spirit of Enterprise* (Chapel Hill: University of North Carolina Press, 1986), p. 254.

22. Nadelhaft, *Disorders*, p. 28, and ' "The Snarls of Invidious Animals" ', in *Sovereign States in an Age of Uncertainty*, ed. R. Hoffman and P. J. Albert (Charlottesville: University Press of Virginia, 1981), p. 68.

23. Nadelhaft, ' "Snarls of Invidious Animals" ', pp. 90–2.

24. D. C. Skaggs, *Roots of Maryland Democracy, 1753–1776* (Westport, Conn.: Greenwood Press, 1973), p. 182.

25. Ibid., pp. 162–3, 184.

26. R. Hoffman, *A Spirit of Dissension* (Baltimore: Johns Hopkins University Press, 1973), p. 169; Skaggs, *Roots of Democracy*, pp. 185–91.

27. Skaggs, *Roots of Democracy*, pp. 192–4; C. Williamson, *American Suffrage from Property to Democracy, 1760–1860* (Princeton, NJ: Princeton University Press, 1960), p. 110.

28. J. T. Main, *The Sovereign States, 1775–1783* (New York: New Viewpoints, 1973), pp. 159–61, 170–1; R. Hoffman, 'The "Disaffected" in the Revolutionary South', in *American Revolution*, ed. Young, p. 292.

29. Main, *Sovereign States*, pp. 166–70; E. P. Douglass, *Rebels and Democrats* (Chicago: Quadrangle Books, 1965 [orig. 1955]), pp. 129–35.

30. E. Countryman, 'Consolidating Power in Revolutionary America: The Case of New York, 1775–1783', *Journal of Interdisciplinary History*, 6 (1976), 659–62.

31. Main, *Sovereign States*, pp. 172–6; E. Countryman, *A People in Rebellion* (Baltimore: Johns Hopkins Press, 1981), p. 169; Douglass, *Rebels and Democrats*, pp. 62–5; Williamson, *American Suffrage*, pp. 107–8.

32. A. F. Kelly, *The Democratic Republicans of New York* (Chapel Hill: University of North Carolina Press, 1967), pp. 17–19.

286     NOTES TO PAGES 136–152

33. B. Bailyn, *The Ideological Origins of the American Revolution* (Cambridge, Mass.: Harvard University Press, 1967), pp. 55–60.

34. W. P. Adams, *First American Constitutions*, 272.

35. Paine, *Common Sense*, in *Tracts of the American Revolution*, ed. M. Jensen (Indianapolis: Bobbs-Merrill, 1967), pp. 406–8.

36. J. Adams, 'Thoughts on Government', in *American Enlightenment*, ed. Koch, p. 247.

37. 'Essex Result', in *Massachusetts*, ed. Taylor, pp. 77–8.

38. Wood, *Creation*, pp. 446–52, 604–6.

39. W. E. Nelson, *Americanization of the Common Law* (Cambridge, Mass.: Harvard University Press, 1975), p. 90.

40. Wood, *Creation*, p. 271.

41. J. N. Rakove, *The Beginnings of National Politics* (Baltimore: Johns Hopkins University Press, 1979), pp. 136–9.

42. Ibid., pp. 148–9.

43. M. Jensen, *The Articles of Confederation* (Madison: University of Wisconsin Press, 1963 [orig. 1940]), p. 254.

44. Rakove, *Beginnings*, pp. 152–4.

45. Ibid., pp. 165–71.

46. Jensen, *Articles*, p. 175.

6  POLITICS IN THE STATES

1. E. Countryman, *A People in Revolution* (Baltimore: Johns Hopkins Unversity Press, 1981), pp. 175–7; J. R. Daniell, *Experiment in Republicanism* (Cambridge, Mass.: Harvard University Press, 1970), pp. 153–62; P. S. Onuf, 'State Making in Revolutionary America', *JAH*, 67 (1980–1), 797–815; R. J. Taylor, *Western Massachusetts in the American Revolution* (Providence: Brown University Press, 1954).

2. J. R. Alden, *The South in the Revolution, 1763–1789* (Baton Rouge: Louisiana State University Press, 1957), pp. 349–60; K. Coleman, *The American Revolution in Georgia, 1763–1789* (Athens: University of Georgia Press, 1958), pp. 89–91; J. E. Selby, *The Revolution in Virginia 1775–1783* (Williamsburg, Va: The Colonial Williamsburg Foundation, 1989), pp. 221–5; R. M. Weir, ' "The Violent Spirit" ', in *An Uncivil War*, ed. R. Hoffman *et al.* (Charlottesville: University Press of Virginia, 1985), pp. 71–4.

3. J. J. Nadelhaft, *The Disorders of War* (Orono: University of Maine Press, 1981), pp. 52–73; J. J. Crow, 'Liberty Men and Loyalists', in *An Uncivil War*, ed. Hoffman *et al.*, pp. 126–7; R. N. Klein, 'Frontier Planters and the American Revolution' in ibid., pp. 60–3.

4. Countryman, *People in Revolution*, p. 238; R. Hoffman, *A*

*Spirit of Dissension* (Baltimore: Johns Hopkins University Press, 1973), pp. 184–9, 196–204, 226–40.

5. R. M. Calhoon, *The Loyalists in Revolutionary America, 1760–1781* (New York: Harcourt Brace Jovanovich, 1973), pp. 388–9, 401–2; Nadelhaft, *Disorders of War*, pp. 81–5.

6. Daniell, *Experiment in Republicanism*, pp. 124–8, 164–79.

7. W. L. Bockelman and O. S. Ireland, 'Internal Revolution in Pennsylvania', *Pennsylvania History*, 41 (1974), 125–60; R. A. Ryerson, 'Republican Theory and Partisan Reality in Revolutionary Pennsylvania', in *Sovereign States in an Age of Uncertainty*, ed. R. Hoffman and P. J. Albert (Charlottesville: University Press of Virginia, 1981), pp. 99–101, 122–7; T. M. Doerflinger, *A Vigorous Spirit of Enterprise* (Chapel Hill: University of North Carolina Press, 1986), pp. 253–5; J. K. Alexander, 'The Fort Wilson Incident of 1779', *WMQ*, 3rd ser., 31 (1974), 590, 608–9; R. L. Brunhouse, *The Counter-Revolution in Pennsylvania* (Harrisburg: Pennsylvania Historical Commission, 1942), pp. 77–9, 111–12, 191–228.

8. Hoffman, *Spirit of Dissension*, pp. 169, 182–95, 206–10, 222–4; P. A. Crowl, *Maryland During and After the Revolution* (Baltimore: Johns Hopkins University Press, 1943), pp. 85–8.

9. C. Williamson, *American Suffrage from Property to Democracy, 1760–1860* (Princeton, NJ: Princeton University Press, 1960), pp. 138–52.

10. R. Walsh, *Charleston's Sons of Liberty* (Columbia: University of South Carolina Press, 1959), pp. 81–4; Nadelhaft, *Disorders of War*, pp. 105–52, 195–211; Klein, 'Frontier Planters', pp. 47–9.

11. R. Isaac, *The Transformation of Virginia, 1740–1790* (Chapel Hill: North Carolina, 1982), pp. 265–7; E. S. Morgan, *American Slavery, American Freedom* (New York: W. W. Norton, 1975), pp. 380–4; A. Kulikoff, *Tobacco and Slaves* (Chapel Hill: University of North Carolina Press, 1986), pp. 300–2, 309, 313; H. J. Eckenrode, *The Revolution in Virginia* (Hamden, Conn.: Archon Books, 1964 [orig. 1914]), pp. 432, 124–5.

12. Selby, *Revolution in Virginia*, pp. 139–41, 145–7, 156–62, 234–5; N. E. Cunningham, Jr, *In Pursuit of Reason* (Baton Rouge: Louisiana State University Press, 1987), pp. 52–63; E. P. Douglass, *Rebels and Democrats* (Chicago: Quadrangle Books, 1965 [orig. 1955]), pp. 287–316.

13. E. Countryman, 'Consolidating Power in Revolutionary America', *Journal of Interdisciplinary History*, 6 (1976), 670–3; and *People in Revolution*, pp. 195, 210, 238–58; A. F. Young, *The Democratic Republicans of New York* (Chapel Hill: University of North Carolina Press, 1967), pp. 32–9.

14. E. J. Ferguson, *The Power of the Purse* (Chapel Hill: University of North Carolina Press, 1961); E. C. Papenfuse, 'The Legislative Response to a Costly War', in *Sovereign States*, ed. Hoffman and Albert, p. 135.

15. C. P. Nettels, *The Emergence of a National Economy, 1775–1815* (New York: Holt, Rinehart & Winston, 1962), pp. 80–4.

16. Ibid., p. 83; I. H. Polishook, *Rhode Island and the Union, 1774–1795* (Evanston, Ill.: Northwestern University Press, 1969), pp. 107–42.

17. Papenfuse, 'Legislative Response', pp. 139–43.

18. R. A. Becker, *Revolution, Reform and the Politics of American Taxation, 1763–1783* (Baton Rouge: Louisiana State University Press, 1980), pp. 6, 116–17, 188, 218, 219–25; Nettels, *Emergence*, p. 31.

19. Becker, *Revolution*, pp. 118–28; R. B. Morris, *The Forging of the Union, 1781–1789* (New York: Harper & Row, 1987), pp. 260–4; D. P. Szatmary, *Shays' Rebellion* (Amherst: University of Massachusetts Press, 1980), p. xiv; F. McDonald, *The Formation of the American Republic* (Harmondsworth, Middx: Penguin Books, 1967 [orig. *E. Pluribus Unum*, Boston: Houghton Mifflin, 1965]), pp. 145–54; J. R. Pole, *Political Representation in England and the Origins of the American Republic* (London: Macmillan, 1966), pp. 227–44; S. E. Patterson, 'The Roots of Massachusetts Federalism' in *Sovereign States*, ed. Hoffman and Albert, p. 55.

20. J. T. Main, *The Sovereign States, 1775–1783* (New York: New Viewpoints, 1973), pp. 319–32; Young, *Democratic Republicans*, p. 62.

21. Main, *Sovereign States*, pp. 322–31; Young, *Democratic Republicans*, p. 63.

22. C. R. Keim, 'Primogeniture and Entail', *WMQ*, 3rd ser., 25 (1968), 550.

23. W. G. McLoughlin, 'Role of Religion', *Essays on the American Revolution*, ed. S. G. Kurtz and J. H. Hutson (Chapel Hill: University of North Carolina Press, 1973), pp. 203–7; 'Return of Ashfield', in *Massachusetts*, ed. R. J. Taylor (Chapel Hill: University of North Carolina Press, 1961), p. 43.

24. F. N. Thorpe (ed.), *Federal and State Constitutions*, 7 vols (Washington, DC: Government Printing Office, 1909), pp. 566–7, 779–80, 1689–90, 1889–90, 2454, 2597, 2636–7, 2788, 2793, 3082, 3085, 3212, 3250, 3255–6, 3814.

25. McLoughlin, 'Role of Religion', pp. 212–33; Selby, *Revolution in Virginia*, pp. 145–7; Isaac, *Transformation*, pp. 278–83; W. G. McLoughlin, *Isaac Backus and the American Pietistic Tradition* (Boston: Little, Brown, 1967), p. 123; T. E. Buckley, *Church and*

*State in Revolutionary Virginia* (Charlottesville: University Press of Virginia, 1977), p. 177–80.

26. McLoughlin, *Isaac Backus*, pp. 143–4; Isaac, *Transformation*, pp. 283–95; Buckley, *Church and State*, p. 175.

27. McLoughlin, 'Role of Religion', p. 227, *Isaac Backus*, pp. 136–66; S. E. Patterson, *Political Parties in Revolutionary Massachusetts* (Madison: University of Wisconsin Press, 1973), pp. 243–4.

28. W. D. Jordan, *White Over Black* (Baltimore: Penguin Books, 1969), p. 302; Kulikoff, *Tobacco and Slaves*, p. 418.

29. Jordan, *White Over Black*, pp. 291–5; Main, *Sovereign States*, pp. 333–40; A. Zilversmit, *The First Emancipation* (Chicago: University of Chicago Press, 1967), pp. 70–108.

30. Jordan, *White Over Black*, p. 345; Zilversmit, *First Emancipation*, pp. 112ff.

31. I. Berlin, 'The Revolution in Black Life', in *The American Revolution*, ed. A. F. Young (DeKalb: Northern Illinois University Press, 1976), pp. 352–60; P. Morgan and M. L. Nicholls, 'Slaves in Piedmont Virginia', *WMQ*, 3rd ser., 46 (1989), 215–17; A. Kulikoff, 'Uprooted Peoples', in *Slavery and Freedom in the Age of the American Revolution*, ed. I. Berlin and R. Hoffman (Urbana: University of Illinois Press, 1986 [orig. Charlottesville: University Press of Virginia, 1983]), pp. 145–80.

32. J. H. Wilson, 'The Illusion of Change', in *American Revolution*, ed. Young, pp. 414–17, 427; M. B. Norton, *Liberty's Daughters* (Little, Brown, 1980), p. xv.

33. J. K. Martin, *Men in Rebellion* (New Brunswick, NJ: Rutgers University Press, 1973), pp. 176–80.

34. Williamson, *American Suffrage*, pp. 92–116; R. J. Dinkin, *Voting in Revolutionary America* (Westport, Conn.: Greenwood Press, 1982), pp. 30–43.

35. J. T. Main, 'Government by the People', *WMQ*, 3rd ser., 23 (1966), 391–407.

36. J. T. Main, *The Upper Houses in Revolutionary America, 1763–1788* (Madison: University of Wisconsin Press, 1967), pp. 230–2, 235–8.

37. S. Brobeck, 'Revolutionary Change in Colonial Philadelphia', *WMQ*, 3rd ser., 33 (1976), 431–2; Martin, *Men in Rebellion*, pp. 14–15, 44–51, 119, 183–9; P. Maier, 'The Charleston Mob and the Evolution of Popular Politics in Revolutionary South Carolina: 1765–1784', *Perspectives in American History*, 4 (1970), 194; C. S. Olton, *Artisans for Independence* (Syracuse, NY: Syracuse University Press, 1975), pp. 79–80; Daniell, *Experiment*, pp. 119–20.

38. J. T. Main, *Political Parties before the Constitution* (New York: W. W. Norton, 1974, [orig. 1973]), pp. 365–407.

39. Main, *Upper Houses*, pp. 238–41.

7 PROBLEMS OF INDEPENDENCE

1. S. E. Morison (ed.), *Sources and Documents Illustrating the American Revolution*, 2nd edn (Oxford: Oxford University Press, 1929), p. 216.

2. D. C. North, *The Economic Growth of the United States, 1790–1860* (New York: W. W. Norton, 1966), pp. 18–19; C. P. Nettels, *Emergence of a National Economy, 1775–1815* (New York: Holt, Rinehart & Winston, 1962), pp. 49–63; M. Jensen, *The New Nation* (New York: Vintage Books, 1965 [orig. 1950]), pp. 191–3.

3. J. J. McCusker and R. R. Menard, *The Economy of British America, 1607–1789* (Chapel Hill: University of North Carolina Press, 1985), p. 374.

4. J. Potter, 'The Growth of Population in America, 1700–1860', in *Population in History*, ed. D. V. Glass and D. E. C. Eversley (London: Edward Arnold, 1965), p. 638.

5. J. A. Henretta, 'The War and Economic Development', in *The Economy of Early America: The Revolutionary Period, 1763–1790*, ed. R. Hoffman *et al.* (Charlottesville: University Press of Virginia, 1988), p. 81; McCusker and Menard, *Economy*, pp. 363–4.

6. J. N. Rakove, *The Beginnings of National Politics* (Baltimore: Johns Hopkins University Press, 1979), pp. 289–91.

7. Rakove, *Beginnings*, pp. 302–3; Nettels, *Emergence*, p. 33.

8. R. B. Morris, *The Forging of the Union, 1781–1789* (New York: Harper & Row, 1987), pp. 52–3.

9. E. J. Ferguson, *The Power of the Purse* (Chapel Hill: University of North Carolina Press, 1961), pp. 239–40.

10. Ibid., pp. 203–4.

11. Ibid., pp. 220–38, 234.

12. Ibid., pp. 234–41.

13. J. L. Davis, *Sectionalism in American Politics, 1774–1787* (Madison: University of Wisconsin Press, 1977), pp. 13, 94–5, 105–8.

14. Jensen, *New Nation*, pp. 338–42; Nettels, *Emergence*, pp. 72–3.

15. F. S. Philbrick, *The Rise of the West, 1754–1830* (New York: Harper & Row, 1965), p. 173; Morris, *Forging of the Union*, pp. 232–6.

16. Davis, *Sectionalism*, p. 124.

17. Philbrick, *Rise of the West*, pp. 82–90.

18. P. S. Onuf, 'Liberty, Development, and Union: Visions of the West in the 1780s', *WMQ*, 3rd ser., 43 (1986), 184–95, 204.

NOTES TO PAGES 192–205

19. Philbrick, *Rise of the West*, pp. 126–7; J. R. T. Hughes, *Social Control in the Colonial Economy* (Charlottesville, Va.: University Press of Virginia, 1976), p. 27.

20. Morris, *Forging of the Union*, pp. 229–32.

21. Jensen, *New Nation*, p. 428.

22. J. L. Davis, 'Political Change in Revolutionary America', in *The Human Dimensions of Nation Making*, ed. J. K. Martin (Madison: The State Historical Society of Wisconsin, 1976), p. 210; D. R. McCoy, 'James Madison and Visions of American Nationality in the Confederation Period', in *Beyond Confederation*, ed. R. Beeman *et al.* (Chapel Hill: University of North Carolina Press, 1987), p. 227.

23. F. McDonald, 'The Anti-Federalists 1781–1789', in *The Reinterpretation of the American Revolution*, ed. J. P. Greene (New York: Harper & Row, 1968), pp. 371–9.

24. Rakove, *Beginnings*, p. 367.

25. G. S. Wood, *The Creation of the American Republic, 1776–1789* (Chapel Hill: University of North Carolina Press, 1969), pp. 76–80.

26. Rakove, *Beginnings*, p. 368–71; R. A. Rutland (ed.), *The Papers of James Madison*, vol. 9 (Chicago: University of Chicago Press, 1975), pp. 348–57.

27. Wood, *Creation*, p. 475.

28. Morris, *Forging of the Union*, pp. 253–4.

29. Ibid., pp. 255–7.

30. Rakove, *Beginnings*, pp. 375–80.

## 8  THE PHILADELPHIA CONVENTION

1. R. Hoffman, *A Spirit of Dissension* (Baltimore: Johns Hopkins University Press, 1973), p. 168.

2. F. McDonald, *Novus Ordo Seclorum* (Lawrence: University Press of Kansas, 1985), pp. 220–1.

3. M. Jensen, *The Making of the American Constitution* (Princeton, NJ: D. Van Nostrand, 1964), pp. 38–9.

4. M. Farrand (ed.), *The Records of the Federal Convention of 1787*, 4 vols (New Haven, Conn.: Yale University Press, 1938), I, 8–9.

5. R. B. Morris, *The Forging of the Union, 1781–1789* (New York: Harper & Row, 1987), p. 268.

6. Cf. G. S. Wood, *The Creation of the American Republic, 1776–1789* (Chapel Hill: University of North Carolina Press, 1969), p. 485.

7. Based on McDonald, *Novus Ordo Seclorum*, pp. 186, 205–9, 214–15.

8. Farrand (ed.), *Records*, I, 20–2.

9. L. Banning, 'The Practicable Sphere of a Republic', in *Beyond Confederation*, ed. R. Beeman *et al.* (Chapel Hill: University of North Carolina Press, 1987), p. 166; Farrand (ed.), *Records*, I, 33.

10. Farrand (ed.), *Records*, I, 48–50.

11. Ibid., I, 242–5.

12. Ibid., I, 291–3.

13. Ibid., I, 313.

14. McDonald, *Novus Ordo Seclorum*, p. 218.

15. Jensen, *Making of the American Constitution*, pp. 57–8.

16. McDonald, *Novus Ordo Seclorum*, p. 236; Farrand (ed.), *Records*, I, 524; M. Farrand, *The Framing of the Constitution of the United States* (New Haven, Conn.: Yale University Press, 1962 [orig. 1913]), pp. 104–6.

17. D. R. McCoy, 'James Madison and Visions of American Nationality in the Confederation Period', in *Beyond Confederation*, ed. Beeman *et al.*, pp. 246–7; Jensen, *Making of the American Constitution*, p. 600.

18. Farrand, *Framing the Constitution*, p. 120.

19. Farrand (ed.), *Records*, II, 76.

20. McDonald, *Novus Ordo Seclorum*, pp. 240, 244, 247; Morris, *Forging of the Union*, p. 287; Farrand (ed.), *Records*, II, 126.

21. Jensen, *Making of the American Constitution*, pp. 72–3; Farrand (ed.), *Records*, II, 177–89.

22. Jensen, *Making of the American Constitution*, pp. 84, 87–8; Farrand (ed.), II, 182; Morris, *Forging of the Union*, p. 284.

23. Jensen, *Making of the American Constitution*, pp. 90–1.

24. Morris, *Forging of the Union*, p. 285.

25. Jensen, *Making of the American Constitution*, pp. 91–4.

26. Ibid., pp. 95–7.

27. Ibid., pp. 97–100.

28. Ibid., p. 101.

29. McDonald, *Novus Ordo Seclorum*, pp. 250–2.

30. Ibid., pp. 253–6; Farrand (ed.), *Records*, I, 97–8; II, 73–5; A. H. Kelly, W. A. Harbison and H. Belz, *The American Constitution: Its Origins and Development*, 6th edn (New York: W. W. Norton, 1983), p. 104.

31. McDonald, *Novus Ordo Seclorum*, p. 256.

32. Farrand, *Framing*, pp. 190–4.

33. Jensen, *Making of the American Constitution*, p. 121; Morris, *Forging of the Union*, pp. 298–300.

34. McDonald, *Novus Ordo Seclorum*, p. 252.

9  THE REVOLUTION COMPLETED

1. H. J. Storing (ed.), *The Complete Anti-Federalist*, 7 vols (Chicago: Chicago University Press, 1981), I, 50.

2. P. S. Onuf, in *Conceptual Change and the Constitution*, ed. T. Ball and J. G. A. Pocock (Lawrence: University Press of Kansas, 1988), pp. 78–82.

3. A. T. Mason (ed.), *The State Rights Debate* (Englewood Cliffs, NJ: Prentice-Hall, 1964), p. 95; S. R. Boyd, *The Politics of Opposition* (Millwood, NY: KTO Press, 1979), pp. 20–1; R. A. Rutland, *The Ordeal of the Constitution* (Boston: Northeastern University Press, 1983 [orig. 1966]), pp. 312–14.

4. J. Madison, A. Hamilton and J. Jay, *The Federalist Papers*, ed. C. Rossiter (New York: New American Library, 1961), pp. 83–4, 280–94.

5. Onuf, in *Conceptual Change*, ed. Ball and Pocock, pp. 78, 91; Rutland, *Ordeal*, p. 312; J. T. Main, *The Antifederalists* (Chicago: Quadrangle Books, 1964 [orig. 1961]), pp. 120–42; Mason (ed.), *State Rights Debate*, pp. 111–14; R. B. Morris, *The Forging of the Union, 1781–1789* (New York: Harper & Row, 1987), p. 307.

6. Rutland, *Ordeal*, p. 135; M. Jensen, *The Making of the American Constitution* (Princeton: D. Van Nostrand, 1964), p. 139.

7. Boyd, *Politics of Opposition*, pp. 20, 40–1. G. S. Wood argues that Lee was probably not the author of the *Letters*, which were published anonymously ('The Authorship of the "Letters from the Federal Farmer?"', *WMQ*, 3rd ser., 31 [1974], 299–308).

8. F. McDonald, *The Formation of the American Republic, 1776–1790* [orig. *E. Pluribus Unum*] (Baltimore: Penguin Books, 1967 [orig. 1965]), p. 210; R. L. Brunhouse, *The Counter-Revolution in Pennsylvania, 1776–1790* (Harrisburg: Pennsylvania Historical Commission, 1942), pp. 200–2.

9. R. D. Brown, 'Shays's Rebellion and the Ratification of the Federal Constitution in Massachusetts', in *Beyond Confederation*, ed. R. Beeman *et al.* (Chapel Hill: University of North Carolina Press, 1987), pp. 122–3.

10. Rutland, *Ordeal*, pp. 106–10.

11. P. A. Crowl, 'Anti-federalism in Maryland', *WMQ*, 3rd ser., 4 (1947), 458–60; Rutland, *Ordeal*, pp. 150–8, 162–9.

12. Main, *Antifederalists*, pp. 221–3.

13. Jensen, *Making of the American Constitution*, p. 145.

14. R. E. Thomas, 'The Virginia Convention of 1788', *Journal of Southern History*, 19 (1953), 72; Main, *Antifederalists*, pp. 225–6; Morris, *Forging of the Union*, pp. 311–13.

15. Main, *Antifederalists*, pp. 234–40; L. G. De Pauw, *The*

*Eleventh Pillar* (Ithaca, NY: Cornell University Press, 1966), pp. 112–17.

16. Main, *Antifederalists*, p. 249.

17. Ibid., pp. 261–8.

18. Ibid., p. 279; F. McDonald, 'The Anti-Federalists, 1781–1789', *The Wisconsin Magazine of History*, 46 (1963), 208.

19. C. M. Kenyon, 'Men of Little Faith', *WMQ*, 3rd ser., 12 (1955), 43.

20. E. C. Burnett, *The Continental Congress* (New York: W. W. Norton, 1964 [orig. 1941]), pp. 703–60.

21. D. C. North, *The Economic Growth of the United States, 1790–1860* (New York: W. W. Norton, 1966 [orig. 1961]), p. 19; S. Bruchey, *The Roots of American Economic Growth 1607–1861* (London: Hutchinson University Library, 1965), p. 99.

22. F. McDonald, *The Presidency of George Washington* (Lawrence: University Press of Kansas, 1974), p. 7; Boyd, *Politics of Opposition*, p. 140–1, 161–2; J. C. Miller, *The Federalist Era, 1789–1801* (New York: Harper & Row, 1960), p. 5.

23. J. R. Howe, Jr., *The Changing Political Thought of John Adams* (Princeton, NJ: Princeton University Press, 1966), pp. 176–8.

24. C. E. Prince, *Federalists and the Origins of the U.S. Civil Service* (New York: New York University Press, 1977), pp. 3–6, 14–18, 269–70.

25. L. W. White, *The Federalists* (New York: Macmillan, 1959), p. 255.

26. McDonald, *Presidency of George Washington*, p. 39; White, *Federalists*, pp. 20–5.

27. White, *Federalists*, pp. 82–5; McDonald, *Presidency of George Washington*, pp. 27–8, 126–7; Miller, *Federalist Era*, p. 172.

28. A. H. Kelly, W. A. Harbison and H. Belz, *The American Constitution*, 6th edn (New York: W. W. Norton, 1983), pp. 162–4.

29. R. A. Rutland, *The Birth of the Bill of Rights, 1776–1791* (Chapel Hill: University of North Carolina Press, 1955), p. 190–217; Kelly *et al.*, *American Constitution*, pp. 121–2.

30. E. J. Ferguson, *The Power of the Purse* (Chapel Hill: University of North Carolina Press, 1961), pp. 292–4, 297–301, 329–30.

31. Ibid., pp. 307–9, 321, 332–3.

32. Ibid., pp. 330–2, 341.

33. Miller, *Federalist Era*, p. 53.

34. McDonald, *Presidency of George Washington*, pp. 145–7.

35. Miller, *Federalist Era*, pp. 55–6; C. P. Nettels, *The Emergence of a National Economy, 1775–1815* (New York: Holt, Rinehart & Winston, 1962), pp. 120–1; McDonald, *Presidency of George Washington*, p. 61.

36. Miller, *Federalist Era*, pp. 58–9; Kelly *et al.*, *American Constitution*, pp. 130–1.

37. Cf. W. N. Chambers, 'Party Development' and P. Goodman, 'First American Party System', in *The American Party Systems*, ed. W. N. Chambers and W. D. Burnham (New York: Oxford University Press, 1967), pp. 7–8, 59.

38. H. J. Henderson, 'Structure and Politics', in *Essays on the American Revolution*, ed. S. G. Kurtz and J. H. Hutson (Chapel Hill: University of North Carolina Press, 1973), p. 160.

39. R. Hofstadter, *The Idea of a Party System* (Berkeley: University of California Press, 1969), p. 53.

40. L. Banning, 'Republican Ideology and the Triumph of the Constitution', *WMQ*, 3rd ser., 31 (1974), 167.

41. N. E. Cunningham, Jr, *The Jeffersonian Republicans* (Chapel Hill: University of North Carolina Press, 1957), p. 13.

42. Ibid., p. 33.

43. Ibid., p. 45.

44. L. Banning, *The Jeffersonian Persuasion* (Ithaca, NY: Cornell University Press, 1978), p. 149n, citing M. P. Ryan and H. J. Henderson.

45. D. H. Fischer, *The Revolution of American Conservatism* (New York: Harper & Row, 1965), pp. 60–71.

# FURTHER READING

The scholarship on eighteenth-century America is extensive. Much of it relates to the colonial period and implicitly assumes that the Revolution came to its climax with the outbreak of war. For many years less attention was paid to the non-military aspects of the Revolution, but this has now changed and numerous excellent studies are appearing. This list is highly selective. Books and articles are normally cited only once; subtitles are generally omitted, except when they include dates. Books in particular often cover a broad chronological period, but are listed in the section to which they predominantly relate.

Further material can be located in the following bibliographies: D. L. Ammerman and P. D. Morgan, *Books about Early America: 2001 Titles* (Williamsburg, Va.: Institute for Early American History and Culture, 1989), R. M. Gephart. *Revolutionary America, 1763–1789* (Washington, DC: Government Printing Office, 1984); J. Shy, *The American Revolution* (Northbrook, Ill.: AHM Publishing, 1973), and E. J. Ferguson, *Confederation, Constitution and Early National Period, 1781–1815* (Northbrook, Ill.: AHM Publishing, 1975). D. L. Smith, *Era of the American Revolution* (Santa Barbara, Cal.: ABC-Clio, 1975) is an annotated selective list of items published after *c.* 1955. Recent publications are noticed in *America: History and Life, Reviews in American History*, The American Historical Association's *Recently Published Articles* and in the journals below.

The *William and Mary Quarterly* 3rd series (cited as *WMQ*) is the outstanding journal of early American history; it includes a number of bibliographical articles. *The Journal of American History* (*JAH*), *Journal of American Studies, Journal of Southern History, Journal of Economic History* and *American Historical Review* (*AHR*) frequently print articles on the Revolutionary era. Articles also appear in other journals, particularly those published by state historical societies.

S. G. Kurtz and J. H. Hutson (eds), *Essays on the American Revolution* (Chapel Hill: University of North Carolina Press, 1973), A. F. Young (ed.). *The American Revolution* (DeKalb, Ill.: Northern

Illinois University Press, 1976), and W. M. Fowler and W. Coyle (eds), *The American Revolution* (Boston: Northeastern University Press, 1979) are valuable collections of original essays. J. P. Greene (ed.), *The Reinterpretation of the American Revolution, 1763–1789* (New York: Harper & Row, 1968) reprints a selection of articles with an extended interpretative introduction.

R. C. Simmons, *The American Colonies* (London: Longman, 1976) is a masterpiece of comprehensive, concise and detailed exposition; W. A. Speck, *British America, 1607–1776* (Brighton: British Association for American Studies, 1985) is a very brief introduction. In J. P. Greene and J. R. Pole (eds), *Colonial British America* (Baltimore: Johns Hopkins University Press, 1984), fourteen scholars discuss the state of scholarship as it stood at the beginning of the 1980s; each essay contains extensive bibliographic notes. D. W. Meinig, *The Shaping of America*, vol 1 (1492–1800) (New Haven: Yale University Press, 1985) provides a geographical perspective. L. J. Cappon *et al.*, *Atlas of Early American History: The Revolutionary Era, 1760–1790* (Princeton, NJ: Princeton University Press, 1976) is excellent. It presents much of the subject-matter of this book visually and includes much very useful source material on which the maps are based.

General descriptions of late colonial society are J. T. Main, *The Social Structure of Revolutionary America* (Princeton, NJ: Princeton University Press, 1965) which emphasises the distribution of property and social hierarchy, and R. Hofstadter, *America at 1750* (New York: Alfred A. Knopf, 1971, and London: Jonathan Cape, 1972) an incomplete but illuminating interpretative discussion. Native Americans are discussed in W. E. Washburn, *The Indian in America* (New York: Harper & Row, 1975) and G. B. Nash, *Red, White and Black* (Englewood Cliffs, NJ: Prentice-Hall, 1974). A. H. Jones, *Wealth of a Nation to Be* (New York: Columbia University Press, 1980) is a treasure house which offers a superb statistical cross-section for 1774 but has wide significance. J. P. Greene, *Pursuits of Happiness* (Chapel Hill: University of North Carolina Press, 1988) interprets social development, as does J. A. Henretta and G. H. Nobles, *Evolution and Revolution: American Society, 1600–1820* (Lexington, Mass.: D. C. Heath, 1987). Articles include R. R. Beeman, 'The New Social History and the Search for "Community" in Colonial America', *American Quarterly*, 29 (1977), 422–43; M. Zuckerman, 'The Social Context of Democracy in Massachusetts', *WMQ*, 25 (1968), 523–44 and 'The Fabrication of Identity in Early America', *WMQ*, 34 (1977), 183–214; J. P. Greene, 'Search for Identity: An Interpretation of the Meaning of Selected Patterns of Social Response in Eighteenth-Century America', *Journal of Social*

298 THE AMERICAN REVOLUTION

*History*, 3 (1970), 189–224, and 'The Social Origins of the American Revolution', *Political Science Quarterly*, 88 (1973), 1–22; and J. A. Henretta, 'Families and Farms: *Mentalité* in Pre-industrial America', *WMQ*, 35 (1978), 3–32. J. M. Murrin has a 'Review Essay' in *History and Theory*, 11 (1972), 226–75. G. H. Nobles, 'Breaking into the Backcountry: New Approaches to the Early American Frontier', *WMQ*, 46 (1989), 641–70 provides a wide-ranging and stimulating introduction to its subject, including consideration of relations with native American communities.

J. J. McCusker and R. R. Menard, *The Economy of British America, 1607–1789* (Chapel Hill: University of North Carolina Press, 1985) sets out those areas of its subject which require further attention and provides a substantial regional and topical description of economic growth with a strong interpretative thesis; it covers demography and aspects of social development as well as production and trade. J. Potter, 'The Growth of Population in America, 1700–1860' in *Population in History*, ed. D. V. Glass and D. E. C. Eversley (London: Edward Arnold, 1965), is very helpful. Brief economic histories are E. J. Perkins, *The Economy of Colonial America* (New York: Columbia University Press, 1980), S. Bruchey, *The Roots of American Economic Growth 1607–1861* (New York: Harper & Row, and London: Hutchinson University Library, 1965), which stresses the social context of its subject, and G. M. Walton and J. F. Shepherd, *The Economic Rise of Early America* (Cambridge, UK: Cambridge University Press, 1979) which stresses the importance of overseas commerce. J. M. Price, 'Economic Function and the Growth of American Port Towns in the Eighteenth Century', *Perspectives in American History*, 7 (1974), 123–89 is a valuable discussion of urban growth. Mark Egnal, 'The Economic Development of the Thirteen Continental Colonies, 1720 to 1775' *WMQ*, 32 (1975), 191–222 offers a broad framework for analysis. A. L. Jensen, *The Maritime Commerce of Colonial Philadelphia* (Madison: University of Wisconsin Press, 1963) and T. M. Doerflinger, *A Vigorous Spirit of Enterprise* (Chapel Hill: University of North Carolina Press, 1986), trace mercantile development in Philadelphia. W. T. Baxter, *The House of Hancock* (Cambridge, Mass.: Harvard University Press), considers a Boston firm and J. B. Hedges, *The Browns of Providence Plantations*, vol. 1 (Providence: Brown University Press, 1952) a Rhode Island firm.

A multitude of excellent local studies exist. For New England they include: K. A. Lockridge, 'Land, Population and the Evolution of New England Society, 1630–1790', *Past and Present*, 39 (1968), 62–80; R. A. Gross, *The Minutemen and Their World* (New York: Hill & Wang, 1976); C. L. Heyrman, *Commerce and Culture* (New

York: W. W. Norton, 1984); C. M. Jedrey, *The World of John Cleaveland* (New York: W. W. Norton, 1979); D. L. Jones, *Village and Seaport* (Hanover, NH: University Press of New England, 1981); B. W. Labaree, *Patriots and Partisans* (Cambridge, Mass.: Harvard University Press, 1975); and M. Zuckerman, *Peaceable Kingdoms* (New York: A. Knopf, 1970). R. E. Brown, *Middle-Class Democracy and the Revolution in Massachusetts, 1691–1780* (Ithaca, NY: Cornell University Press, 1955) pursues a distinctive thesis as its title implies, and must be treated with caution. R. L. Bushman, *From Puritan to Yankee* [on Connecticut] (Cambridge, Mass.: Harvard University Press, 1967), C. S. Grant, *Democracy in the Connecticut Frontier Town of Kent* (New York: Columbia University Press, 1961), B. C. Daniels, 'Economic Development in Colonial and Revolutionary Connecticut: An Overview', *WMQ*, 37 (1980), 429–50, and 'Connecticut's Villages Become Mature Towns . . . 1676–1776', *WMQ*, 34 (1977) 83–103.

The middle colonies are analysed in P. U. Bonomi, 'The Middle Colonies: Embryo of the New Political Order' in A. T. Vaughan and G. A. Billias (eds), *Perspectives in Early American History* (New York: Harper & Row, 1973) and D. Greenberg, 'The Middle Colonies in Recent American Historiography', *WMQ*, 36 (1979), 396–427. New York is considered in P. U. Bonomi, *A Factious People* (New York: Columbia University Press, 1971) and S. B. Kim, *Landlord and Tenant in Colonial New York* (Chapel Hill: University of North Carolina Press, 1978). T. L. Purvis, 'High Born, Long-Recorded Families: Special Origins of New Jersey Assembly-men, 1703–1776', *WMQ*, 37 (1980), 592–615 is useful. Studies of Pennsylvania society are less common than those of its politics. They include J. E. Illick, *Colonial Pennsylvania* (New York: Scribner, 1976); and J. T. Lemon, *The Best Poor Man's Country* (Baltimore: Johns Hopkins University Press, 1972).

There is now some excellent work on the South. It includes, for the Chesapeake Bay area, A. C. Land, 'Economic Base and Social Structure: The Northern Chesapeake in the Eighteenth Century', *Journal of Economic History*, 25 (1965), 639–654, and 'Economic Behaviour in a Planting Society', *Journal of Southern History*, 33 (1967), 469–85; A. Kulikoff, *Tobacco and Slaves* (Chapel Hill: North Carolina University Press, 1986) and D. C. Skaggs, *Roots of Maryland Democracy, 1753–1776* (Westport, Conn.: Greenwood Press, 1973). Virginia is considered by E. S. Morgan, *American Slavery, American Freedom* (New York: W. W. Norton, 1975), R. Isaac, *The Transformation of Virginia, 1740–1790* (Chapel Hill: University of North Carolina Press, 1982), R. E. and B. K. Brown, *Virginia, 1705–1786* (East Lansing, Mich.: Michigan State University Press,

1964), R. R. Beeman, *The Evolution of the Southern Back Country* (Philadelphia: University of Pennsylvania Press, 1984) and T. H. Breen, 'Horses and Gentlemen', *WMQ*, 34 (1977), 239–57, 'The Culture of Agriculture' in D. D. Hall *et al.* (eds), *Saints and Revolutionaries* (New York: W. W. Norton, 1984) and *Tobacco Culture* (Princeton, NJ: Princeton University Press, 1985). H. T. Lefler and W. S. Powell, *Colonial North Carolina* (New York: Scribner, 1973), R. A. Ekirch, *'Poor Carolina', Politics and Society in Colonial North Carolina, 1729–1776* (Chapel Hill: University of North Carolina Press, 1981), R. M. Weir, *Colonial South Carolina* (Millwood, NY: KTO Press, 1983) treat the lower South. E. Countryman, 'Stability and Class, Theory and History', *Journal of American Studies*, 17 (1983), 243–50 reviews new work on the eighteenth-century South. F. S. Philbrick, *The Rise of the West 1754–1830* (New York: Harper & Row, 1965) and J. M. Sosin, *The Revolutionary Frontier 1763–1783* (New York: Holt, Rinehart & Winston, 1967) discuss the West.

For urban development see C. Bridenbaugh, *Cities in Revolt* (New York: Alfred A. Knopf, 1955) and G. B. Nash, *Urban Crucible* (Cambridge, Mass.: Harvard University Press, 1979); G. B. Warden, *Boston, 1689–1776* (Boston: Little, Brown, 1970); C. and J. Bridenbaugh, *Rebels and Gentlemen* (New York: Oxford University Press, 1962 [orig. 1942]) and sections of S. B. Warner, Jr, *The Private City* (Philadelphia: University of Pennsylvania Press, 1968) on Philadelphia, and S. G. Wolf, *Urban Village* (Princeton, NJ: Princeton University Press, 1977) on Germantown.

Much attention has been given recently to the poor and exploited. Slavery is considered by W. D. Jordan, *White over Black* (Chapel Hill: University of North Carolina Press, 1968) and R. B. Davis, *The Problem of Slavery in Western Culture* (Ithaca, NY: Cornell University Press, 1966) and *The Problem of Slavery in the Age of Revolution, 1770–1823* (Ithaca, NY: Cornell University Press, 1975) as well as many of the local studies listed above; W. M. Wiecek describes 'The Statutory Law of Slavery and Race in the Thirteen Mainland Colonies of British America' in *WMQ*, 34 (1977), 258–80. Unfree whites are discussed by D. W. Galenson, *White Servitude in Colonial America* (Cambridge, UK: Cambridge University Press, 1981). D. L. Jones, 'The Strolling Poor: Transience in Eighteenth-Century Massachusetts', *Journal of Social History*, 8 (1975), 28–54, G. B. Nash, 'Urban Wealth and Poverty in Pre-Revolutionary America' and G. B. Warden 'Inequality and Instability in Eighteenth-Century Boston: A Reappraisal' both in *Journal of Interdisciplinary History*, 6 (1976), 545–84 and 585–620 respectively, R. A. Mohl, 'Poverty in Early America . . . New York

City', *New York History*, 50 (1969), 5–27; J. K. Alexander, *Render Them Submissive: Responses to Poverty in Philadelphia, 1760–1800* (Amherst, Mass.: University of Massachusetts Press, 1980); B. G. Smith, 'The Material Lives of Laboring Philadelphians, 1750–1860', *WMQ*, 38 (1981), 163–202 and 'Inequality in Late Colonial Philadelphia . . .', *WMQ*, 41 (1984), 629–45; G. A. Stiverson, *Poverty in a Land of Plenty* [Tenancy in Maryland] (Baltimore: Johns Hopkins University Press, 1977), L. Simler, 'Tenancy in Colonial Pennsylvania: The Case of Chester County', *WMQ*, 43 (1986), 542–69.

Religion is discussed both comprehensively and sympathetically by P. V. Bonomi, *Under the Cope of Heaven* (New York: Oxford University Press, 1986); see also T. L. Smith, 'Congregation, State, and Denomination: The Forming of the American Religious Structure', *WMQ*, 25 (1968), 155–76 and A. Heimert, *Religion and the American Mind From the Great Awakening to the Revolution* (Cambridge, Mass.: Harvard University Press, 1966). Education is discussed in L. A. Cremin, *American Education: The Colonial Experience 1607–1783* (New York: Harper & Row, 1970) and K. A. Lockridge, *Literacy in Colonial New England* (New York: W. W. Norton, 1974).

L. W. Labaree describes *Royal Government in America* (New York: Frederick Ungar, 1958 [orig. 1930]) and B. C. Daniels (ed.), *Town and County* (Middletown, Conn.: Wesleyan University Press, 1978) describes local government. B. Bailyn, *The Origins of American Politics* (New York: A. Knopf, 1968) is a major analysis of the difference between constitutional theory and actual political behaviour. C. Williamson, *American Suffrage from Property to Democracy 1760–1860* (Princeton, NJ: Princeton University Press, 1960) and R. J. Dinkin, *Voting in Provincial America* (Westport, Conn.: Greenwood Press, 1977) explore the extent of the colonial franchise. All but two of the essays in B. C. Daniels (ed.), *Power and Status: Officeholding in Colonial America* (Middletown, Conn.: Wesleyan University Press, 1986) concern the eighteenth century. E. M. Cook Jr., *The Fathers of the Towns* (Baltimore: Johns Hopkins University Press, 1976) and R. M. Zemsky, 'Power Influence and Status. . .' *WMQ*, 26 (1969), 502–20 discuss local and colony political behaviour in Massachusetts. C. S. Sydnor, *Gentlemen Freeholders* (Chapel Hill: University of North Carolina Press, 1952) remains the best description of political behaviour in Virginia; it has been reprinted as *American Revolutionaries in the Making* (New York: Collier Books, 1962). R. M. Weir, 'The Harmony we were Famous for', *WMQ*, 26 (1969), 473–501 is concerned with South Carolina. J. P. Greene, 'The Role of the Lower Houses of Assembly in

Eighteenth-Century Politics', *Journal of Southern History*, 27 (1961), 451–74, and *The Quest for Power* (Chapel Hill: University of North Carolina Press, 1963) examine the increasing power of southern legislatures.

V. L. Parrington, *Main Currents in American Thought*, vol. 1 (New York: Harcourt, Brace, 1927) is the classic progressive interpretation of American intellectual development for the colonial period. See also C. L. Rossiter, *Seedtime of the Republic* (New York: Harcourt, Brace & World, 1953). C. B. Cowing, *The Great Awakening and the American Revolution* (Chicago: Rand McNally, 1971), is a good general intellectual history. H. F. May, *The Enlightenment in America* (New York: Oxford University Press, 1976), D. H. Meyer, *The Democratic Enlightenment* (New York: Capricorn, 1976), H. S. Commager, *The Empire of Reason* (New York: Doubleday, and London: Weidenfeld & Nicolson, 1978) discuss various aspects. M. G. White explores *The Philosophy of the American Revolution* (New York: Oxford University Press, 1978) and A. Koch, *Power, Morals and the Founding Fathers* (Ithaca, NY: Cornell University Press, 1961) is concerned with political application; Koch, 'Pragmatic Wisdom and the American Enlightenment', *WMQ*, 18 (1961) 313–29 and Bailyn, 'Political Experience and Enlightenment Ideas in Eighteenth-Century America', *AHR*, 67 (1962), 339–51 discuss the relationship between ideas and politics; E. S. Morgan discusses 'The Puritan Ethic and the Coming of the American Revolution', *WMQ*, 24 (1967), 3–18 and 'The American Revolution Considered as an Intellectual Movement' in *Paths of American Thought*, ed. A. M. Schlesinger, Jr, and M. G. White (Boston: Houghton Mifflin, 1963, and London: Chatto & Windus, 1964). L. W. Labaree considers *Conservatism in Early American History* (New York: New York University Press, 1948).

G. Dargo, *Roots of the Republic* (New York: Praeger, 1974) treats some of the Constitutional background, P. K. Conkin considers political principles in *Self-Evident Truths* (Bloomington: Indiana University Press, 1974) and E. S. Morgan discusses popular sovereignty in *Inventing the People* (New York: W. W. Norton, 1988). R. G. Adams, *Political Ideas of the American Revolution*, 3rd edn (New York: Barnes & Noble, 1958 [orig. 1922]) is still useful.

Discussion of political ideology throughout the Revolutionary era is presently dominated by debate over the nature of republicanism. J. T. Kloppenberg, 'The Virtues of Liberalism: Christianity, Republicanism and Ethics in Early American Political Discourse', *JAH*, 74 (1987), 9–33 discusses several threads. B. Bailyn, *The Ideological Origins of the American Revolution* (Cambridge, Mass.: Harvard University Press, 1967) is the reigning synthesis presently under attack. H. T.

Colbourn, *The Lamp of Experience* (Chapel Hill: University of North
Carolina Press, 1965) discusses the revolutionaries' historical reading. R. E. Shalhope, 'Toward a Republican Synthesis', *WMQ*, 29
(1972), 49–8 and 'Republicanism and Early American Historiography', *WMQ*, 39 (1982), 334–56; I. Kramnick, 'Republican
Revisionism Revisited', *AHR*, 87 (1982), 629–64 are attempts to
survey the field. J. Appleby offers a liberal market-oriented alternative; among her writings are 'Liberalism and the American Revolution', *New England Quarterly*, 49 (1976), 3–26, 'The Social Origins
of American Revolutionary Ideology', *JAH*, 64 (1978), 935–58, and
'Republicanism in Old and New Contexts', *WMQ*, 43 (1986), 20–
34; she has also edited a special issue of *American Quarterly*, 37
(1985). M. Jensen (ed.), *Tracts of the American Revolution: 1763–
1776* (Indianapolis: Bobbs-Merrill, 1967) is a useful collection of
contemporary pamphlets.

The problems and challenges facing colonial America on the eve
of Revolution are often discussed primarily, though not entirely, in
the context of separation from Britain. They are treated in many of
the works cited previously. In addition, B. Bailyn, 'The Central
Themes of the American Revolution', J. P. Greene, 'An Uneasy
Connection' [i.e. with Britain] and R. Berthoff and J. M. Murrin,
'Feudalism, Communalism and the Yeoman Freeholder', all in
Kurtz and Hutson (eds), *Essays on the American Revolution*, Greene,
R. L. Bushman and M. Kammen, in R. M. Jellison (ed.), *Society,
Freedom and Conscience* (New York: W. W. Norton, 1976) are all
perceptive essays, as are articles by G. B. Nash, E. Countryman,
M. L. M. Kay, J. Ernst, D. Hoerder and R. Hoffman, in Young
(ed.), *The American Revolution*, which takes a radical stance. Other
general studies are K. A. Lockridge *Settlement and Unsettlement in
Early America* (Cambridge, UK: Cambridge University Press, 1981)
which discusses a crisis of political legitimacy and 'Social Change
and the Meaning of the American Revolution', *Journal of Social
History*, 6 (1973), 403–39. M. M. Egnal and J. A. Ernst offer 'An
Economic Interpretation of the American Revolution' in *WMQ*, 29
(1972), 3–32. M. Egnal, *A Mighty Empire* (Ithaca, NY: Cornell
University Press, 1988) interprets the Revolution in terms of
colonial elites' interest in western development. R. M. Weir, 'Who
Shall Rule at Home: The American Revolution as a Crisis of
Legitimacy for the Colonial Elite', *Journal of Interdisciplinary His-
tory*, 6 (1976), 679–700 and P. Maier, 'Popular Uprisings and Civil
Authority in Eighteenth-Century America', *WMQ*, 27 (1970), 3–35
are also good.

Local studies of New England are largely incorporated in the
general narrative of the onset of war. The standard work on New

York from 1760 to 1790 is now E. Countryman, *A People in Revolution* (Baltimore: Johns Hopkins University Press, 1981), though C. L. Becker, *The History of Political Parties in the Province of New York 1760–1776* (Madison: University of Wisconsin Press, 1960 [orig. 1909]) remains valuable. For other colonies see W. L. Bockelman and O. S. Ireland, 'The Internal Revolution in Pennsylvania: An Ethnic-Religious Interpretation' *Pennsylvania History*, 41 (1974), 125–59; R. A. Ryerson, 'Political Mobilization and the American Revolution: The Resistance Movement in Philadelphia 1765–1776', *WMQ*, 31 (1974), 565–88; J. H. Hutson, 'An Investigation of the Inarticulate: Philadelphia's White Oaks', *WMQ*, 28 (1971), 3–25; J. Lemisch and J. K. Alexander, 'The White Oaks, Jack Tar and the Concept of the Inarticulate', *WMQ*, 29 (1972), 109–43. J. Lemisch, 'Jack Tar in the Streets: Merchant Seamen in the Politics of Revolutionary America', *WMQ*, 25 (1968), 371–407; C. S. Olton, 'Philadelphia's Mechanics in the First Decade of Revolution 1765–1775', *JAH*, 59 (1972), 311–26; C. A. Barker, *The Background of the Revolution in Maryland* (New Haven: Yale University Press, 1940); D. C. Skaggs, 'Maryland's Impulse Toward Social Revolution 1750–1776', *JAH*, 54 (1968), 771–86; Isaac, *The Transformation of Virginia 1740–1790* and 'Evangelical Revolt: The Nature of the Baptists' Challenge to the Traditional Order in Virginia, 1765–1775', *WMQ*, 33 (1974), 345–68; T. W. Tate, 'The Coming of the Revolution in Virginia', *WMQ*, 19 (1962), 323–43; E. G. Evans, 'Planter Indebtedness and the Coming of the Revolution in Virginia', *WMQ*, 19 (1962), 511–33; M. Egnal, 'The Origins of the Revolution in Virginia', *WMQ*, 37 (1980), 401–28; J. P. Whittenburg, 'Planters, Merchants and Lawyers; Social Change and the Origins of the North Carolina Regulation', *WMQ*, 34 (1977), 215–38; R. N. Klein, ' "Ordering the Backcountry": the South Carolina Regulation', *WMQ*, 38 (1981), 661–80.

Studies of the pre-Revolutionary period that are particularly pertinent to the main theme of this book include *The Development of A Revolutionary Mentality* (1972) published by the Library of Congress, Washington, DC; P. Maier, *From Resistance to Revolution* (New York: Alfred A. Knopf, 1972 and London: Routledge & Kegan Paul, 1973) which discusses radical opposition; L. G. DePauw, 'Politicizing the Politically Inert', in Fowler and Coyle (eds), *American Revolution* uses social science theory to present an interesting thesis. J. P. Reid, *In A Defiant Stance* (University Park: Pennsylvania State University Press, 1977) which examines the use of legal procedures to frustrate British policy in Massachusetts, R. Champagne, 'Liberty Boys and Mechanics of New York City, 1764–1774', *Labor History*, 8 (1967), 115–35 and 'New York's Radicals and the Coming of Independence' *JAH*, 51 (1965), 21–40; B. Freedman, 'The Shaping of Radical Consciousness in Provincial New York' *JAH*, 56 (1970), 781–801; R. D. Brown, *Revolutionary Politics in Massachusetts . . . 1772–1774* (Cambridge, Mass.: Harvard University Press, 1970); B. W. Labaree, *The Boston Tea Party* (New York: Oxford University Press, 1964); R. L. Bushman, *King and People in Provincial Massachusetts* (Chapel Hill: University of North Carolina Press, 1985); D. O. Lovejoy, *Rhode Island Politics and the American Revolution, 1760–1776* (Providence: Brown University Press, 1958); B. Mason, *The Road to Independence, The Revolutionary Movement in New York, 1773–1777* (Lexington, Ky: University of Kentucky Press, 1966); R. A. Ryerson, *The Revolution is Now Begun* (Philadelphia: University of Pennsylvania Press, 1978) which discusses radical committees in Philadelphia between 1765 and 1776; C. S. Olton, *Artisans for Independence* (Syracuse, NY: Syracuse University Press, 1975) goes through the Revolutionary era, as does J. R. Alden, *The South During the Revolution* (Baton Rouge: Louisiana State University Press, 1957). C. Bridenbaugh, *Mitre and Sceptre* (New York: Oxford University Press, 1962) discusses the disturbing impact on the colonies of proposals to establish an American bishopric and R. Isaac, 'Religion and Authority. . .', *WMQ*, 30 (1973), 3–36 discusses the established church in Virginia. Other useful works are listed in the previous section.

The most authoritative general study of the coming of the Revolutionary War is M. Jensen, *The Founding of a Nation* (New York: Oxford University Press, 1968) but it covers only the period 1763–76. I. R. Christie and B. W. Labaree, *Empire or Independence, 1760–1776* (Oxford: Phaidon Press, 1976) traces both sides of the Anglo-American dispute with considerable success. R. W. Tucker and D. C. Hendrickson, *The Fall of the First British Empire* (Baltimore: Johns Hopkins University Press, 1982) is a hardheaded discussion of British policy, and I. R. Christie, *Crisis of Empire* (London: Edward Arnold, 1966) sets out and comments on British policy from 1754 to 1783. Full lists of books and articles concerned with the rebellion against Britain can be found in the bibliographies listed above; they include works on the Stamp Act crisis, the Townshend duties crisis, Boston Massacre and Boston Tea Party, etc.

The growth of what retrospectively can be termed American nationalism can be traced in C. Bridenbaugh, *The Spirit of '76* (New York: Oxford University Press, 1975); J. M. Bumsted, ' "Things in the Womb of Time": Ideas of American Independence, 1633 to 1763,' *WMQ*, 31 (1974), 533–64; P. A. Varg, 'The Advent of

Nationalism, 1758–1776', *American Quarterly*, 16 (1964), 169–81; M. Savelle, 'Nationalism and Other Loyalties in the American Revolution', *AHR*, 67 (1962), 901–23 and R. L. Merritt, *Symbols of American Community: 1735–1775* (New Haven: Yale University Press, 1966). The immediate crisis is discussed in D. Ammerman, *In the Common Cause: American Response to the Coercive Acts of 1774* (Charlottesville: University Press of Virginia, 1974); J. G. Marston, *King and Congress: The Transfer of Political Legitimacy 1774–1776* (Princeton, NJ: Princeton University Press, 1987). The decision to declare independence is considered in J. R. Pole, *The Decision for American Independence* (London: Edward Arnold, 1975), J. H. Hutson, 'The Partition Treaty and the Declaration of American Independence', *JAH*, 58 (1972), 877–96 and J. N. Rakove, 'The Decision for American Independence', *Perspectives in American History*, 10 (1976), 215–75. Thomas Paine, *Common Sense* (1776) is brilliant; its significance is examined in W. D. Jordan, 'Familial Politics: Thomas Paine and the Killing of the King 1776', *JAH*, 60 (1973), 294–308. For very different readings of the Declaration of Independence see C. L. Becker, *The Declaration of Independence* (New York: Alfred A. Knopf, 1922) and G. Wills, *Inventing America* (New York: Doubleday, 1978). See also other studies of the first Continental Congress (below).

Many books discuss the war in general, its campaigns, battles and generalship. R. Middlekauf, *The Glorious Cause* (New York: Oxford University Press, 1982) is one of many good narratives of the war though disappointingly orthodox on other aspects of the Revolution. D. Higginbotham, *The War of American Independence: Military Attitudes, Policies and Practices 1763–1789* (New York: Macmillan, 1971) is broader in its concerns and in many respects superior. H. H. Peckham, *The War for Independence* (Chicago: University of Chicago Press, 1958) is a brief account; his *The Toll of Independence* (Chicago: University of Chicago Press, 1974) is very important since it demonstrates that American casualties were far higher than had been supposed. P. Mackesy, *The War for America, 1775–1783* (London: Longman, 1964) is an excellent study from a British perspective. Higginbotham has edited essays on important aspects of the war under the title *Reconsiderations on the Revolutionary War* (Westport, Conn.: Greenwood Press, 1978). R. Hoffman and P. J. Albert (eds), *Arms and Independence* (Charlottesville: University Press of Virginia, 1984) contains useful essays on both sides of the war. E. W. Carp, *To Starve the Army at Pleasure* (Chapel Hill: University of North Carolina Press, 1984) discusses administration, and R. Buel, Jr, *Dear Liberty: Connecticut's Mobilization for the Revolutionary War* (Middletown, Conn.: Wesleyan University

Press, 1980) examines the great strain imposed by the war on one state.

The standard diplomatic history is now J. R. Dull, *A Diplomatic History of the American Revolution* (New Haven: Yale University Press, 1985); R. B. Morris, *The Peacemakers* (New York: Harper & Row, 1965) describes the treaty ending the war. G. Lanctot, *Canada and the American Revolution, 1774–1783* (Toronto: Clarke Irwin, 1967) covers an important issue.

Much attention has recently been directed to the war as a civilian experience. See J. Shy, *A People Numerous and Armed* (New York: Oxford University Press, 1976), C. Royster, *A Revolutionary People at War* (Charlottesville: University Press of Virginia, 1979), J. K. Martin and M. E. Lender, *A Respectable Army* (Arlington Heights, Ill.: Harlan Davidson, 1982), R. Hoffman and P. J. Albert (eds), *Arms and Independence* (Charlottesville: University Press of Virginia, 1984), L. D. Cress, *Citizens in Arms* (Chapel Hill: University of North Carolina Press, 1982), R. Hoffman, *et al.* (eds), *An Uncivil War: The Southern Backcountry During the American Revolution* (Charlottesville: University Press of Virginia, 1985), R. Middlekauff, 'Why Men Fought in the American Revolution', *Huntington Library Quarterly*, 43 (1980), 135–48, and J. Lemisch, 'Listening to the Inarticulate', *Journal of Social History*, 3 (1969), 1–29, which discusses the resistance of American prisoners to British attempts to induce them to repudiate their loyalty to the United States. A. F. Young, 'George Robert Twelves Hewes (1742–1840)', *WMQ*, 38 (1981), 561–623 traces the impact of the Revolution on a Boston shoemaker.

Loyalism is described and analysed in W. H. Nelson, *The American Tory* (New York: Oxford University Press, 1961), and at length in R. M. Calhoon, *The Loyalists in Revolutionary America* (New York: Harcourt Brace Jovanovich, 1973). E. Wright (ed.), *Red, White and True Blue* (New York: AMS Press, 1976), P. H. Smith, *Loyalists and Redcoats* (Chapel Hill: University of North Carolina Press, 1964) and W. Brown, *The King's Friends* (Providence: Brown University Press, 1965) discuss particular aspects. C. Van Tyne, *The Loyalists in The American Revolution* (New York: Macmillan, 1902) is old but useful. Their numbers are also analysed in P. H. Smith, 'The American Loyalists. . .', *WMQ*, 25 (1968), 258–77. B. Bailyn, *The Ordeal of Thomas Hutchinson* (Cambridge, Mass.: Harvard University Press, 1974) is a brilliant biography of a leading figure. A. Y. Zimmer, *Jonathan Boucher* (Detroit: Wayne State University Press, 1978), and with A. H. Kelly, 'Jonathan Boucher: Constitutional Conservative', *JAH*, 58 (1972), 897–922 discusses an expatriate clergyman who returned to England; see also C. Berkin,

*Jonathan Sewall* (New York: Columbia University Press, 1974).
Among local studies are J. Potter, *The Liberty We Seek* (Cambridge,
Mass.: Harvard University Press, 1983); J. Clark, 'The Problem of
Allegiance in Revolutionary Poughkeepsie' in D. D. Hall *et al.* (eds),
*Saints and Revolutionaries* (New York: W. W. Norton, 1984) and
B. G. Merritt, 'Loyalism and Social Conflict in Revolutionary
Deerfield Massachusetts', *JAH*, 57 (1970), 277–89.

G. S. Wood, *The Creation of the American Republic, 1776–1787*
(Chapel Hill: University of North Carolina Press, 1969) is a
commanding and brilliant general interpretation of the internal
Revolution, though its conclusions have not gone unchallenged. F.
McDonald, *The Formation of the American Republic 1776–1790*
(Baltimore: Penguin Books, 1967; originally published as *E.
Pluribus Unum* [Boston: Houghton Mifflin, 1965]) covers the whole
period. J. T. Main, *The Sovereign States 1775–1783* (New York:
New Viewpoints, 1973) covers all except national aspects of domestic affairs but A. Nevins, *The American States During and After the
Revolution 1775–1789* (New York: Augustus M. Kelley, 1969 [orig.
1924]) is much more detailed, though its economic analysis is out-
dated. R. Hoffman and P. J. Albert (eds), *Sovereign States in an Age
of Uncertainty* (Charlottesville: University Press of Virginia, 1981)
includes individual essays on the major states.

The state constitutions are helpfully treated analytically by W. P.
Adams, *The First American Constitutions* (Chapel Hill: University of
North Carolina Press, 1980); W. C. Webster, 'Comparative Study
of the State Constitutions of the American Revolution', *American
Academy of Political and Social Science: Annals*, 9 (1897), 380–420 is
still useful. J. R. Pole, *Political Representation in England and the
Origins of the American Republic* (London: Macmillan, 1966) discusses Massachusetts, Pennsylvania and Virginia as well as national
developments in relation to British constitutionalism, and P. S.
Onuf, 'State Making in Revolutionary America', *JAH*, 67 (1980–1),
797–815 analyses Vermont. F. M. Green considers *Constitutional
Developments in the South Atlantic States 1776–1860* (Chapel Hill:
University of North Carolina Press, 1930). E. P. Douglass, *Rebels
and Democrats* (Chicago: Quadrangle Books, 1955 [orig. 1955])
discusses the constitution-making process in terms of conflict between conservatives and radicals. Works on the federal constitutions
are listed below. Other discussions can be found in the general
works (above) and local studies (below).

R. J. Dinkin analyses state elections in *Voting in Revolutionary
America* (Westport, Conn.: Greenwood Press, 1982); J. T. Main
traces significant changes in *The Upper House in Revolutionary
America* (Madison: University of Wisconsin Press, 1967) and

'Government by the People: The American Revolution and the Democratization of the Legislatures', *WMQ*, 23 (1966), 391–407; and J. K. Martin, *Men in Rebellion* (New Brunswick, NJ: Rutgers University Press, 1973) argues that important changes took place among the governing elites.

General essays and studies on the internal Revolution include: R. Buel, Jr., 'Democracy and the American Revolution', *WMQ*, 22 (1964), 165–90; G. S. Wood, 'Rhetoric and Reality in the American Revolution', *WMQ*, 23 (1966), 3–32 and *Representation in the American Revolution* (Charlottesville: University Press of Virginia, 1969); M. Jensen, 'Democracy and the American Revolution', *Huntington Library Quarterly*, 20 (1957), 321–41 and 'The American People and the American Revolution', *JAH*, 57 (1970), 5–35; T. W. Tate, 'Social Contract in America 1774–1787: Revolutionary Theory as A Conservative Instrument', *WMQ*, 22 (1965), 375–91; C. M. Kenyon, 'Republicanism and Radicalism in the American Revolution', *WMQ*, 19 (1962), 153–82.

J. F. Jameson, *The American Revolution Considered as a Social Movement* (Princeton, NJ: Princeton University Press, 1926) is the classic exposition of its subject. F. B. Tolles published '. . . A Re-Evaluation' in *AHR*, 60 (1954), 1–12. Other studies include R. B. Morris, 'Class Struggle and the American Revolution', *WMQ*, 19 (1962), 3–29 and *The American Revolution Reconsidered* (New York: Harper & Row, 1967), M. Jensen, *The American Revolution Within America* (New York: New York University Press, 1974) and C. C. Bonwick, 'The American Revolution as a Social Movement Re-visited', *Journal of American Studies*, 20 (1986), 355–73. S. Lynd has published a collection of his essays as *Class Conflict: Slavery and the United States Constitution* (Indianapolis: Bobbs-Merrill, 1967). The social implications of tax policy are considered in R. A. Becker, *Revolution, Reform and the Politics of American Taxation* (Baton Rouge: Louisiana State University Press, 1980).

Local studies of Revolutionary New England include J. R. Daniell, *Experiment in Republicanism* (Cambridge, Mass.: Harvard University Press, 1970) and L. W. Turner, *The Ninth State* (Chapel Hill: University of North Carolina Press, 1983) on New Hampshire; W. Pencak, *War, Politics and Revolution in Provincial Massachusetts* (Boston: Northeastern University Press, 1981); S. E. Patterson, *Political Parties in Revolutionary Massachusetts* (Madison: University of Wisconsin Press, 1973), Van Beck Hall, *Politics without Parties* (Pittsburgh: University of Pittsburgh Press, 1972), R. J. Taylor, *Western Massachusetts in the American Revolution* (Providence: Brown University Press, 1954), J. L. Brooke, 'To the Onset of the People: Revolutionary Settlements and Civil Unrest in Western

Massachusetts, 1774–1789', *WMQ*, 46 (1989), 425–60 and R. A. East, 'The Massachusetts Conservatives in the Critical Period' in *The Era of the American Revolution*, ed. R. B. Morris (New York: Columbia University Press, 1939); I. H. Polishook, *Rhode Island and the Union, 1774–1795* (Evanston, Ill., Northwestern University Press, 1969), J. P. Kaminski, 'Democracy Run Rampant: Rhode Island on the Confederation' in *The Human Dimensions of Nation Building*, ed. J. K. Martin (Madison: University of Wisconsin Press, 1976).

The middle states are discussed in E. Countryman, 'Consolidating Power in Revolutionary America: The Case of New York 1775–1783', *Journal of Interdisciplinary History*, 6 (1976), 645–77; A. F. Young, *The Democratic Republicans of New York* (Chapel Hill: University of North Carolina Press, 1967); S. Lynd and A. F. Young, 'After Carl Becker: The Mechanics and New York Politics, 1774–1801', *Labor History*, 5 (1964), 215–76; D. P. Ryan, 'Landholding, Opportunity and Mobility in Revolutionary New Jersey', *WMQ*, 36 (1979), 571–92, E. Foner, *Tom Paine and Revolutionary America* (New York: Oxford University Press, 1976), R. L. Brunhouse, *The Counter-Revolution in Pennsylvania, 1776–1790* (Harrisburg: Pennsylvania Historical Commission, 1942), S. Rosswurm, *Arms, Country and Class* (New Brunswick, NJ: Rutgers University Press, 1987) which discusses the political role of the Philadelphia 'lower sort'; O. S. Ireland, 'The Crux of Politics: Religion and Party in Pennsylvania, 1778–1789', *WMQ*, 42 (1985), 453–75, J. K. Alexander, 'The Fort Wilson Incident of 1779', *WMQ*, 31 (1974), 589–612; and S. V. Salinger, 'Artisans, Journeymen and the Transformation of Labor in Late Eighteenth Century Philadelphia', *WMQ*, 40 (1983), 165–91 and 'Colonial Labor in Transition: The Decline of Indentured Servitude in Late Eighteenth-Century Philadelphia', *Labor History*, 22 (1981), 165–91.

Work on the South includes P. A. Crowl, *Maryland During and After the Revolution* (Baltimore: Johns Hopkins University Press, 1943), and R. Hoffman, *Spirit of Dissension: Economics, Politics and the Revolution in Maryland* (Baltimore: Johns Hopkins University Press, 1973). J. E. Selby, *The Revolution in Virginia* (Williamsburg, Va: Colonial Williamsburg, 1988) is the first major narrative of its type since the Progressive interpretation in H. J. Eckenrode, *The Revolution in Virginia* (Hamden, Conn.: Archon Books, 1964 [orig. 1916]). J. T. Main, 'The One Hundred', *WMQ*, 11 (1954), 354–84 discusses leading planters of the 1780s. N. K. Risjord, *Chesapeake Politics, 1781–1800* (New York: Columbia University Press, 1978) is solid and detailed. J. J. Nadelhaft, *The Disorders of War* (Orono: University of Maine Press, 1981) discusses South Carolina, and R.

Walsh, *Charleston's Sons of Liberty* (Columbia: University of South Carolina Press, 1959) and P. Maier, 'The Charleston Mob and the Evolution of Popular Politics in Revolutionary South Carolina: 1765–1784', *Perspectives in American History*, 4 (1970), 171–96 discuss the activities of non-aristocrats. K. Coleman treats *The American Revolution in Georgia 1763–1789* (Athens: University of Georgia Press, 1958).

Economic developments are traced in C. P. Nettels, *The Emergence of A National Economy 1775–1815* (New York: Holt, Rinehart & Winston, 1962) and C. L. Ver Steeg, 'The American Revolution Considered as an Economic Movement', *Huntington Library Quarterly*, 20 (1957), 361–72, and R. Hoffman *et al.* (eds) *The Economy of Early America: the Revolutionary Period 1763–1790* (Charlottesville: University Press of Virginia, 1988). O. and M. F. Handlin, 'Revolutionary Economic Policy in Massachusetts', *WMQ*, 4 (1947), 3–26, M. Jensen, 'The American Revolution and American Agriculture', *Agricultural History*, 63 (1969), 107–27, J. F. Shepherd and G. M. Walton, 'Economic Change after the American Revolution. . .', *Explorations in Economic History*, 13 (1976), 397–422, and R. A. East, *Business Enterprise in the American Revolutionary Era* (New York: Columbia University Press, 1938) discuss various aspects.

The position of labour during the Revolution is discussed by H. Wellenreuther and others in *Labor History*, 22 (1981) and 24 (1983) and many of the local studies cited above. T. E. Buckley, *Church and State in Revolutionary Virginia 1776–1787* (Charlottesville: University Press of Virginia, 1977) and W. G. McLoughlin, *Isaac Backus and the American Pietistic Tradition* (Boston: Little, Brown, 1967) discuss religion in its political context. The contributions of women – and their continued subordination – are discussed by L. K. Kerber, *Women of the Republic* (Chapel Hill: University of North Carolina Press, 1980), M. B. Norton, *Liberty's Daughters* (Boston: Little, Brown, 1980), and in R. Hoffman and P. J. Albert (eds), *Women in the Age of the American Revolution* (Charlottesville: University Press of Virginia, 1989). B. Quarles, *The Negro in the American Revolution* (Chapel Hill: University of North Carolina Press, 1961), D. J. MacLeod, *Slavery, Race and the American Revolution* (Cambridge, UK: Cambridge University Press, 1974), and I. Berlin and R. Hoffman (eds), *Slavery and Freedom in the Age of the American Revolution* (Charlottesville: University Press of Virginia, 1983) discuss the condition of African Americans; A. Zilversmit, *The First Emancipation* (Chicago: University of Chicago Press, 1967) traces the abolition of slavery in the North. D. L. Robinson, *Slavery in the Structure of American Politics: 1765–1820* (New York:

Harcourt Brace Jovanovich, 1971) has useful chapters on the Revolutionary period. The impact of the Revolution on native Americans, blacks and women is also considered in *The American Revolution*, ed. Young, and *The American Revolution*, ed. Fowler and Coyle.

Other important themes are considered by W. E. Nelson, *The Americanization of the Common Law* (Cambridge, Mass.: Harvard University Press, 1975), J. H. Kettner, *The Development of American Citizenship* (Chapel Hill: University of North Carolina Press, 1978), L. W. Levy, *Emergence of a Free Press* (New York: Oxford University Press, 1985); K. Silverman, *A Cultural History of the American Revolution* (New York: Thomas Y. Crowell, 1976), and J. J. Ellis, *After the Revolution: Profiles of Early American Culture* (New York: W. W. Norton, 1979).

National politics have been extensively explored, J. N. Rakove, *The Beginnings of National Politics* (Baltimore: Johns Hopkins University Press, 1979) is the most illuminating discussion of the Continental Congress from 1774 to its demise in 1789, though E. C. Burnett, *The Continental Congress* (New York: Macmillan, 1941) remains a useful narrative. M. Jensen, *The Articles of Confederation* (3rd printing, Madison: University of Wisconsin Press, 1959 [orig. 1940]) is still the standard work on the first federal constitution, though its Progressive stance has been overtaken by later interpretations of the Revolution. H. J. Henderson demonstrates the existence of voting blocs in 'The Structure of Politics in the Continental Congress' in Kurtz and Hutson (eds), *Essays,* and *Party Politics in the Continental Congress* (New York: McGraw-Hill, 1974). Financial issues throughout the era are brilliantly dissected in E. J. Ferguson, *The Power of the Purse* (Chapel Hill: University of North Carolina Press, 1961). Sectional divisions are emphasised in J. L. Davis, *Sectionalism in American Politics: 1774–1787* (Madison: University of Wisconsin Press, 1977).

The 1780s are covered in a number of books. Though M. Jensen, *The New Nation* (New York: Alfred A. Knopf, 1950) remains important as a Progressive interpretation, R. B. Morris, *The Forging of the Union: 1781–1789* (New York: Harper & Row, 1987), though uneven, is now the standard work on the 1780s. B. F. Wright, *Consensus and Continuity 1776–1787* (Boston: Boston University Press, 1958) emphasises continuity. F. W. Marks III, *Independence on Trial* (Baton Rouge: Louisiana State University Press, 1973) discusses foreign relations. D. P. Szatmary, *Shays' Rebellion* (Amherst: University of Massachusetts Press, 1980) deals with the major crisis of the decade, while C. Matson and P. S. Onuf, 'Toward a Republican Empire: Interest and Ideology in Revolutionary

America', *American Quarterly*, 37 (1985), 496–531, and Onuf, 'Liberty, Development, and Union: Visions of the West in the 1790s', *WMQ*, 43 (1986), 179–213 are highly sophisticated discussions, and J. T. Main, *Political Parties Before the Constitution* (Chapel Hill: University of North Carolina Press, 1974) analyses a political phenomenon that became central during the 1790s. General works, particularly those on Congress, the West and finance are also useful, as are many local studies cited previously.

F. McDonald, *Novus Ordo Seclorum* (Lawrence: University of Kansas Press, 1985) is sophisticated and the best single work on formation of the US Constitution of 1787, though it is analytical rather than narrative. A more straightforward approach can be found in M. Jensen, *The Making of the American Constitution* (Princeton, NJ: Van Nostrand, 1964) which provides an excellent brief exposition of the background and debates. See S. N. Katz for 'The Origins of American Constitutional Thought', *Perspectives in American History*, 3 (1969) 474–90, and C. C. Bonwick, 'English Principles and American Constitutionalism' in *Studies in US Politics*, ed. D. K. Adams (Manchester, UK: Manchester University Press, 1989). M. Farrand, *The Framing of the Constitution of the United States* (New Haven, Conn.: Yale University Press, 1913), C. Warren, *The Making of the Constitution* (Cambridge, Mass.: Harvard University Press, 1921), and C. L. Rossiter, *1787: The Grand Convention* (New York: Macmillan, 1966) set out the proceedings of the Philadelphia Convention. Now that C. A. Beard, *An Economic Interpretation of the Constitution of the United States* (New York: Macmillan, 1913) no longer carries weight, the background to the constitution can be explored in R. Beeman *et al.* (eds), *Beyond Confederation* (Chapel Hill: University of North Carolina Press, 1987) and L. W. Levy (ed.), *Essays on the Making of the Constitution*, 2nd edn (New York: Oxford University Press, 1987); intellectual aspects are considered in P. Eidelberg, *The Philosophy of the American Constitution* (New York, Free Press, 1968). A. H. Kelly, W. A. Harbison and H. Belz, *The American Constitution*, 6th edn (New York: W. W. Norton, 1983) is an excellent constitutional history; its first eight chapters cover the period to 1800.

The vigour of the struggle over ratification is also visible in the scholarly argument. The *Federalist* papers have been printed in many editions, and are dissected in a collection of Douglas Adair's essays edited by T. Colbourn as *Fame and the Founding Fathers* (New York: W. W. Norton, 1974) and by G. Wills, *Explaining America* (New York: Doubleday, and London: Athlone Press, 1981). R. A. Rutland *The Ordeal of the Constitution* (Norman: University of Oklahoma Press, 1966) is a narrative; L. G. De Pauw, *The*

*Eleventh Pillar* (Ithaca, NY: Cornell University Press, 1966) discusses ratification in the crucial state of New York. Anti-Federalist
opposition was dismissed in C. Kenyon 'Men of Little Faith', *WMQ*,
12 (1955), 3–43 but has been more sympathetically treated by H. J.
Storing, *The Complete Anti-Federalist*, vol. I. *What the Antifederalists
were For* (Chicago: University of Chicago Press, 1981) and S. R.
Boyd, *The Politics of Opposition* (Millwood, Conn.: KTO Press,
1979). J. T. Main, *The Antifederalists* (Chapel Hill: University of
North Carolina Press, 1961) provides a social analysis, R. A.
Rutland, *The Birth of the Bill of Rights, 1776–1791* (Chapel Hill:
University of North Carolina Press, 1955) is also useful.

Establishment of the new federal government during the 1790s
can be traced in J. C. Miller, *The Federalist Era* (New York: Harper
& Row, 1960) and R. Buel, Jr., *Securing the Revolution* (Ithaca, NY:
Cornell University Press, 1972). L. D. White, *The Federalists* (New
York: Macmillan, 1948) has much useful material on administrative
developments, while F. McDonald examines *The Presidency of
George Washington* (Lawrence: University of Kansas Press, 1974).
C. E. Prince, *The Federalists and the Origins of the United States Civil
Service* (New York: New York University Press, 1977) illuminates
the use of political patronage; Ferguson, *Power of the Purse* illumin-
ates Hamilton's financial programme. See also biographies of
Washington by D. S. Freeman, Jefferson by N. E. Cunningham, and
Hamilton by B. Mitchell, T. P. Slaughter, *The Whiskey Rebellion*
(New York: Oxford University Press, 1986) is good.

The development of parties has attracted considerable attention.
M. Borden, *Parties and Politics in the Early Republic 1789–1815*
(New York: Thomas Y. Crowell, 1967; London: Routledge & Kegan
Paul, 1968) is a brief introduction. The background is explored in
Main, *Political Parties before the Constitution* and from a more
theoretical perspective in R. Hofstadter, *The Idea of a Party System*
(Berkeley: University of California Press, 1969). Other good studies
are J. Charles, *The Origins of the American Party System* (New York:
Harper & Row, 1961 [orig. 1956]), W. N. Chambers, *Political
Parties in a New Nation* (New York: Oxford University Press, 1963)
and P. Goodman, 'The First American Party System' in *The
American Party Systems*, ed. W. N. Chambers and W. D. Burnham
(New York: Oxford University Press, 1967). D. H. Fischer, *The
Revolution of American Conservatism* (New York: Harper & Row,
1965) traces the fate of the Federalist party and N. E. Cunningham,
*The Jeffersonian Republicans* (Chapel Hill: North Carolina Press,
1957) the Republicans. L. Banning, *The Jeffersonian Persuasion*
(Ithaca, NY: Cornell University Press, 1978), D. R. McCoy, *The
Elusive Republic* (Chapel Hill: University of North Carolina Press,

1980), and J. Appleby, *Capitalism and a New Social Order* (New York: New York University Press, 1984) explore ideological issues. R. M. Bell, *Party and Faction in American Politics* (Westport, Conn.: Greenwood Press, 1973) uses roll-call analysis to trace party activity in the House of Representatives.

There are biographies of all the leading Revolutionaries and many secondary figures. They include D. S. Freeman on *George Washington*, 7 vols (New York: Scribners, and London: Eyre & Spottiswoode, 1948–57), P. Smith, *John Adams*, 2 vols (Garden City, NY: Doubleday, 1962), J. R. Howe, *The Changing Political Thought of John Adams* (Princeton, NJ: Princeton University Press, 1966), E. Wright, *Franklin of Philadelphia* (Cambridge, Mass.: Harvard University Press, 1986) and D. S. Malone, *Jefferson and His Times*, 6 vols (Boston: Little, Brown, 1948–81), M. D. Peterson, *Thomas Jefferson and the New Nation* (New York: Oxford University Press, 1970) and N. E. Cunningham, *In Pursuit of Reason* (Baton Rouge: Louisiana State University Press, 1981) on Jefferson; I. Brant, *James Madison*, 6 vols (Indianapolis: Bobbs-Merrill, 1941–61), R. Ketcham, *James Madison* (New York: Macmillan, 1971), G. Stourzh, *Alexander Hamilton and the Idea of Republican Government* (Palo Alto, Cal.: Stanford University Press, 1970), B. Mitchell, *Alexander Hamilton*, 2 vols (New York: Macmillan, 1957–62) and concise edn (New York: Oxford University Press, 1976); C. L. Ver Steeg, *Robert Morris* (Philadelphia: University of Pennsylvania Press, 1954) and G. Seed, *James Wilson* (Millwood, NY: KTO Press, 1978). P. Maier, *The Old Revolutionaries* (New York: Alfred A. Knopf, 1980) provides miniature biographies of Samuel Adams and other secondary radical politicians. The papers of major figures are being published in modern letterpress editions.

# INDEX

Adams, Abigail (1744–1815), 171
Adams, John (1735–1826), and
  Articles, 147; in Continental
  Congress, 87, 118, 119;
  diplomat, 102, 187, 201; on
  equality, 127; Federalist party,
  249, 250; on government, 116,
  118, 119, 127, 130, 133, 139–40;
  and independence, 76, 80, 88,
  91, 93, 118; nature of
  Revolution, 2–3, 4; nature of
  union, 7; *Thoughts on
  Government*, 133, 134, 139
Adams, Samuel (1722–1803), and
  independence, 74–5, 76, 77, 80,
  87, 88, 91; parties, 245; US
  Constitution, 202, 227
Administration of Justice Act, 78
African Americans, 10, 210;
  distribution, 20–1; free blacks,
  33, 47, 168, 172; immigration,
  19; and War, 112, 167–70,
  178; *see* slavery; anti-slavery
  movement
agriculture, 22, 23, 26–9, 32–3,
  36–7; changes in
  upper South, 28, 58; pre-war
  recession, 56–7; effect of war on,
  114, 115, 180; Philadelphia
  Convention, 203, 212
Alamance, Battle of the, 61–2
Albany, NY, 30, 107
Albany Congress, 69, 81
All Hallows Parish, Md, 57–8
alliance, French, 106, 107, 108,
  109–10
amendment process, Articles, 149;
  US Constitution, 213–14

America, British central, 67
American Philosophical Society,
  49, 68
American Prohibitory Act, 89, 91
ancient constitution, *see under*
  constitution, British
Andover, Mass., 30
Anglicans, *see* Church of England
Anglo-Saxon constitution, *see under*
  constitution, British
Annapolis Convention, 199
Annapolis, Md, 79, 232
Anne Arundel County, Md, 133, 232
Anti-Federalists, 223–33, 234,
  236, 246; campaigns, 226–31;
  ideology, 223–5; tactics, 225–6
anti-slavery movement, 168–70,
  178, 198
Appalachian mountains, 6, 12, 15,
  21, 70, 164, 181, 189
Appleby, Joyce, 54
aristocracy: American, 42, 45,
  140–2, 176, 196, 197, 204–5,
  223–5; English as social model,
  39–40, 41–2, 45, 65
army, American, 115, 130, 145,
  202, 233; casualties, 113; and
  civilians, 111–12; and Congress,
  102; formed, 88; mutinies, 108,
  183; outbreak of war, 84, 86;
  problems of, 92, 106, 108, 113,
  183; recruitment, 86–7, 88, 112,
  132–3; reduction, 183; service in,
  92, 95, 113; suppression of
  loyalism, 97; *see also* War of
  Independence
army, British, behaviour of, 111,
  115; in colonies, 71, 74, 75, 79;

316

British colonial policy: and
American liberty, 70, 71;
American views of, 67, 70–1,
72–3, 74, 75, 77, 78, 79; coming
of War, 60–1, 78–9, 82, 83; after
Great War for Empire, 70–7;
Intolerable Acts, 78–9; and
native Americans, 71; taxation,
71–3, 74; and western lands, 71
British Empire: and American
ideology, 51–2; as community,
39, 42, 66, 67, 80, 84, 96–7, 101;
and Continental Congress, 89;
disintegration of, 86–7, 88, 91–5;
Galloway's Plan of Union, 81–2;
after Great War for Empire,
69–70; Loyalists' view of, 96–7,
101; *see also* British colonial
policy; individual colonies; War
of Independence
Brown family, 99
Brown, John (1736–1803), 76
Brown, Joseph (1733–85), 49
Brown University, 49
Bryam, George (1731–91), 129
Bunker Hill, battle of, 87
Bull, William 1710–91), 99
Burgoyne, John (1722–92), 107
Burnaby, Andrew (?1734–1812),
68
Burke, Thomas (*c.*1747–83), 147–8
Byrd, William (1674–1744), 41

Calvert proprietory estates, 44;
family, 162, 163
Calvinism, 49, 50–1, 62–3
Cambridge, Mass., 88, 117, 125
Camden, battle of, 108
Canada: addressed by First
Continental Congress, 82; in
empire, 67, 70; French colonial
growth, 17; government, 70, 79;
Loyalists, 97; Quebec Act, 79;
refusal to join Revolution, 90–1;
in war, 90–1, 107; *mentioned*, 2,
12, 194
Cannon, James (1740–82), 127,
129

capitalism, 54, 55
Carlisle peace mission, 107
Carroll, 'Barrister', Charles, 133
Carroll of Carrollton, Charles
(1737–1832): wealth of, 32;
Quebec, 90; pessimism, 96; Md
constitution, 132; Md politics,
150, 155, 165; Philadelphia
Convention, 202
Carter family, 38
Champlain, lake, 87, 187
Charles river, Mass., 87
Charleston, SC, 28, 30, 34, 37,
131, 132; coming of Revolution,
73, 78; Loyalists, 98, 153;
politics, 155, 156, 174;
ratification, 228; and War, 87,
108, 114, 132, 151
charters, colonial, 5, 44, 78, 119,
120, 122, 124
Chase, Samuel (1741–1811), 76,
90, 201, 227, 231
Chatham, William Pitt, earl of
(1708–78), 83
Chauncy, Charles (1705–87), 63
Chebacco, Mass., 113
Cherokee Indians, 61
Chesapeake Bay, 14, 17, 18, 133;
economy, 23, 25, 29, 33, 57;
loyalism, 98, 132; ratification,
232; slavery, 34; tenants, 36, 64;
in war, 109; *see also* upper South
Church of England, Anglicans:
disestablishment, 157, 165–7;
establishment, 42, 43, 44, 60;
loyalism, 100; proposed
bishopric, 77; in states, 46–7, 60,
77, 128, 130, 153
churches: denominations, 42–4;
disestablishment, 157, 165–7,
217–18; educational role, 48;
and politics, 41–2, 166; as social
units, 38; *see also* individual
denominations; liberty, religious;
religion
Circular Letter, Massachusetts,
74–5
Citation Act, NY, 152

324 INDEX

judiciary: colonial, 44, 45, 48, 60,
74; federal, 205, 206, 211,
214–15, 217, 219, 220, 238;
states, 138, 139, 160
Judiciary Act, 238
juries, 48, 60, 79

Kentucky, 21, 181, 189–90, 233,
252
Kenyon, Cecelia M., 233 [sic
spelling]
King, Rufus (1755–1827), 190, 202
King's Mountain, battle of, 109
Kingston, NY, 151
Knox, Henry (1750–1806), 113,
181

labourers, 114, 126, 128, 135
Lamb, John (1735–1800), 73
Lancaster, Pa., 34
land: and Articles, 147, 148;
availability, 6, 57–8, 65, 189;
cession to Congress, 188, 189,
191; prices, 33, 148; riots, 61;
sales, 190, 192, 193; speculators,
15, 26, 29, 71, 163–4; state
claims, 147, 148; titles, 60, 61;
see also west
Land Act (1796), 192
Land Ordinance (1785), 8, 191–2
landless whites, 34–5, 47, 99, 135
Laurens, Henry (1724–92), 59, 76,
112, 131
Laurens, John (1754–82), 112
Lee, Arthur (1740–92), 42, 106
Lee family, 38, 42, 48
Lee, Richard Henry (1732–94): in
Continental Congresses, 80, 87,
89, 93, 118; Philadelphia
Convention, 210; ratification,
224, 225, 226, 228, 231
Lee, William (1739–95), 42
legislatures, colonial, 44, 45–6, 48,
60, 61, 72, 73, 74, 76, 78
legislatures, state, 122–4, 130, 134,
136, 137, 139–41, 142, 173, see
also lower houses; upper houses,
states

Letters from a Farmer in
Pennsylvania, see under
Dickinson, John
Letters of a Federal Farmer, 226
Lexington, battle of, 1, 4, 84, 86,
95
Lexington, Mass., 24
liberty: Bill of Rights, 238–9;
Declaration of Independence, 94;
definition, 53–5; ratification,
223–5; 230; religious, 53, 130,
146, 156–7, 165–7, 198; in
states, 126, 132, 136–7;
threatened by Britain, 70–1, 72,
76; US Constitution, 218–19,
148, 150
Lincoln, Benjamin (1733–1810),
108, 194, 236
Livingston family, 38, 40, 163
Livingston, Robert R.
(1746–1813), 95, 181, 189
Livingston, William (1723–90), 102
localism, 176–8, 196, 198, 199,
229, 230, 232–3, 238
Locke, John (1632–1704), 49, 52,
53, 54–5, 202
Long Island, NY, 34
Louisburg, NS, 67
Louisiana Purchase, 12
lower houses, colonial, 44, 45–6,
47–8, 78, 119, 130, 131, 139–40
lower orders: advancement, 156,
157–8, 171–8; aspirations, 64–5;
128, 129, 132, 154, 155–6, 178;
and elites, 59, 65, 154–5, 158,
250; and Great Awakening,
62–5; loyalism, 99; Philadelphia
Convention, 201; politicised, 3, 6,
72–3, 80, 85, 95, 111–13; price
controls, 104, 154; ratificaion,
226–7; Shays's Rebellion, 161–2;
state constitutions, 123, 126–8,
133, 134; taxation, 160–2; and
war, 95, 111–14; see also equality
lower South, 14, 28, 33, 34, 38, 98,
108–9, 232; see also Georgia;
North Carolina; South Carolina;
South

professional men, 35–6, 47, 164, 173, 202
progress, possibility of, 50; *see also* pessimism
property, 47, 52, 126, 128, 134, 177, 178; distribution of, 31–2; and franchise, 46–8, 131–6, 141–3, 172, 173, 176; lower orders and, 65, 134–5, 143; Philadelphia Convention, 203, 208, 211, 219, 231; RI and, 198; in west, 189, 192, 193
proprietorship: Maryland, 44, 162, 163, 164; Pennsylvania, 40, 44, 59–60, 128, 152, 154, 162, 164, 245
protestantism, 43–4, 50–1, 62–3, 68, 165; *see also* individual denominations
Providence, RI, 34, 58, 68, 80, 104, 115, 140, 245
provincial congresses: and the Association, 83, 88; draft constitutions, 118, 119, 122; exercise authority, 91, 92, 116, 117, 127; Mass., 84, 86, 117; NY, 8, 92, 94, 135
Prussia, 187
puritanism, 50–1, 52

Quakers (Society of Friends), 43, 44, 68; and loyalism, 98, 100, 152; in Pennsylvania politics, 61, 128, 130; and slavery, 168
qualifications for office, 47; *see also* suffrage
Quartering Act 1765, 74
Quartering Act 1774, 79
Québec: capture, 67, 69; government of, 71; rejects Revolution, 90; *see also* Canada
Quebec Act, 79, 90
Queen's County, NY, 98
quit rents, 61, 164

racialism, 38, 65, 156, 167, 169–70
radicals, English, 51, 202
Rakove, Jack N., 82

Ramsay, David (1749–1815), 79
Randolph, Edmund (1753–1813), 203, 205–6, 210, 215, 244
Randolph family, 38
Rappahannock river, 14, 37
ratification (of US Constitution): Philadelphia Convention, 206, 215–16, 221; process, 222–33, 234; social divisions, 231–3
Rawdon, Lord Francis (1754–1826), 113
real whigs, *see* radicals, English
reconciliation, American hopes of, 87, 89, 93, 118
redemptioners, *see* indentured servants
Regulator movement, 61–2, 134, 189
religion, 6, 42–4, 46–7, 63–4, 98, 100, 157, 165–7, 217–18; *see also* individual denominations; liberty, religious
representation: in Articles, 145, 146–7; in colonial assemblies, 45–6, 61; at Philadelphia Convention, 205–6; in state constitutions, 137, 143; in US Constitution, 205–9; *see also* Articles of Confederation; Continental Congress; franchise
republicanism, 1–2, 3, 5, 10, 116: and social hierarchy, 52–3, 197; theory, 51–3; 120–1, 124, 125–6, 127, 136–7, 139–40, 196, 197, 198; and US Constitution, 204, 209–10, 223–5; in west, 191, 193
Republican party, 248–51
Republican Society (Pa.), 130–1, 153–4, 246
resistance to British policy, colonial, 71, 72–83
Revenue Act 1764, *see under* Sugar Act
Revenue Act 1766, 73
Revenue Act 1767, *see under* Townshend Duties

Revolutionary debt: Hamiltonian
programme, 240–2; Morris
programme, 182–3, 184–5, 195;
nationalist movement, 195;
origin, 103–6, 159, 160; party
formation, 248; and Philadelphia
Convention delegates, 203; and
ratification, 231
Revolutionary war, *see* War of
Independence
Rhode Island, 102, 236: and
Articles, 183; Charter, 4, 44,
119, 120, 122; as colony, 13,
16, 17, 21, 40, 43, 44; coming
of Revolution, 69, 76, 80;
financial problems, 158, 159–60,
198; forming government, 5, 119,
122; independence, 92; loyalism,
97, 162; parties, 177;
Philadelphia Convention, 198,
201; population, 17, 21, 152;
post-war trade, 186;
primogeniture, 165; ratification,
222, 226, 228, 230, 235; religion,
165, 166; slavery, 168, 169; war,
86, 112
rice and indigo, 22, 28, 37, 56, 114,
180
Ridgely, Charles, 160
Rittenhouse, David (1732–96), 49,
127
Robinson scandal, 59
Rochambeau, Jean, comte de
(1725–1807), 109
Rockingham, Charles Watson-
Wentworth, marquess of
(1730–82), 73, 110
Rocky mountains, 12
Rogerenes, 43
Roman Catholics, 42–3, 100, 165;
church in Canada, 79, 90;
suffrage, 46
Ross, George (1730–79), 129
Rowley, Mass., 30
Rush, Benjamin (1745–1813), 2–3,
4, 127, 147
Russian Revolution, 10
Rutgers University, 49

Rutledge, Edward (1749–1800),
93, 95
Rutledge, John (1739–1800):
Philadelphia Convention, 202,
205, 210, 215; South Carolina
politics, 118, 131, 138, 150
Ryerson, Richard A., 128

St John's College, Annapolis, 155
St Thomas Jenifer, Daniel of
(1723–90), 160
Salem, Mass., 30, 58, 79, 115,
117
Sandemanians, 43
Saratoga, NY, 107, 194
Savannah, Ga., 30, 86, 108
Schuyler family, 40, 163
Schuyler, Philip (1733–1804), 96,
113, 157, 195, 233
Scotch Irish, 18, 19, 20, 43, 58;
Pennsylvania politics, 128, 129,
130, 153
Scots, 19, 20, 99; loyalism, 98, 99,
100
Scott, John Morin (*c.*1730–84),
135
Seabury, Samuel (1729–96), 100
Sears, Isaac (1730–86), 73
Second Continental Congress, *see
under* Continental Congress
Secret Committee [of Congress],
102
sectionalism, 188, 190, 194, 204,
208, 247
Senate, US, *see* Congress, US
Senates, for states *see* upper
houses, states
separation of powers, 5, 8–9, 44–6,
138; state constitutions, 137,
138–9, 142; US Constitution,
210, 214, 219, 220; *see also* state
constitutions; individual states
Separatists, 43
Seven Years War, *see* Great War
for Empire
Sewall family, 99
Shays, Daniel (*c.*1747–1825),
161–2